Twist&Build

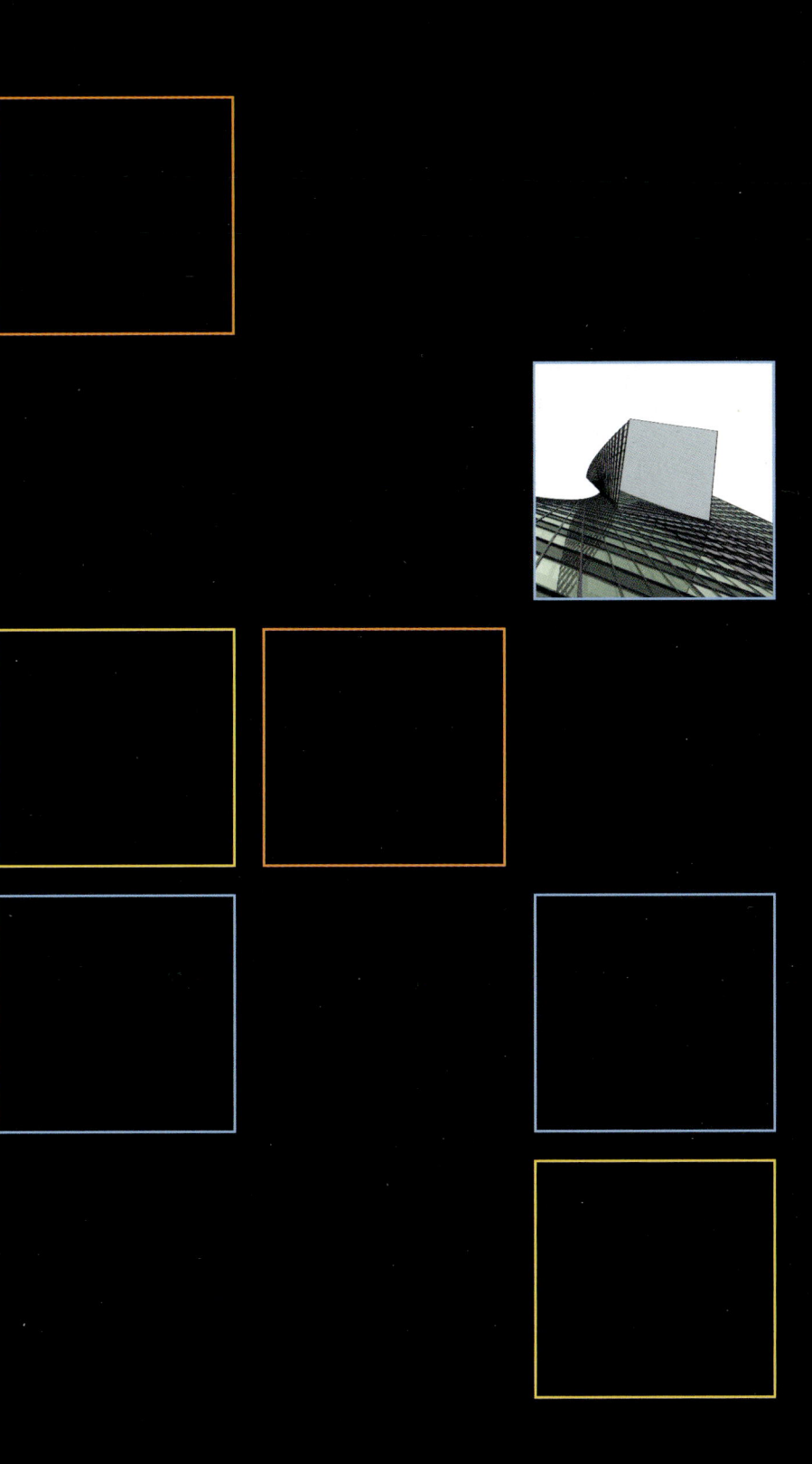

Karel Vollers **Twist&Build**
creating non-orthogonal
architecture

010 PUBLISHERS, ROTTERDAM 2001

Credits
Translation by Lynn de Graaf and Brenda Vollers-King
Design by Jan van Mechelen (ZEE, Rotterdam)
Prepress by Philip Brands (Antenna-men, Rotterdam)
Printed by Lecturis, Eindhoven

ISBN 90 6450 410 5

Acknowledgment

During the past eight years, while working on this project, the seasons have passed rapidly. I often wondered whether I should continue, to sit inside my office behind a computer, in fact generations of computers, spending most of my time on cumbersome every-day work. I was hardly building anything, and working like this seemed an expensive hobby. Year after year I realized I had hardly spent any time sailing on my boat, and had continued to work through most of the holidays.

But I considered myself lucky to be able to follow a personal interest, through an economic aberration which allowed me to increase the mortgage on my house. Discovering shapes, developing new technologies, and working with people whom I admired, is very inspiring. Sometimes it is their work, often their attitude or character, that I simply enjoy to be in contact with. For their financial support, I thank Wim van den Berg (Reynolds) and Hans Köhne (vnc), and for their technical support Han van Herwijnen (Reynolds), Hans van Blokland (Van Tetterode) and Rob Nijsse (abt). Many others who have provided highly professional advice and support are not mentioned here, but have been named in this report. They can be assured of my gratitude.

I feel most grateful to Sir Norman Foster who responded after I sent him information about my work in 1995. He commented that I had 'opened up some very interesting fields of technical study and aesthetic debate'. Rem Koolhaas gave me a similar reply. It was a great inspiration that architects whom I greatly admire, thought my work worthwhile. Their comments again helped me to continue for years.

Gobel Hellevoort has made the computer drawings from the very beginning. Our discussions of architectural aspects, and the pictures which he created with great feeling and ability, were most inspiring. I thank him very much for his help.

Private life and profession tend to mix, which is not always easy. My friends helped me to continue the search for a more sensuous environment. Many gave their view on how to keep 'the good work' going, especially Marianne Peretti, Jane Edwards, Marie-Louise Spronck and my wife Ana. Their practical and balanced opinions sustained me in my aim to produce a sound, artistic result.

The advice of my promotors, professors Jan Brouwer and Mick Eekhout, was of great tactical importance, and I am indebted to the Faculty of Architecture of the University of Technology Delft for enabling me to pursue this study in recent years.

To conclude, this project would not have been possible without my Mum - which I agree sounds logical. Always supporting me loyally, she was relieved every time a perspective dawned that my work might bring in money at last, but was also content to see me enjoy pursuing ideals.

Karel Vollers

Contents

DESCRIPTION OF THE RESEARCH ASSIGNMENT
The design and production of a façade system for ruled surfaces.

MOTIVATION
The background to this research project is a fascination for the expressive and lyrical aspects of curved lines and surfaces. In order to make these shapes generally applicable in buildings, an integrated system had to be designed for the constituent parts, particularly for glass and its frame.

DESCRIPTION OF THE PROJECT
To produce, by means of an interaction between material research and building design, a clear description of the transforming and application potential of twisted façades and their components.
To produce a 1:1 prototype of a twisted window frame with twisted glass.

Introduction

Introducing computers into the building industry in the early eighties gave rise to an explosion of design and production options. Initially, the computer was brought into action to automate certain aspects of the building process. It reduced costs of labour, increased production speed and minimized human error. The influence on the design of buildings was limited: structures remained orthogonal and were mostly character-ized by a frequent repetition of components, both in façades and ground plans. With all storeys being copies of the ground floor, their geometry was often called 2.5D. Almost at the same time, relatively cheap and easy modelling programmes became available. Some architects took an interest in freely transformed volumes, or 'blobs'. An important incentive to develop such shapes was that with the increasingly flush fin-ish of façades (often due to economics), visual expression of planes and contours got more attention. An obvious next step was to give buildings an additional value by mod-elling, 'molding' them like a clay object, thus exploiting and accentuating curvatures. Since 1990, the attention of a number of leading architects has been focused on twist-ed surfaces. They share many spatial qualities with freely doubly-curved surfaces, but are far easier to construct. Various renowned architects currently apply them in their buildings, including Frank Gehry (the Guggenheim Museum in Bilbao, Spain) and Kas Oosterhuis (the salt-water part of the 'Waterland Neeltje Jans' exhibition pavilion in Zeeland, the Netherlands). The notion 'twisting' covers many types of transformation, but until now the typological terminology has been too unspecific; besides, most con-temporary architects are no longer used to describing surfaces mathematically. Consequently, designer, architect, constructor, as well as manufacturer experience this notion as confusing, and, in practice, avoid the use of such geometry.

Until now, twisted surfaces have only been realized in wood, steel, masonry or concrete, but not yet in glass. With this material only, twisted planes could be approxi-mated, namely by embellishing (=facetting) with flat planes. The industry was not able to deliver twisted, let alone freely doubly-curved glass for an acceptable price and at short notice. A production process had simply not yet been developed.
The problems with which one is confronted must be dealt with integrally:

- there is hardly a market demand as yet (because the product is completely new);
- the building volumes of the first projects, are far too small to allow the develop-ment costs to be written off;
- the series of elements, for instance glass sheets, are too small to allow them to be offered at an acceptable price;
- the development time accepted in current projects is too short;
- manufacturers must be found to launch new, not yet existing products on the market at an acceptable price;
- the product transformations and applications are still unfamiliar.

This research project is intended to give insight into design and production options. Applications in urban settings, building design as well as technically and economically feasible material processing are interactive in this thesis. On the one hand, buildings were designed with large scale application of transformed materials. On the other

13

hand, techniques were developed, in consultation with many experts, to transform materials according to the geometry for which we expect a demand.

New transformations of façade structures are initially very time-consuming and therefore expensive. In order to arrive at products that can be tendered at realistic market prices, the link was made with industrial production processes. These were subsequently innovated. Industrial co-operations were initiated, resulting in the launch onto the market of products with guaranteed quality.

The integration of various disciplines is pre-eminently the task of the architect. It is probably one of the most important parts of the development process and very time-consuming. It was difficult to find a financier to integrate the various building parts. As a rule, manufacturers only wanted to invest in the development of their own products and were unwilling to invest in an integral approach. The window frame system developer was more generous and visionary; the firm gave a steady support throughout. Architectural institutions that were supposed to financially stimulate developments, in their turn did not want to subsidize product development. The broadness of this research, sometimes contributed to finding financial funds, because any subject could be connected to it. Just as often though, it was a hindrance because there was always some reason for refusing aid.

Financial means to pay advisers and manufacturers for their work and expenses were lacking in this research. By presenting them with attractive building designs, together with financially and technically feasible possibilities of new transformed materials, they were encouraged to believe in the market value of products and techniques that they themselves had to invest in.

The sequence of the design activities was not a usual one and varied per building model. Since there was no deadline, nor any kind of commission, it was possible to strive for a result that was not dominated by the usual economic, political or social processes. Therefore the various aspects of torsion could be tuned to each other at various planning levels.

The approached builders, manufacturers, investors and designers, all authorities in Dutch industry, showed great interest in the project. They sensed the potential and adventure of a new development, and understood that by radical innovations, not just products, but also urban living and working space would become very different, with as yet unknown shapes.

All participants in this project are innovative and economically strong. They were selected because of their ability to guarantee the quality of the final product. Since they would only invest in development of building parts or buildings, if this was realistic with regard to manufacturing, costs, spatial characteristics, and use, some buildings were worked out in detail and the consequences of twisted façades for various building aspects were described. By exactly defining the components that deviate from the ones in common buildings (structure, façade cleaning equipment, connection of inner walls to the façade, airco systems), the planning and cost-technical insecurities of a new geometry were reduced to acceptable quantities.

From the many aspects that were studied, new schedules, shapes and theories arose. Many of them are new, although with hindsight they are simple and even obvious. Several of the aspects noticed and described in general terms, have not yet been elaborated. They should be regarded as starting points for further research.

The project resulted in a prototype of a twisted façade component. This concept, the components of which were described as far as geometry and connection requirements are concerned, provides the participating industries with a model within which their respective contributions can be optimized. Production costs are considerably lower, now that only the geometry of exemplary models needs to be adjusted. The participants, but also companies of either related or different industry sectors, may suggest alternatives based on their particular expertise, and so perhaps innovate the prototype radically. It offers architects a view on a new product, so that they can design new applications for it and by so doing, instigate a demand.

01

RESEARCH AND CONTEXT

The subject of twisted façades touches on many aspects. The transformation has a long history and can be found on many scales, ranging from town planning, through architecture, products of everyday use, to molecules. The choice for torsion when designing a building is deliberate, for practical, technical and aesthetical reasons. This chapter starts with a brief description of various aspects that were, or will be, influencing architectural design with twisted surfaces. It continues with technological aspects of torsion, and the process of innovation in the context of market demand. Subsequently objectives of this study are defined and a framework is put up for industrial production of a twisted window frame with twisted glass. The description of the process of research by design is illustrated with a diagram that shows the designs that were made to conclude each stage.

CONTEXT OF TWISTED CONSTRUCTIONS

TORSION AND TOWN-PLANNING

It is only during the last few decades that large twisted surfaces have been applied in architecture. What may be large in architecture, is still small on an urban level. Twisted surfaces can play a part on this scale e.g. in a district, when they are used as:

1   Landscape elements. This may be a spatially transformed plaza or a park, serving as a connection or a separation between town-districts.

2   Points of orientation. A twisted building may be a beacon in the landscape that emphasizes directions. Buckled or curved façades, may point in two directions, but a twisted surface adds two extra ones, because of the rotation. Therefore a twisted shape will frequently be used to mark a bend in the road (or in a waterway), a fork or an intersection from a great distance.

3   Common shape characteristics. They may, for instance, interrelate groups of objects. A twisted street wall, may be a series of buildings of which the twisted façades are aligned. Town-planning prerequisites may, next to alignment or building height, additionally enforce a roofline, which is not parallel to the alignment. As a rule, however, the design of buildings will not be laid down in such a compelling manner.

Tilla Duriuex Park, Berlin, Germany
(DS-landscape-architects 1995-2001)

Plan in Amsterdam, The Netherlands
(Fenna Haaksma Wagenaar 1998)

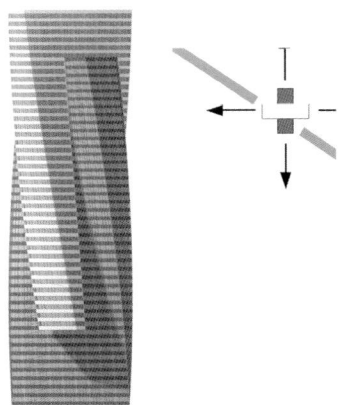

The Tilla Durieux Park is levelled off with a twisted field of grass, measuring 25 x 500m. It simultaneously serves as a park and a plaza. Two corners, stick out 5 m above streetlevel. On a path that cuts through the park half way, are seven 21 m long see-saws. Their oscillating movements recall the characteristic rotation of straight lines of the field surface. Because of the torsion, the view from the park changes from a westward into an eastward direction. The rising banks change the atmosphere in adjacent streets gradually from closed-in to open and vice versa.

Perspective 90° twisted tower (Karel Vollers 1996)

Perspective 66° twisted tower (Karel Vollers 1997)

In the Amsterdam plan an office building with a twisted façade flanks the twisted square (110 x 300 metres). Because of its large dimensions, the square is the direct link at street level, and both an urban element – a parking area – and an architectural element – a roof.

Both designs of towers (above) show a characteristic application of a twisted shape: two urban directions are connected. From a great distance one can see that the direction of the ridge, that for example is parallel to one road, turns towards the direction of the foot of the building, which is parallel to the other.

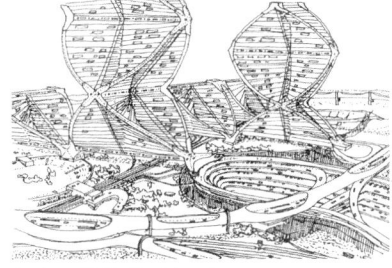
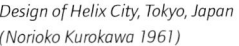

Design of Helix City, Tokyo, Japan
(Norioko Kurokawa 1961)

Villes Cosmiques (Iannis Xenakis 1964)

The three-dimensional mega structure of the rigorous design of Kurokawa offered, at a town planning level, a regulating framework for the rapidly increasing population, with its inherent streams of traffic, and built-up areas. Within the circular traffic system that concentrates housing and bundles activities, are buildings that fan out. [1-1]

Composer/architect Iannis Xenakis in 1964 presented his Utopian project for 'cosmic' cities; it was 5 kilometres in height. The various assembled sheaves (bundles of straight lines) form a visual unity by their shape. [1-2]

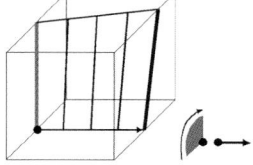

Twisted surface

TORSION AND ARCHITECTURE

A twisted surface can be described in various ways:

- **According to the conventional definition** it is a surface composed of straight lines, where adjacent lines are not parallel (in that case it would be a planar or a single-curved surface), nor do they intersect (then it would be a planar or a conical surface).
- **According to the definition developed in this project** it is a surface built up from lines by shifting and rotation, whereby one component of the rotation direction is perpendicular to the shifting direction (see drawing).

Because a twisted surface is built up from straight lines ('rules'), it is also named a 'ruled surface'. 'Torsion' and 'twisting' will be used in this study interchangeably. A twisted surface cannot be developed (unrolled) without stretching or shrinking. A twisted panel cannot be unrolled without fully stretching or buckling it. It would be possible with a cylindrical or conical panel, because when they are bent, the one outer side will be compressed and the other outer side stretched, and there will be a neutral in-between layer where no change of length occurs. With materials of low elasticity, like steel or glass, twisting is a more complex process than bending, because of these changes.

Twisting considerably increases the possibilities of expression in architectural shapes. Associations that can be conjured up with simpler surface shapes, for instance surfaces curved in one direction, are enriched by the additional rotation of its lines. Instead a 'clinical' straight shift of a line, twisting surfaces introduces curves. It is economically interesting when this type of transformation has practical advantages, for instance if double-curving results in a higher material rigidity (less use of material), or a smaller outside surface (less consumption of material and energy). But before realizing such a functional use, this research shows that the material transformations are feasible and that a smoothly twisted façade will acquire an additional value in its manifestation. This has not been demonstrated ever before in glass.

Torsion is not a new kind of transformation. Twisted surfaces have been applied for a long time, often for functional reasons, as in a spiral staircase when the flush finish below the steps resulted in a twisted ceiling. It prevented the head from knocking against protruding edges and improved the flow of forces between steps.

Twisted profiles (usually strips and bars) were applied in metal fencing and machines, sometimes for structural reasons, sometimes for their ornamental value. Ornamental

ruled surfaces can also be found in furniture, forged silverware and stuccowork, respectively made out of materials like wood, silver or lime. Often parts of sculptures are twisted; chiselling or smearing may form ruled surfaces.

An early example of torsion can be found in the jointed stone rib system of a staircase in the Hradcany Castle in Prague, a specimen of Late Gothic work dating from 1500. The twist of the ribs is a consequence of the intersection of complex planes. [1-3]

Liane Lefaivre and Alexander Tzonis described underlying aspects of transformation in the Renaissance in 'The Question of Autonomy in Architecture'. They state that the method of creating distance from the architectural object by drawing, of foregrounding and systematizing its visual structural attributes, helped both promoting the idea of an austere traditional order in buildings and instigating 'by-products', such as experiments with shapes by manipulating perspective. Methods already used by cartographers for mapping forms from one plane to another and from one system of coordinates to another were systematically analyzed. The orthogonal matrix that had underlined the norms of regularity and symmetry became less rigid. It is as if the traditional order became elastic, bent, compressed, stretched. The humanist efforts to legitimize the emerging absolutist states during the end of the fifteenth century by emphasizing regularities, eventually found an antipode in distortion. Distortion tells by picturing how form emerges arbitrarily from under the ruling of conventions of representation, in the same mood as Machiavelli, Montaigne, or Erasmus observe, how the states of law and order result from arbitrary power and how limited their legitimacy is. It mirrored the aggressive bourgeois doctrine of individualism. The problem of how to save the order of the plan in the face of site anomalies seems similar to a different problem: the orthogonally inscribed form of a balustrade climbing up onto the inclined plane of a stair. In the drawing, abacus and base block of the baluster are cut into trapezia or triangular prisms. Caramel de Lobkowitz in his 'Architectura Civil Recta y Obliqua' opposed this hybrid solution and thought the imperatives of consistency and completeness of formal Renaissance architecture obliged one to transform such balusters. The grid was bent so that the angle of its axes matched the sloping angle of the stair. As an isolated figure, the form seems distorted, but as part of a system it is regular. [1-4]

An example of a stair with balusters following a similar transformation, can be seen in Le Chateau de Benouville, Normandie, France (± 1770-80), designed by Claude Nicolas Ledoux. The top side of the handrail is twisted. [1-5]

Staircase Hradcany Castle, Prague

Hybrid solution for balusters

Corinthian capital, 'Architectura Civil Recta y Obliqua'

Twisted balusters, Le Chateau de Benouville

An isolated early use of torsion, (origins nor year of making are known to the author), is the shaping of church spires in the Beaugeois, Pays de Loire (France). All spires are different. [1-6]

Support roof truss
(Victor Horta 1898-1901)

Ruled surfaces with cross,
Crypt Colònia Güell (Gaudí 1908-1914)

Balconies Casa Battló
(Gaudí 1904-1906)

After Classicism, around 1900 a culmination occurred with regard to free geometry, particularly in shapes of the artistic trends of Art Nouveau and Jugendstil. The curves were inspired by growth in nature, as can be seen in the home of architect Victor Horta where parts of the roof truss construction wind around a column like ivy. The support structure is an assembly of steel profiles with an ornamental as well as a structural function. The various kinds of surfaces within the profiles flowingly blend together. Horta was not after the application of a particular type of twisted surface. Instead he wanted to reflect a naturally grown shape. Like animal tentacles the profiles feel their way into a space to be newly cultivated. It reflected the new age. Space became more accessible to man: aeroplanes, steam vessels, cars and trains started to conquer the world.

Parallel to this, in Barcelona, a group of architects with Antonio Gaudí as its exponent, developed a style in which the curves stirred mystic associations. Gaudí was a rationalist with a perfect skill. [1-7] From 1884 onwards he studied and used ruled surfaces. In contrast to many functionalist architects after him, he usually introduced so many variations to the main shape that structural aspects were overshadowed through multiplicity of added symbolic expressions. As an example, in the crypt of the Colònia Güell, ruled surfaces would also not have been noticed as such, had Gaudí not given some intersecting rules their own colour. [1-8]

For the balconies of Casa Battló, he 'forged' various components into a coherent whole, by transforming them in a similarly free manner.

Adziogol lighthouse

Port of Kobe Tower

Sydney Center Point Tower

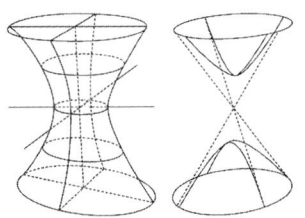

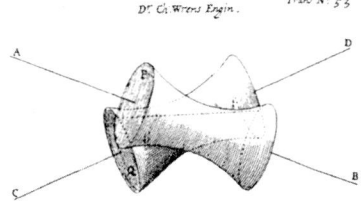

Revolution of the hyperbola   *Two hyperboloids (Wren)*

In contrast with free-shaped ruled surfaces like in Gaudí's work, hyperboloids feature a great regularity, and therefore, usually a repetion of components. A hyperboloid is an open surface generated by revolving a hyperbola about either one of its axes. In mathematics the form was long known before Christopher Wren (UK), in the 17th century, discovered that the hyperboloid of one sheet could also be constructed from straight lines. This discovery was of great importance to the practical use of the shape. One of the first known applications of the hyperboloid was an engine for a grinder of aspherical lenses designed by Wren in 1667. The Russian engineer Suchov and the Spanish architect Antonio Gaudí independently studied the potential of ruled surfaces in the late 19th century. They both used the hyperbolic paraboloid in their constructions. Because of the double symmetry, a hyperboloid has, at any point of the surface, two intersecting straight lines. Suchov realized that the hyperboloid offered pre-eminent solutions for tower-like buildings. In 1896 he built his first tower in the form of a hyperbolic lattice at the Russian Exhibition in Nizni Novgorod (water tower, 25.6 m high, container for 10 m3). In the years to follow the hyperboloid was used for the construction of hundreds of water towers, lighthouses and high voltage masts throughout Russia. [1-9]

The form and success of Suchov's towers did not remain unnoticed. Early in the 20th century the hyperboloid was used for the first time for the concrete shell of a cooling tower (already in 1916, designed by Van Iterson and Kuyper in Heerlen, the Netherlands). Through this application, the hyperboloid gained worldwide publicity.

Reservoir at Horta de Ebro, detail
(Pablo Picasso)

In 1959 the shape was first used as a load bearing structure for a building. The Port of Kobe Tower (Kobe, Japan) is approximately 100 metres high. Its hyperboloid lattice provides both horizontal and vertical stiffness and stability to the five-storey office building in the top of the tower. The cylindrical core of the building is used for vertical transport and has no structural function.

Six years later, in 1965, the Sydney Center Point Tower was completed. This 250 m high tower derives its horizontal strength and stability from a hyperboloid lattice, acting under tension. Steel cables are tensed between foundation and central core. Thus the core is part of both horizontal and vertical load bearing systems. As the lattice elements are under tension, they can be very thin. At some distance the lattice is hardly visible, leaving the spectator a construction with excessive slenderness.

At the beginning of the last century, artists touched lightly on the phenomenon of torsion. In 1920 Tatlin designed the 400 m high Monument commemorating the Third International. The inclined columns along the spiralling path to the speaker's platform resemble an asymmetrically twisted shape. But with the diagonals in between them, it is a facetted surface constructed from triangles.

From 1920 onward, Kurt Schwitters made various 'Merzbauten'. The first of the series is in his home in Hannover, Germany. The shapes were in a continuous flux. The shadows suggest that in the enlarged detail, the stalactite-like lath was twisted.

But neither the later works of Tatlin, nor those of Kurt Schwitters pay direct attention to geometrical, spatial or associative characteristics of torsion. [1-10] The fact that ruled surfaces are time-consuming in modelling as well as in defining and building, may be the reason.

Also the art of painting, for instance the Cubism painting 'Summer' by Georges Braque, (1908) and 'Reservoir at Horta de Ebro' by Pablo Picasso (1909), portray twisted surfaces, but they are not indicating an awareness of a specific surface type either.

In contrast, since the Great War sculptors, like the Constructivists Naum Gabo and Pevsner, sought the experience of complex transformed surfaces. They wanted to express a reality in which nature and modern techniques would unite. To them, surfaces and volumes were a rhythmically combined action of straight lines. In Pevsner's drawing Naissance de l'Universe, 1934, ruled surfaces appear; they were a theme he varied on for the rest of his life, mainly in sculptures, e.g. Construction for an airport, 1935. Naum Gabo started applying ruled surfaces in 1934. He was inspired

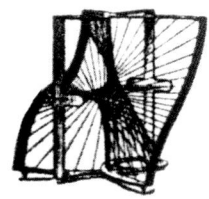 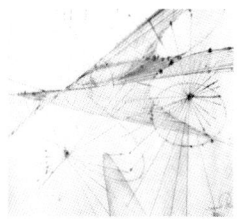 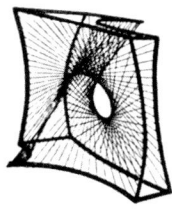 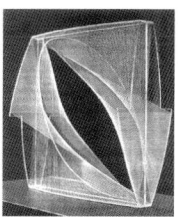

by wire models, as can be seen in Linear Construction no. 1, Variation, 1942-43. [1-11] These turned twisted surfaces into graphics and were common illustrations in the professional journals of mathematicians by the end of the nineteenth century. The flowingly progressing field of simple straight threads combined sensual aspects with the image of technology and science. The great layering of 'surfaces' provided strongly varying patterns.

Mathematical model, Katalog 1892

Naissance l'Universe (Antoine Pevsner)

Mathematical model in Institut Henri Poincaré

Linear Construction no.1, Variation (Naum Gabo)

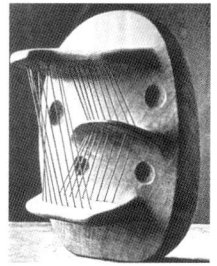

Head (Henri Moore)　　　Inclining figure with wires (Henri Moore)

Wire models, as published in Walter Dyck's, 'Katalog mathematischer und mathematische-physikalische Modelle, Apparate und Instrumente' (1892 München, Germany), became generally known in the arts when the photographs Man Ray took of wire models in the Institut Poincaré were published in 'Cahiers d'Art' (issues 1 and 2, 1936). [1-12]
Henri Moore discovered similar models in the Science Museum in London in 1935. In sculptures he combined wires with massive volumes, e.g. Head, 1938 and Reclining figure with wires, 1939. [1-13]

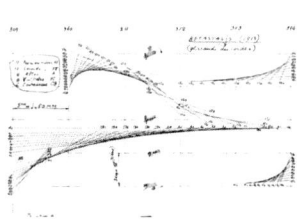 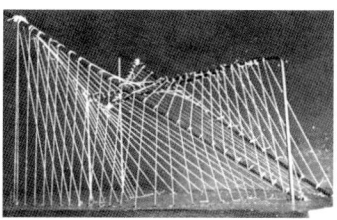  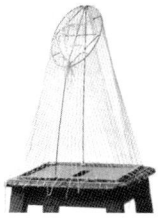

Musical composition
(Iannis Xenakis)

Wire model Philips Pavilion
(Le Corbusier-Xenakis)

Philips Pavilion

Wire model
Firminy church
(Le Corbusier)

Occasionally other forms of artistic expression, for instance music, inspired the use of ruled surfaces. Composer and architect Xenakis translated the glissandi from his music into wire models for buildings. They bore great similarities to the shape of the Philips Pavilion that

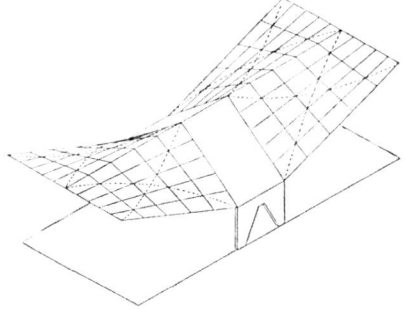

he and Le Corbusier created in 1958 for the World Exhibition in Brussels. [1-14]

The Firminy Church, that Le Corbusier designed in 1961, was less exuberant, but of no less interest as a geometrical shape. He viewed this as a new archetype because it was based upon a gradual merging between square and circle by means of straight lines. (Computer transformation of one figure into the other is now called 'morphing'). The form of the church can also be seen as four blending conoidal surfaces. [1-15]

Not only geometrical shapes can be transformed in this way; also associations linked to shapes can be related to each other. In the fifties, the general public was also fascinated by wire models. Many made objects from boards, nails and thread, to hang on the walls at home. Similar figures were drawn with the Spiro graph. They may have been symbols for aerospace technology with orbit trajectories of sputniks and capsules.

Experimental umbrella (Felix Candela)   *High Life textile factory (Felix Candela)*

In 1929 the French civil engineer Laffaille studied the construction of concrete hyperbolic paraboloid vaults. The hyperboloid had been applied as a whole by Suchov in his open steel tower structures. Gaudí often shaped brick vaults along the lines of a segment of a hyperboloid. These surfaces, also called hypars, offered practical advantages, as they feature straight lines in two directions. Laffaille's first prototype of a hypar shaped concrete roof was built in Dreux, France 1934. [1-16] In the thirties several other European engineers experimented with concrete vaults too, and published their findings in professional magazines. Soon architects started to apply vaults, among them Eduardo Toroja, e.g. the cantilevering double-curved canopy at the Hippodrome de la Zarzuela in Madrid (1935).

Felix Candela, born in Madrid, in 1939 emigrated to Mexico. He gained world-wide recognition with extremely thin and light, concrete vaults that were coupled with

refined detailing. The illustration shows twenty-five workman who mounted an experimental umbrella for a deflection test (1954). Almost all vaults he built (he acted as the contractor too) were hypars. Among many other factories, churches and houses, are the High Life textile factory, Coyoacan, D.F. (1954-55) and the N.S. de Soledad Church in Mexico, 1956. [1-17]
Structural architects like Nervi and Breuer have applied hypars since 1953. At first small surfaces, for instance the entrance canopy of the Unesco building in Paris (1957) and subsequently increasingly larger ones, like the roof over the San Francisco Church in Muskegon, Michigan USA in 1961. In their 'technical' design style, the processing of a geometrically simple basic shape was clearly recognizable.

University Entrance canopy
(Marcel Breuer)

San Francisco Church
(Marcel Breuer)

Railway station,
(K. van der Gaast)

University Waterworks Beerenplaat, (W. Quist, Bouma, Loof)

Twisted structures were not, however, suitable for repetition of rectangular office spaces, or inexpensive housing required in the post-war period. The structural advantages of vaults were often outweighed by the extra costs due to the geometric complexity and the large amount of work to produce them. Despite much attention paid by the professional press, hypars have only been sporadically applied in the Netherlands. There they are mainly to be found in civil engineering projects and public buildings, like the railway station at Tilburg, NL (1965) and the Public Water Supply Company Beerenplaat in Rotterdam, NL (1959).
In South America, where building costs are low because of cheap labour, they are still regularly applied to cover public transport junctions and market halls. By contrast, during the seventies in Europe, hypars became more and more a symbol of indeed glorious, but bygone times.

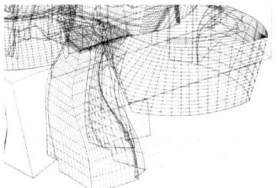

Neue Statsgalerie

(James Stirling and M. Wilford)

Guggenheim Museum

(Frank Gehry)

Wire drawing

In that period a powerful development of computer drawing and modelling pro-grammes for ship building and aircraft construction took place. After some years of delay, this software became available to the building industry. By the eighties, they offered architects an enormous freedom to visualize complex shapes. The interest in new design opportunities was considerable, particularly when smooth detailing of façades (smaller surface area, less material, less energy consumption and easier maintenance), caused the orthogonal shapes to be perceived as increasingly mono-tonous. The attention to expression of curved façades and their contours increased. Many architects wanted to model in 3D, with a total freedom of shape. Ruled sur-faces were initially said to be obsolete, because they limited geometry by straight lines. After developing skill in detailing of complex shapes, however, designers understood that ruled surfaces were affordable, but that irregular doubly-curved surfaces could only be produced on a small scale or at high cost.

In the Neue Statsgalerie in Stuttgart, Germany (1977-82), designed in Post-Modernist style, a twisted surface was created as a distinctive feature. The twisted window sits next to the entrance. The narrowing of the path along the parapet is compensated by an upward widening of the space, as the façade slopes backward at the corner. Planar glass sheets, each basically differing in size, were measured on the spot and then manufactured in the factory; wooden window frames were made to measure with help of tapering inserts. Dimensioning was complex for architects in those days, but nowadays many have access to the necessary equipment.

Manufacturing doubly-curved surfaces, however, requires a lot of manual labour, which is contradictory to the pursuit of a modern image. As for their realization, they do not attune to the newest technologies. The irregular geometry and cumbersome building methods, make these designs look rather more like the work of an artist, than of an engineer. Because doubly-curved shapes are expensive to manufacture, ruled surfaces are often preferred.

With the Guggenheim Museum in Bilbao, 1991-1997, Frank Gehry drew global atten-tion to curved shapes. The building is built up integrally of transformed volumes. The different surface types in the façades blend together fluently. Most of them, like the stone-cladded surfaces, are just flat and singly curved. But some parts of the glass and titanium cladded façades are basically twisted. The glass ones, however, are facetted with flat triangular glass sheets. The titanium ones are made by pressing

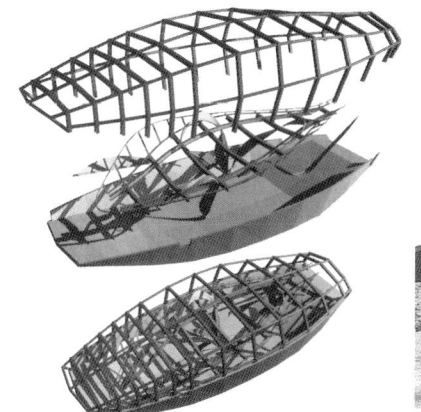
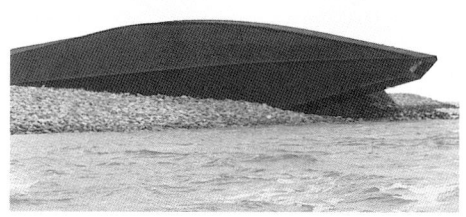

Waterland Neeltje Jans

(Kas Oosterhuis)

(rumpling) the panels into shape. Titanium panels can be very thin. Corrosion on the folds hardly decreases their life span, as the material is very durable. The expensive shiny metal is seldom applied and looks chic in this application. The volumes and their curvatures are emphasized by the varying light reflections. In the course of time a scale enlargement had occurred. Where in Art Nouveau profiles seemed to feel like tentacles into the interior, Gehry seems to let volumes react to the exterior, to the urban setting. With the museum, he also drew attention to the fact that twisted window frames and glass were not yet available.

The Exhibition Pavilion of the salt water part of the 'Waterland Neeltje Jans', NL, 1997, carries the shaping of a hollow volume even further. Not only its exterior, but also its floor is twisted. The skin is composed of corrugated steel sheets. Elongation and shrinking were achieved by transforming the sheets. The whole is covered with sprayed-on synthetic insulation. Striking are the folds in the surface which, like 'streamlines' in a car, allow one to 'read' the double-curved shape and oversee its geometry. The floor is in situ made concrete.

In the past, many (often leading) architects have presented a multitude of applications of ruled surfaces. With the introduction of CAD-CAM systems, design and production possibilities increased. This development is progressing so rapidly that designers and draughtsmen with mathematical skills are hard to find. Alongside the designers' desire to give a different expression to their work, there is a growing need to optimize the building shape with the help of 3D transformed surfaces, and thus minimize material and energy consumption, wind load, etcetera.

In order to provide insight into shaping possibilities, the geometrical and material-technical aspects of twisted façades in this research have been described in a simple diagram. Furthermore, applications in design have been shown to increase the market for new products, and to give project developers and contractors insight into realization costs. The samples will be convincing now there is co-operation between the industries that market them.

TORSION AND THE LANGUAGE OF SHAPE

The association incurred by the notion 'twisting' or 'turning', is not necessarily a positive one. The meaning of 'turning', may be good as well as bad. 'To give something a turn' often means to introduce an unexpected change; this may be a constructive action. To 'twist' something, on the other hand, for instance the truth, is usually not considered the right thing to do. This explanation of the notion is similar in other European languages.

The 'Bouwkundig Woordenboek' (a Dutch Architectural Dictionary) describes the entry 'to twist' as follows: twisting occurs particularly in bars on the outside of windows, against burglars. These are metal bars, consisting of a rod with a square, rectangular or round cross-section. [1-18] It is somewhat awkward when trying to explain the meaning of twisting, to immediately talk about burglars, although at the same time any type of fencing will imply some association with 'safety and security'.

The 'Bouwkundig Vertaalboek' (a Dutch English Architectural Dictionary) translates the Dutch word for torsion into: 'to twist and to distort. [1-19] The word 'twist' has different meanings: a quarrel, but also a yarn of doubled threads. When it comes to a story with a twist, it may mean that it has an unexpected, refreshing and positive change in development, but it may also mean a yarn with an unpleasant and bad turn: a nasty twist. This elasticity always appears with the connotation of twist. To distort means to deform and is used in the compound of distorting truth, but usually it is a technical description.

In German, 'to twist' in the 'Bouwkundig Vertaalboek' is translated to: tordieren, verdrehen, verdrillen, verkrümmen, verwinden, ringen. These descriptions are technical in nature and, to a certain extent, have the same unpleasant connotation as the Dutch word. The French translations are: tordre, torquêre. Torquêre means to turn, to turn around, to torture. The association with the notion to torture is particularly interesting: tying up and strangling with a powerful and unavoidable turn enlivens the image of twisting. How could an executioner carry out a proper investigation without a thumbscrew?

In the well-known dance of the sixties, 'the twist', various sections of the body turned on the longitudinal axis. The partners' body positions and time of twisting were synchronous, but they did not touch each other. [1-20] It was the dance of the young, free-

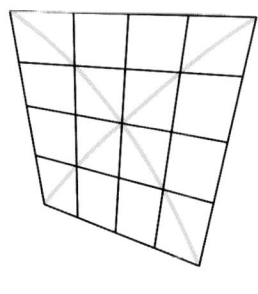

ing themselves from conventions and, certainly in their view, it had a positive connotation. The dance, as well as architecture, deals with the laws of gravitation in a light-hearted manner. One might well expect that ballet and dance, as a staging of movement and the interaction of bodies, together with the additional twisting, will acquire an increasing number of shape parallels in architecture.

The 'twist' – the extra effect that turning the surface adds to visual experience – is partly due to the apparent greater depth. A flat surface may be regarded as a surface formed by the shift of a straight line. In a twisted surface a turn has been added to this shift through which perspective distortions seem to occur: there is not one vanishing point on the horizon to which, as in a common façade, all horizontal straight lines are directed. The resulting alienation in perspective experience is probably one of the reasons why the connotation 'twisting the truth' was given to the term 'twisting'.

Within the twisted surface itself, visual effects occur which suggest distortion of a normal building: the corners seem to be drawn away from each other or, on the contrary, to be pushed towards each other. In the visual experience, such a surface may, therefore, express compression as well as expansion, or indeed both at the same time, for instance in a hypar where the one diagonal is concave and the other is convex. Both associations are evoked by the same manipulation. The intensity of the experience depends on the degree of twisting. It can be read from the diagonals: if one is slightly curved it may be a 'tasty' twist, but if it is too strongly curved, the shape may seem threatening. The surface may then 'squeeze' the space or be transformed in such a way that it almost 'cracks', or is about to 'burst open'.

The examples of torsions around us are countless. In many houses with a spiral staircase, the bottom of the stairs is plastered into a twisted ceiling. The phenomenon twisting is not limited to a man-made environment, but is part of nature as well. The geometrical shape, for instance, can be found in the bearer of the genetic characteristics, the DNA molecule. Bridging connections maintain two twisted 'shapes' (helices), coupled to each other. In phthalocyanine, individual molecules stack up spontaneously (in this case to the right, a Z-twist, as opposed to an S-twist) and form a kind of corkscrew stair of their own accord. The steps search for each other and form short, twisted little fibres, one-thousandth of a millimetre in length. Such stairs are built up from flat, circular molecules that can be stacked easily. They seem to be useful in their application in

Twisting person

  (Chubby Checker)

Many vanishing points in

  twisted tower perspective

  (Karel Vollers)

Diagonals curved in

  opposite directions

hair gel, in materials with an unusual optical appearance or for the stabilization of unstable elements, for instance to 'imprison' more volatile molecules in empty cavities of their structure. Such applications of twisted surfaces are just as unexpected and diverse as the ones in architecture.

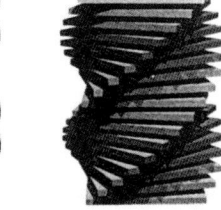

Montana perfume   *DNA molecule   Pile of books*

There are many everyday examples: in shops, books or cans are sometimes stacked to form a helicoid, resembling a model of a twisted tower. In the Netherlands, the 'wokkel' is the popular name for this rotating shape. The name is derived from the brand name of a Dutch savoury snack. The name became popular when an advertising campaign for a spiral crisp coincided with the propulsion into space of the Dutch astronaut W. Ockels. The 'wokkel' became the household name for a rotating shape. In this study the 'wokkel' shape is given a more international name: 'twister'.

Some types of macaroni are 'twisters'. Because of their shape, the pieces hardly touch each other and, they are less inclined to stick together. Also, the larger surface provides more hold for the sauce. Geometry like this can also be applied in architecture: twisters, which are close together, can be mutually positioned in such a way that they combine a large outside surface (light and air entries) with high density and variations in view.

The twister usually has an equal, roughly rectangular cross-section all over its longitudinal axis. A screw bolt, on the other hand, has a roughly round diameter with a notch for the thread. With a tapering screw, often a twisted shape, the diameter decreases to a single point. The screw enters the material because it forces itself in by means of rotation; in addition, the profile produces a high pull out resistance. These physical qualities of consumer items may well be associated with the building, if such shapes are used in architecture.

When buttering bread, the movement of the knife will often leave a twisted impression because of the motion of the wrist. Twisting as a movement can also be seen when a baby tries to turn over. It turns the upper body, but leaves the lower body lying because it does not yet have sufficient strength or coordination to steer the muscles. [1-21] The child wishes to do something, reaches out for something and twists the body in its length.

Brazilian girls with 'dental floss' bikinis

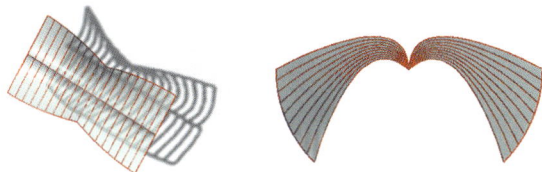

Associative geometry: twisted surface with repetition of curves (see Chapter 4)

In consumer items, the tactile qualities of the shape - the invitation to touch it physically and 'with the eye' invoked by sensual associations - will often instigate the application of twisted surfaces. A twisted object is in contact with its surroundings. They may in fact have been the cause of twisting, or reacting to it. When caressing someone's body, following a 'straight' or a curved line, one would not do justice to the 'feeling' if one did not allow one's hand to turn with the curve of the stroked body: most of the hand would end up floating in the air. Since geometry creates certain associations, the term 'associative geometry' is useful. When drawing with the computer, the meaning of this term is different: 'a system that consists of geometry and parameter objects, that can be formed into dependency relations' (see Chapter 5).

The described experiences are important. The naturalistic comparison is a major means of communicating about the meaning of curved shapes. Likewise, architecture often deals with sentiments or personal experiences. The naturalistic comparison therefore is a considerable source of inspiration when designing. If architects avoid the associations with nature, this enforces a variation in the established language of shape. As a starting point for design, the deviation implies naturalistic shape. In the course of time, as people get used to archetypical shapes, like cubes or spheres, new predominant connotations may arise. They will always be related to the way people experience shapes.

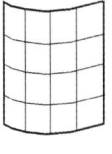 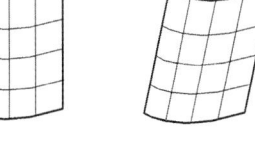 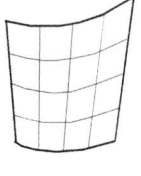 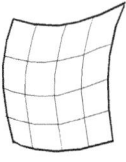

Curve   *Inclined and single-curved*   *Twisted*   *Freely double-curved*

DEVELOPMENTS IN INDUSTRY

APPROXIMATING ALTERNATIVES IN TWISTED FAÇADES

As far as production complexity is concerned, twisted surfaces can be positioned in-between developable and double-curved surfaces. With their rules they connect to single-curved surfaces. At the same time, because of the additional turning of these rules, they show similarities with freely double-curved surfaces. When applying a window frame system, twisted and double-curved surfaces both have mullions and transoms coming together from three directions at ever changing angles. In addition glass sheets, in the length of transoms and mullions, meet the profiles under a varying angle of incidence. This also holds true for single-curved surfaces, of which the straight lines meet orthogonal building structures under varying angles of incidence e.g. when cylindrical façades are sloping. Because the window pane must fit the profile at a varying angle, it has to be twisted. At the outset of this research project, a window frame system for a twisted façade had not yet been developed, nor had anyone ever made twisted glass with window proportions. To date, only façade structures have been realized in which some of the constituent parts are straight, flat or unwindable. None of the systems applied so far offers a solution for connecting a building wall or column to a twisted surface, that is simple to produce.

Facetting as an alternative for 3D transformation

Quadrangular flat panels Neue Stats Galerie, Stuttgart (James Stirling)   *Quadrangular panels Metro-entrance, Paris*   *Triangular panels Guggenheim Museum, Bilbao (Frank Gehry)*

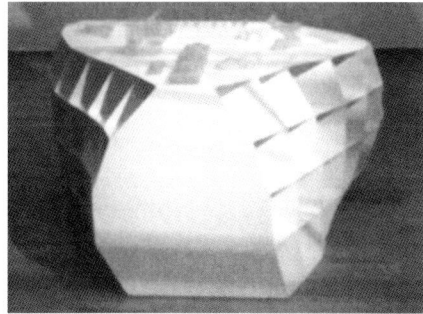

In the past, smooth ruled surfaces could only be made in concrete, steel or timber. *Gallery table (Greg Lynn)*
In glass they were to be approached by facetting with flat sheets. In facetting, many
variants are possible with flat or curved panels and with twisted panels too. With a
layered façade build-up, it is possible to economize by combining flat interior panels
with twisted exterior ones. If facetting is possible without deviating too much from
the really twisted version, this will be opted for because, so far, it is cheapest.

On many scales (doubly) curved surfaces are now approached by facetting, sometimes
as a canopy, sometimes as an entire building façade. Usually it is done with triangular
or quadrangular planar glass. Triangular sheets can always be connected to the
required shape. With quadrangular panels this is not always the case. A disadvantage
of the application of two triangular glass sheets is that together they have a considerably longer edge, than one quadrangular one. This can be the reason for merging two
triangles into a hypar shape, thus facetting a double-curved surface with ruled ones.
For an installation in the Henie Onstad Kunstsenter (Oslo, Norway) Greg Lynn in 1995
designed, a pedestal for models, which resembles a multi-story building. [1-22]
Its double-curved façades are facetted with straight lines that connect to walls and
floors. In contrast, the Guggenheim Museum consists mainly of hollow volumes.
The upright rules of its façades mostly do not connect up with the building structure
nor with internal walls. [1-23]

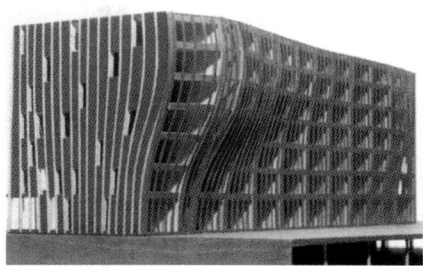

Appartment building, Almere, NL (R. van Zuuk, 1999-)

This appartment building has an orthogonal superstructure. The facades are double-
curved, but as the curvature is very big, they can be facetted with either planar or
hypar-shaped glass panels. As the mullions protrude from the surface, the difference

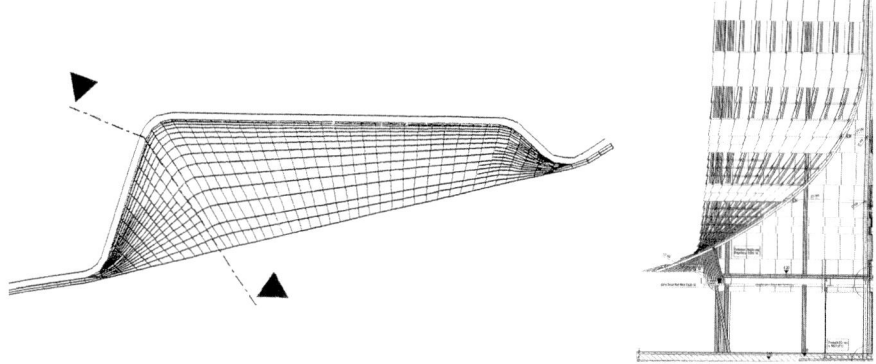

will probably not be perceivable.

When facetting, varying distances occur between adjacent quadrangular glass panels. There are several ways to solve this problem, for instance:

- Separating the glass sheets and leaving the joint open. By allowing the panels to overlap, natural drainage can be created.
- Applying a medium that compensates for the connection gaps, for instance a window frame with varying grooves.

In this design, produced by Octatube Space Structures in Delft, the Netherlands in 1998, a facetted double-curved shape was made from relatively small quadrangular flat glass sheets with photovoltaic cells. The joints were left open.

Flat glass panels and twisted profiles

Multimedia library at the Gambetta Square, Orleans (Lyon-du Besset)

In the bay window of the multimedia library in Orleans, France 1995, the cylindrical shape was approximated by means of facetting with triangular planar glass. The sheets can be coupled to flat bands between straight horizontal transoms. The mullions form buckled lines and have angled connections with the transoms. In order to make a continuous groove for the sheets, and line up the profiles smoothly on the inner side of the façade, they are twisted, though not sufficiently to connect them in true alignment. A rubbery sealing profile absorbs variations in connection between straight panel edges and twisted profiles. The bay window's horizontal borders connect to the building easily because they can remain straight. This system does not provide a solution for connecting partitioning walls to the twisted profiles inclining sideways.

Developable glass sheets and twisted profiles

Ford Research Centre, Aken,
Germany, 1998
(Carbonell-Figueras)
Façade construction by
Bellapart Engineering,
Barcelona, Spain

The curtain wall is an unwindable surface. [1-24] The transoms are horizontal. The bent glass meets the horizontal surface through the transoms, at varying angles of incidence. In order to make a constant connection, the curved transoms are slightly twisted. The angle of incidence varies so little, that twisting by hand was sufficient. The transoms have a glazing profile on the outside to prevent the panes from falling down. The aluminium mullions are straight. The differences caused by the varying angle of incidence of the glass along the mullion, are absorbed by a sealed joint. On the outside, the vertical seams between the panes are just sealed.

Twisted (metal) surfaces and twisted profiles

Waterland Neeltje Jans, Fresh water segment (Lars Spuybroek 1997). A thin corrugated metal plate was applied as the outside cladding of the freshwater section of exhibition pavilion Waterland Neeltje Jans, the Netherlands. By transforming the corrugation, it could be stretched and buckled in order to take on the twisted shape. The steel IPE profiles, functioning as roof girders, were sufficiently torsion-elastic to be transformed by hand. The profiles were bent in the required shape, just like a strip of paper. The differences from the developable surface to an actual twisted shape were acceptable here. The corrugated steel is supported by profiles. Therefore sideways bending of IPE profiles, due to non-absolute torsion, was compensated for by adding a small transformation to the cladding during assembly. When assembling prefabricated glass panes, trusses must be transformed more precisely, otherwise they won't fit.

Waterland Neeltje Jans,
Fresh water segment, NL
(Lars Spuybroek)

The choice between a twisting and facetting

There are several arguments for twisting:

- Optical perfection. With slight twisting, the difference to an approximation by facetting with small flat elements will hardly be perceivable. But a relatively large rotation, with rough facetting of flat surfaces, will be clearly visible. In that case twisting of plates will give a very smooth and perfect appearance. The qualitative assessment is closely connected to the required identifying image for clients: technical perfection with attention for detail, great skill in the application of materials (as a symbol for market control), and refinement in expressive design

- Optimum technical construction, because as far as production, sealing and connection tolerance are concerned, the various parts will connect accurately. This results in better control of measurement during production and assembly. Introduction of approximation tolerances because of facetting is unfavourable, because these will be added to production and assembly tolerances.

- Improved production technology. If production is based on exact dimensions, one intermediate stage in design can be omitted. Describing measuring routines is simpler if exact dimensions can be maintained. Not every part will have to be calculated and described separately.

- Smaller number of different connections. A simplification of the production of one part, e.g. the straightening of an element to make it easier to produce, often causes problems when executing 3D façades. Changes are discovered later in the building process. In non-orthogonal connections, changing a length or an angle has more far reaching implications than in rectilinear or flat elements: all elements are defined in three directions and have specific production problems

- Simple measuring. It is advantageous when for all elements only the 'reference dimensions' (the dimensions of an absolute twisted surface) have to be taken into account. This will increase the interchangeability of the adjacent elements and there is no cumulation of dimensional deviations in connections. When the geometry of one element deviates from the reference surface, adjacent elements must be adjusted and sometimes also those adjacent to them. Thus, each component acquires additional requirements that need to be checked when agreed connection tolerances would be exceeded because of changes in adjacent elements.

Should it be necessary to incur extra costs to produce a twisted façade, the mentioned arguments must offer sufficient additional value.

Twisted surfaces versus free double-curved
Twisted façade structures are expensive. Neither the glass, nor its frame is a common building product. Twisting of materials is, in fact, currently avoided. Twisting surfaces, however, is considerably easier than double-curving them, if the presence of rules in the surface can be used. A mold of straight bars can be made for the warm bending of glass at relatively low cost.

Theoretically, new factories can be built, specifically designed for producing double-curved glass sheets. Twisted glass sheets could also be produced there. However, this requires very steep investments. To optimize the final product, all connecting double-curved parts would also have to be produced according to new production methods. Important considerations for manufacturers for not having taken that step so far, are that necessary logistics, production and assembly methods are different from the current ones. Therefore, the necessary investments imply great risks. Market demand may indeed be latently present, but the probably long introductory period has to be bridged. Furthermore, insight into the money involveed and development trajectories is as yet insufficient.

MARKET DEMAND AND INVESTMENTS IN DEVELOPMENT

Here we have the good old chicken-and-egg problem. Many architects would love to build double-curved shapes, but cannot convert this wish into actual commissions for manufacturers because, prior to this research, these typical products, in particular glass and window frames, were not available on the market. Architects have to deliver on short notice, while building product prices must be guaranteed within limited bounds. Manufacturers will not state a cost price in advance for a double-curved façade part, with accurate details, due to uncertainty of the development trajectory. They calculate such high-risk surcharges in their quotes, that the resulting price is too high for potential consumers. Furthermore, because profits of twisted and double-curved elements will only occur in case of integral implementation, manufacturers of adjacent elements must enter the market simultaneously. If one kind of building components cannot yet be transformed, it will lead to facetted connections to twisted parts and thus to a less ideal (more expensive) product. It is harder to attach a flat glass sheet to a double-curved car body than a sheet that yields to the shape.

Directors of large glass manufacturing companies are selected for their managerial qualities but their training gives them insufficient insight into the architectural potential of double-curved façades. If others do not provide them with this knowledge, and there is no clear proven market demand, there is no reason for them to run risks by spending a lot of money on new developments. Generally they prefer to optimize the production of bulk products, and the quality and application of existing ones. In case of uncertainty, they will leave the development of new products to others, and later copy them, or apply for a licence when there is a proven market.

Particularly the far-reaching monopolization of the glass industry had a restraining influence on the development of new shapes in architecture. Parent companies have concentrated research effort and directed it towards optimizing material quality (reflection) and logistics. They present their subsidiary companies with sophisticated assured production methods. In their turn these subsidiary companies concentrate on marketing, processing and logistics, leaving the development of new products to the parent company.

The remaining, relatively small, independent companies usually only employ a few specialists with knowledge of material development. Guarding quality of already commissioned work and innovating products for which a requirement exists, leaves them little time for developing a new production line. Even if costs could remain low, further development into a well guaranteed product takes time, something they are often short of.

A computer-controlled production line of heat-strengthened double-curved glass is much more expensive to establish than an installation to warm and bend glass. Besides, the greater output of glass sheets with a tempering furnace implies specific logistics and marketing. Only when a production line is computerized, will the production costs decrease and become acceptable to an extended market. Until then, the market will remain small. This product's main advantage is that one can ask a high price, because of its exclusiveness.

Companies invest little in new glass technology, but lose large market shares because the general public has become bored with flat, reflecting façades. The importance of the capability to deliver double-curved glass is also underestimated. Often, only a small part of the façade will be double-curved and a large adjacent surface of planar glass can be sold in the same deal. Apparently, manufacturers prefer to lose a large market share to other façade materials, e.g. natural stone, concrete or brick parapets, rather than incur expenses for a product for which demand is uncertain in advance.

By structurally glazing a double-curved façade, the development of window frames or concrete panels can be omitted. Therefore this would seem to be a time-saving step. In addition to the advantage of transparency, frameless glazing has the disadvantage of a poor connection to fire-resistant or sound-proof walls.

Each of the façade elements has specific advantages, such as wind and water-proofing or making opening parts. Moreover, by including window frames, it is possible to use a different type of glass that is easier to transform: annealed (warm bent) glass. The investments for the production of bent glass are considerably lower than for heat-strengthened bent glass. With this material the market can be tested at low costs and will probably take off. Later, bent glass may well provide a market share of its own. Furthermore, laminated annealed glass, has explicit advantages, particularly when applied to inclined surfaces. Disadvantages are high chances of breaking through unequal solar heating and low assembly tolerances.

'Science is looking at reality with interest and wonder, whether it is realistic or fictive.' dr. Mathijs Prins, TU Delft 1999

THE RESEARCH PROJECT

The objective of this project was to acquire insight into the feasibility of twisted constructions in the building industry. For this purpose a metaphorical framework that unites architectural and technological studies, was needed. In order to test the results, a real framework was aimed at, consisting of an industrially produced twisted window frame with twisted glass.

Transformation possibilities were described on various scales, and simultaneously the chances for integral applications in building models and components were examined. Neither the ultimate goals, nor the conditions the designs had to meet, were fixed.

Making twisted surfaces is elucidated from the perspective of a development in architecture from flat surfaces to freely double-curved surfaces. In line with this, the details and production of twisted façade elements are developed as an intermediate step towards the development of double-curved elements.

CONTEXT	OBJECT	
	Determined	Variable
Determined	Design Research	Studying Design
Variable	Typological research	Designing Study

The study followed specific trajectories for the separate products. No time-limit was set; the only objective was the final product. Time, in the current building process, is hardly ever abundant for designers and manufacturers. Since the author was largely footing the bill, there was nobody to stop the process, for reasons of an exceeded time-limit. The author's financial independence, which he himself considers an economic anomaly, saw to it that no participant sub-interests would send him in an undesired direction. Because the author bore the largest part of the coordination investments, the costs for participating parties were relatively low in the beginning. This was an important condition for them to participate in developing entirely new products. Having to earn the money to keep the project going, considerably delayed the process.

After preliminary research, the study was divided into four parts (CAD-CAM, Concrete, Window framing system, Glass). Four teams were formed, and coordinated by the author during the initial stages. This implied that during preliminary investigations not all uncertainties were known to all participants, who therefore could not be put off by them. It also meant that the author was continuously at the centre of activities, and that he was the only one who knew everything. In the course of events the coordination was delegated to, and in a natural way taken over by the participants. This was in line with the intention to make the participants responsible for the developments in their respective field of study, because they were the ones who had to introduce the products onto the market.

Industry has limited knowledge of complex three-dimensional measuring of twisted constructions. They meet today's market demand and, with regard to geometrical transformation, this is not very complex yet. For this reason the author provided the industries with the measuring data of the various components, often with indications for the transformation of materials - at hand or yet to be developed – and development schedules.

In contrast to the great freedom in his research, the author integrated sub-studies into concrete results (feasible building models) at the end of various development stages. This helped him to keep his feet on the ground. It also kept the industries interested. Every time plans surpassed the expectations of industries, they lost interest and everything came to a standstill. Initially, when the author worked on one subject, for example geometry, other themes were put on hold (for example the design of the mold for the glass). It took a few years for the process to gain momentum. The participants wanted to exploit their investments. Their activity will increase with market demand.

To test the market and stimulate the use by architects, it is advantageous to show a prototype of a twisted window frame with glass, even if it is not yet suitable for all applications. Optimizing production and quality, as well as addition of other components will follow automatically.

To be able to coordinate and integrate the developments in sub-fields, much specialist knowledge was acquired but, due to the broadness of the working field, neither in-depth theoretical foundation, nor completeness was the aim.

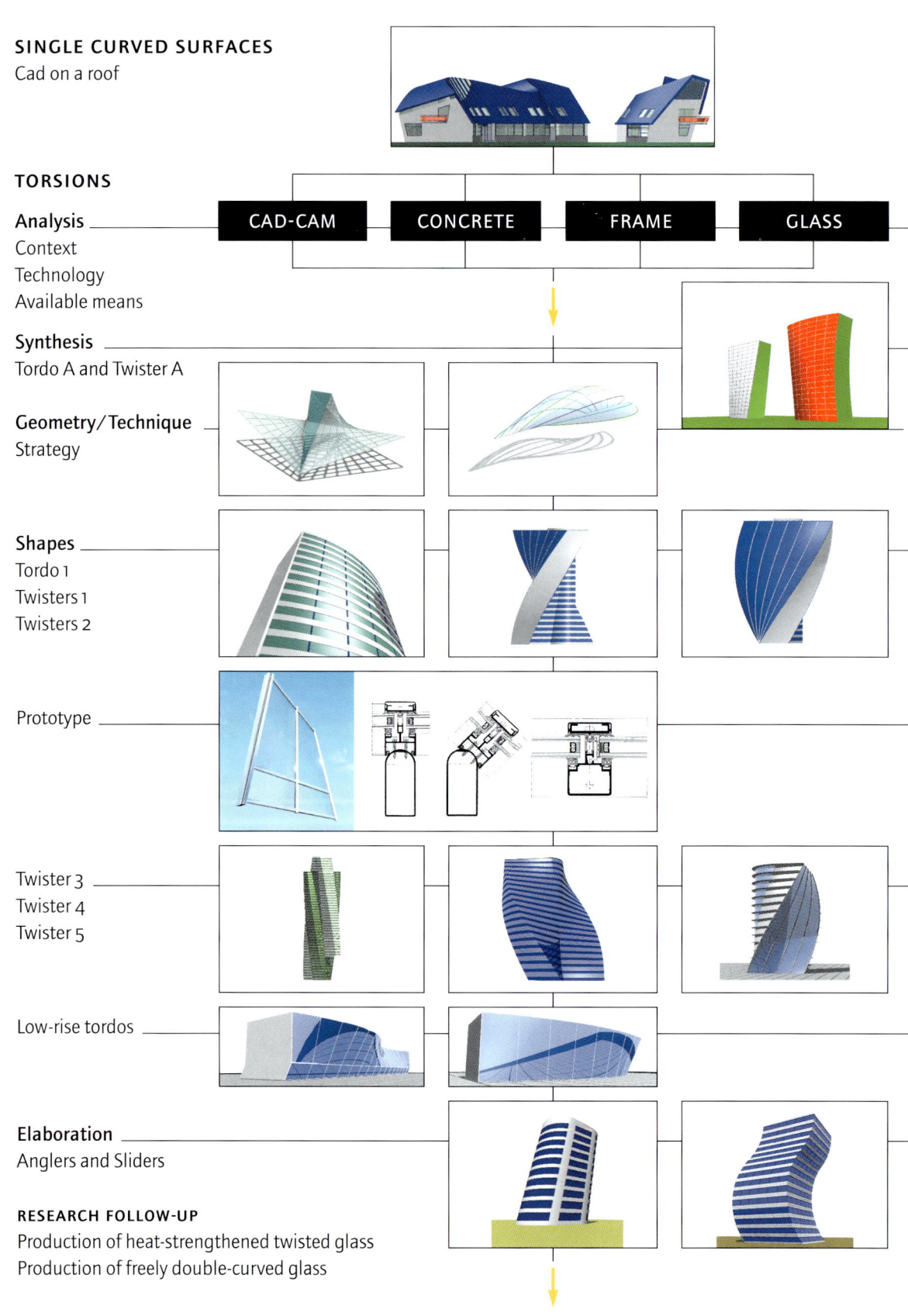

SINGLE CURVED SURFACES
Cad on a roof

TORSIONS

Analysis
Context
Technology
Available means

| CAD-CAM | CONCRETE | FRAME | GLASS |

Synthesis
Tordo A and Twister A

Geometry/Technique
Strategy

Shapes
Tordo 1
Twisters 1
Twisters 2

Prototype

Twister 3
Twister 4
Twister 5

Low-rise tordos

Elaboration
Anglers and Sliders

RESEARCH FOLLOW-UP
Production of heat-strengthened twisted glass
Production of freely double-curved glass

PHASING OF THE RESEARCH

SINGLE CURVED LINES AND SURFACES
Preliminary research
Study of geometry resulted in a housing model and the elaboration of its construction.
Selection and purchase of hardware and software.

TORSIONS
Analysis
Description of motivation and objectives.
Inventory of the use of torsion in architecture and other fields of science.
Analysis of geometry, and technical problems of drawing.
Synthesis
Typological scheme for twisted surfaces.
- Plan on how to direct industrial developments.
- Initiation of teams to innovate the various products.
- Design of pilot building models Tordo A and Twister A.
Elaboration of geometry
Design of shape classification scheme, based on icons.
Technique
Industrial co-operations were initiated.
Shapes
Prototype 0 *Production of a large, hot molded, slightly twisted glass sheet and aluminium profiles. Subsequently another singular glass panel was produced and fitted into the assembled Twist window frame.*

Building model Tordo 1 *As the feasibility of twisting the building components had not been proved yet, for all parts the option was left open to make them straight or flat.*

Building models Twisters 1 and 2 *To demonstrate use for the produced twisted building parts, Twister 1 and 2 were designed. They feature larger series of façade elements than Tordo 1, and their panels are twisted stronger.*

Prototype 1 *This window frame is fitted with four hot molded glass sheets and the Twist framing system.*

Building model Twister 3 *To simplify production, and lower the costs, a higher building model 3 was designed with even more repetition, but with a smaller torsion per element than Twisters 1 and 2.*

Prototype 2 *Mock-up of façade of Twister 3 with heat-strengthened glass sheets and cold-bent window frames.*

Building model Twisters 4 and 5 *A more complex building shape (built of twisted and cylindrical surfaces) is combined with a mirror symmetrical structure.*

Low-rise tordos *Featuring small series of elements, they show the reflections of the various kinds of twisted facades.*

Elaboration of new applications
'Anglers' and 'Sliders'. Elaborating usage of new products: twisted window profiles. New kinds of buildings can be realized with for example cylindrical façades.

RESEARCH FOLLOW-UP
Improving production of warm transformed twisted glass. Developing heat-strengthened twisted and freely double-curved glass.

02

FRAME OF REFERENCE

'Frame of reference' is an inventory of the use of ruled surfaces in the arts and in architecture. In various fields, the phenomenon of twisting has been studied and applied simultaneously. These may be artistic disciplines like jewelry design, ceramics, sculpture, music, painting, virtual media, but also technically oriented fields, like the shipping and car industry. Sometimes the developments in a field show a clear sequence, sometimes they are parallel to or alternating with others. In the following text, a great diversity in the use of twisted surfaces is shown. Many more interesting projects with ruled surfaces have been erected all over the world. They are not contained in this inventory, due to shortage of time and limited available information.

Some applications were provided with a short explanation of geometrical and/or architectural properties. To avoid repetition several aspects were given specific names.

RULED SURFACES IN THE ARTS

'Tea-time' and detail,
Jean Metzinger

Several cubist painters portray twisted surfaces, (Georges Braque in 'Summer', 1908, Pablo Picasso in 'Reservoir at Horta de Ebro, 1909, Jean Metzinger in Tea-time, 1911) but they are not indicating an awareness of a specific surface type. Probably they did not wish to make their already complex images, that united various views in one image, even more difficult to interpret by applying unusual kinds of surfaces.

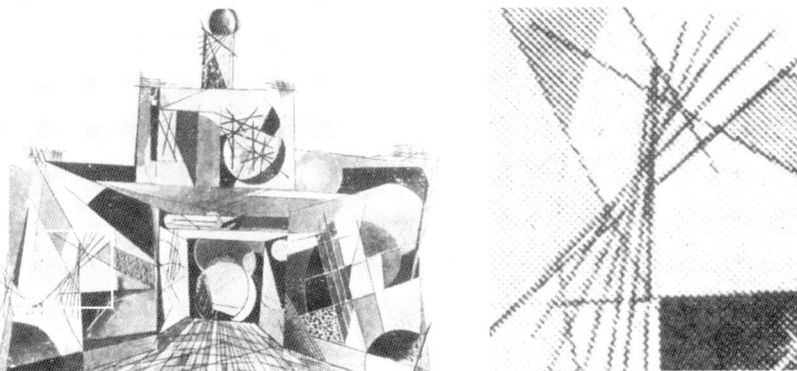

Project Palace of Labour, with detail from the drawing, 1919 (Alexandre Rodtchenko)

In 1920 Russian Constructivists proclaimed that space is not determined by volume, that spatial effects cannot be represented by massive shapes and that works of art are based on dynamic rhythms. [2-1] In their vision, perspectives of ruled surfaces, where rules or lines disappeared behind each other through rotation and translation, reflected movement and space better than, for instance, the literally moving space in Calder's works of art. [2-2] Like the Futurists, they thought it necessary to express in their work the latest insights in technical and scientific developments. They didn't want to turn away from nature, but instead were eager to use ruled surfaces for reflecting the forces that shape natural forms and in this way realize new physical events. The essence of life was approached through abstractions. In this process life and mathematical laws do not exclude each other; they are interwoven. Growth and form are inseparable. They always depend on the same regularities. The shape of an aeroplane is no less natural than that of an egg. Although referring to the regularities in nature, they worked intuitively. In this way natural life would be expressed more purely than naturalistic art could ever do. [2-3]

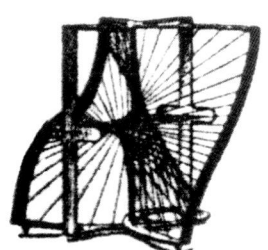
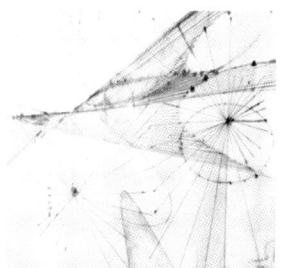
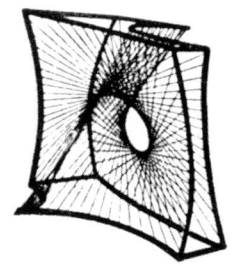

From 1936 onward the Constructivist Antoine Pevsner designed sculptures with ruled surfaces. Just like, for instance, Henry Moore and Barbara Hepworth, he concentrated for a while on the relationship between fields of wires (that reflected transparent ruled surfaces), and double-curved volumes. In doing so, he anticipated the application of this geometry in architecture. This drawing from 1934 suggests twisted surfaces of which the ends connect to geometrical figures like (parts of) circles and ellipses. The 'Construction for an airport' of 1935 is composed of flat surfaces, but shows striking similarities with the line pattern of ruled surfaces.

Mathematical model, Katalog 1892

Naissance de l'Universe, 1933 (Antoine Pevsner)

Mathematical model Institut Poincaré, Paris

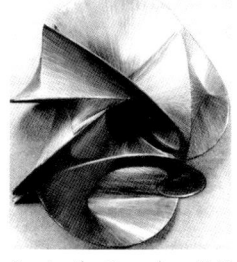
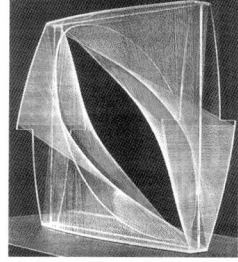
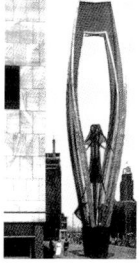

Construction Dynamique, 1947 (Antoine Pevsner)

Linear Construction no. 1, Variation, 1942-43 (Naum Gabo)

Sculpture: Bijenkorf, 1957 (Naum Gabo)

The wire models must have been a revelation to Naum Gabo. Their patterns gave rise to a combination of associations: techniques, nature and sensual aspects. They linked up perfectly to what he had tried to express in the preceding years. Since 1936 he showed his perception of space in models that were characterized by a great transparency and interaction of parts. The surfaces were defined by a succession of lines. Instead of enclosing space with intersecting planes, he avoided fixed angles between surfaces and transformed them to blend into one another. A reversal of inside and outside occurs, as in the Möbius ring. He wanted to show continuity and life, rather than infinity. Dutch art historian Pierre Janssen on Gabo: 'We search and grope in space, like Naum Gabo in thin nylon threads that are light and emptiness, suggesting nothing and yet having a life of their own'. [2-4]

The structure of Gabo's sculpture outside the Bijenkorf Store in Rotterdam, the Netherlands is inspired by trees and their growth. At the corners steel tubes with a square section twist 90°. The architectural scale of this object, produced in steel and concrete, is deliberate.

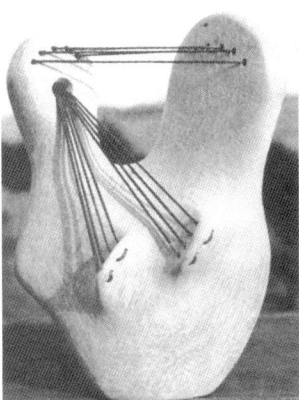

Mother and child, 1938

(Henri Moore)

In 1936 Henry Moore participated in the International Exhibition of Surrealism in London. From 1937 onwards he worked for 'Circle', a magazine published by J.L. Martin, Ben Nicholson and Naum Gabo. Historian Erich Neumann wrote the following about Henri Moore's work: While the similarity of the Great Mother figure to the neolithic figures from France is certainly striking, Moore goes beyond the archetypical pattern by providing the overarching mother figure with a child. In spite of its independence, the child remains intimately connected with the mother. The crossbeam joining the two is an expression of the indissoluble unity that has always preoccupied Moore. The separate masses of material are joined to one and another by the interconnecting strings in such a way that the living current of relationship becomes visible, and psychological truth becomes concrete fact. The streams connecting the child's eyes with those of the mother are like ghostly, spiritual bridges, immaterial yet visible. They form the upper horizontals of the structure. Simultaneously a current of desire, like lines of force, streams from the mouth of the child to the mother's breasts, whose incorporal yet dynamic presence sets up the diagonal connection that puts life into the conjoined masses of mother and child. [2-5]

Delphi, 1955 (B. Hepworth)   *Bryher II, 1961 (B. Hepworth)*

In the sculpture 'Delphi' by Barbara Hepworth, a volume with a chestnut coloured exterior has a fine wire mesh connecting the pale inner surfaces. An open and a closed shape are interrelated. The mesh catches the attention like a web and then leads it to the volume around it. In 'Bryher II', the wires connect the contours of the two sides. Two 'transparent' surfaces, a perforated and a stringed one, combine. [2-6]

In the forties, Lippold made installations with structures of shining wires: 'weightless' sculptures that flooded the space. They now seem forerunners of the spatial figures that are created with laser beams, although because of the used prisms, the latter are in fact cones, not ruled surfaces.

Installation: Flight, 1962

(R. Lippold)

Mathematical models increasingly take part in our understanding of reality. The lower and upper surface of the ring of Möbius blend together by twisting the strip. Escher combined mathematical reasoning with great skill and craftsmanship. With his typical use of relativities, convex lenses, perspective variations, gliding reflections and rhythmical repetitions, he unsettled the world as we know it. Most of his work is about the admiration for the regularities that the space around us holds. He was amazed that only few people, if any, were struck in the same way he was, by what they saw around them, however objective or impersonal most of his subjects seemed to him. [2-7]

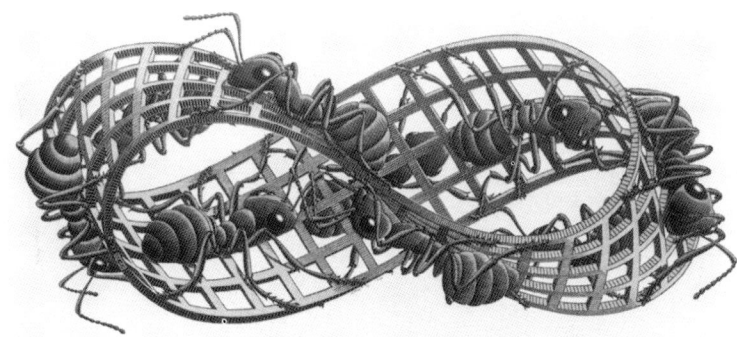

Woodcut: Ring of Möbius II, 1963, (M.C. Escher)

RULED SURFACES IN ARCHITECTURE

In this description the applications of twisted surfaces are grouped according to their geometrical composition. Some designs look 'technical', because of a proud display of geometry, structure and material optimization. Their overall shape is clearly defined and the structural parts, after assembly, determine the final image. The newly generated forms by their pronounced contours and unusual slender constructions, have a modern appearance. It is art by engineers. Other designs look 'free-associative'. Also developed with great skill, these are often composed of many differently transformed surfaces and many different materials. Their images evoke a great number of associations, of which the naturalist ones are predominant. The materials support this classification: concrete, often painted white and showing the straight lining of shuttering, looks more 'technical' than warm-coloured finely facetted masonry. In the seemingly simple geometry of concrete vaults, the 'rules' are often easy to recognize. In contrast, masonry or cladding with stone or metal panels, is often applied to create complex transformed surfaces of a smaller scale. As the notion 'free-associative' or 'technical' is subjective and generic, the division in this inventory was based on geometry, not on materials.

The tools available when drawing with the computer, may be taken as a basis to distinguish building components and volumes. Some manipulations induce archetypal building shapes. This study concentrates on ruled surfaces, the twisted shapes based on 'shifting' and 'rotating' a straight line, but some shapes that evolve from only 'shifting' a figure along inclined straight and curved lines, are shown as well. They are called 'extruders' and feature many similarities with volumes with ruled surfaces. Spheres result from 'rotating'. They are sufficiently well known not to be elaborated here.
In the scheme, surfaces that do not connect with rules to an orthogonal grid, received the adjective 'free'. When a conoid connects with its rules to an orthogonal grid, it is given the adjective 'ortho', and if a hypar does, it is named 'tordo'. If a building has planar and one or more ortho-hypar shaped façades, it is called a 'tordo' too.

The inventory of the use of ruled surfaces in architecture starts with non-enveloping building parts (for example: balustrades, columns). Subsequently flexible surfaces and building volumes are shown.

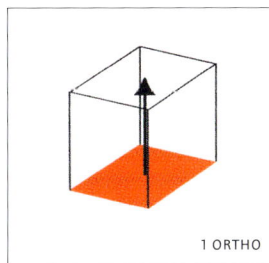

1 ORTHO

2 ANGLER

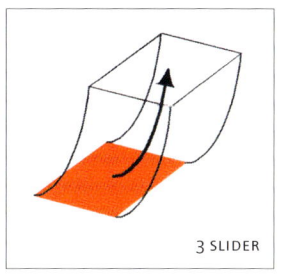

3 SLIDER

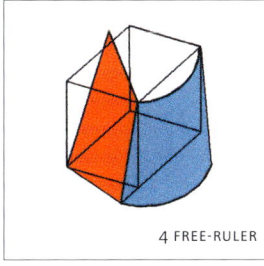

4 FREE-RULER

5 ORTHO-RULER

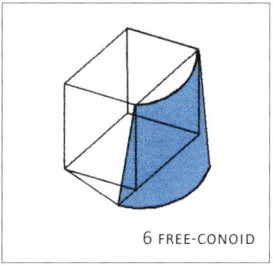

6 FREE-CONOID

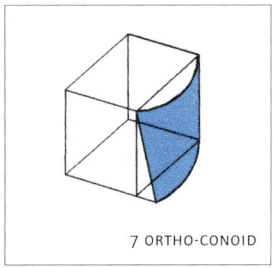

7 ORTHO-CONOID

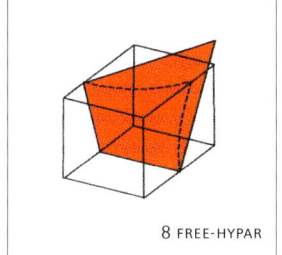

8 FREE-HYPAR

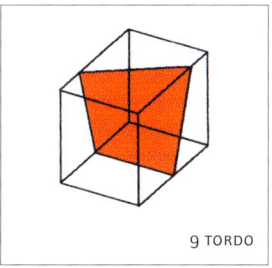

9 TORDO

10 TWISTERS

11 ROTO-TWISTER

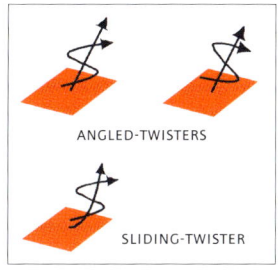

ANGLED-TWISTERS

SLIDING-TWISTER

The following (building) volumes are distinguished and their features noted:

MIXERS

various kinds of surfaces (single- or double-curved)

EXTRUDERS

1 ORTHO *drawn by shifting ground plans along a vertical line*

2 ANGLER *ditto, along an inclined straight line*

3 SLIDER *ditto, along a 2D curve*

RULERS

4 FREE-RULER *with ruled surfaces (conoid and hypar)*

5 ORTHO-RULER *ditto, of which some connect with their rules to an orthogonal grid*

6 FREE-CONOID *one or more conoids, of which at least one does not connect with rules to an orthogonal grid*

7 ORTHO-CONOID *ditto, of which all connect with rules to an orthogonal grid*

8 FREE-HYPAR *one or more hypars, of which at least one does not connect with rules to an orthogonal grid*

9 TORDO *one or more hypars, of which all connect with rules to an orthogonal grid*

10 TWISTERS *a repetition of twisted façade elements in vertical direction*

11 ROTO-TWISTER *a repetition of twisted façade elements in horizontal direction, while floor plans differ on each level*

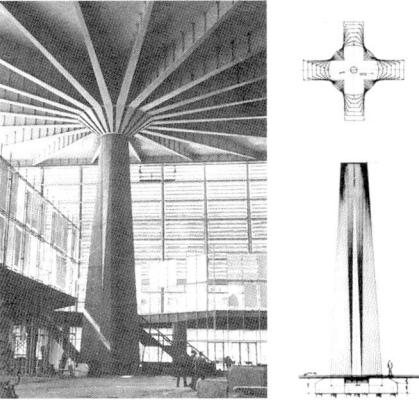

Column with varying diameter,
1961 (P.L. Nervi)

Soliton Gate, 1993
(C. Jencks)

TWISTED NON-ENVELOPING BUILDING PARTS

Many columns and vaults in the Sagrada Familia, Barcelona, (1883-), have been constructed with ruled surfaces. By for example connecting different cross-sections of a column with straight lines, fluent transitions in its shape result. In a similar way, the shape is defined of the 20 metres high concrete columns in the Palace of Labour, built in Turin for the Italia '61 Exhibition in 1961. Straight lines connecting the cross-shaped base to a circular top, result in conoid sides. The shaping reflects the flow of stresses. The column is rigidly connected to the foundation.

Sinuous balustrade, 1972 (O. Niemeyer)

The Oscar Niemeyer Cultural Centre is located at the head of a windy harbour in Le Havre, France; the entrance and an adjoining shopping area are recessed in a vast concrete plaza. The Centre offers a sheltered area below street level. Like a lazy whirl wind, a balustrade composed of twisted surfaces twirls downwards with the ramp.
In the Soliton gate fossyles on the edges with a field of twisted steel strips, resemble waves rippling around stones in shallow water. 2-8

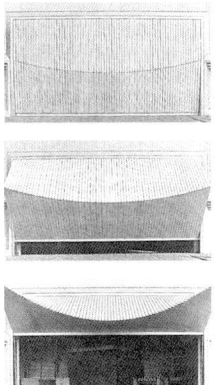

FLEXIBLE ORTHO-RULED SURFACES

A twisted surface can be made by interconnecting linear elements. As soon as the linear elements obtain a width, like a lamella, a facetted approximation of a twisted surface will result. The shape may remain variable by leaving the joints entirely open or by making the joints flexible, for instance with sealant.

The architect/engineer Santiago Calatrava has designed various building elements that can be transformed in an unusual manner. Because of the curved groove straight through the lamelle, flat expedition doors of Emsting Warehouse can transform into a twisted canopy. He also designed fan-like roofs that can change shape. 2-9

Canopy/door, respectively in opened and closed position, Emsting Warehouse, Coesfeld, Germany 1983-1985

FREE AND ORTHO-CONOIDS

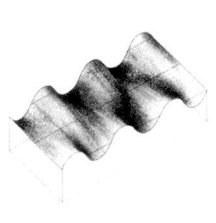
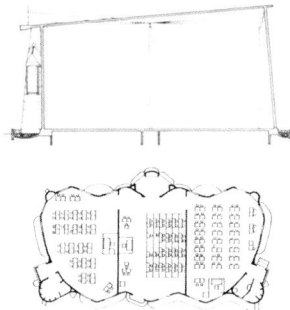

School at Sagrada Familia Cathedral, Barcelona, Spain, 1909-1910 (Gaudí)

The classic example of early applications of twisted surfaces in architecture can be found in Barcelona, Spain. The roof is composed of straight beams, that rest on a steel girder in the middle and at the ends on walls. The sine shaped beam-ends differ in height at one side of the building, and the other beam-ends have the same shape, but are shifted half a wavelength. The roof is an 'ortho-conoid' because of the connection with an orthogonal ground plan. The external brick walls are also sinuous and twisted. Due to the curving of the relatively thin surfaces, the building is very stable. It features several kinds of surfaces, and therefore is classified as a 'mixer'. 2-10

Living quarters, Lambertsville,
New Yersey, US, 1960
(Jules Gregory)

The sinuous roof of Gaudís' school became an archetype in architecture, and was copied in the living quarters designed by Jules Gregory (US) and in the Nederlands Dans Theater in Den Haag, 1977, by O.M.A., NL. The roof of the latter was constructed of corrugated steel that by its profiling, allowed the surface to be compressed or lengthened to allow surface twisting.

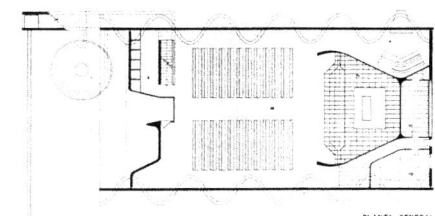

PLANTA GENERAL

Parish church Atlantida (Uruguay), 1958 (Eladio Dieste)

Eladio Dieste made use of locally available cheap labour and materials, and developed vaulted structures of reinforced bricks. In the past bricks were only used for structures under compression: walls, columns or domes. By applying internal reinforcement he made the bricks also suitable for structures under tension, like he did in this church with its many joints and finely faceted double-curved surfaces. The quality of the natural light is also due to the floodlight along the self-supporting twisted walls and double-curved vaulted roofs. By applying the same material everywhere, even the smallest parts become part of the whole. The building has a rectangular structure with six naves. The double-curved vaulted roof and the conoidal wall surfaces are equal each time. The walls are 'ortho-conoid' but, due to the double curving of the roofs, the building as a whole, is a 'mixer'. 2-11

FREE-HYPARS AND TORDOS
Free hypars and tordos as building volumes
Hypars (hyperbolic paraboloid surfaces) have rules in two directions and are therefore easier to define and produce than twisted surfaces with rules in only one direction. **Tordos** are hypars that connect to an orthogonal building structure. **Free-hypars** feature rules rotating in two directions.

Entrance canopy,
UNESCO building, Paris,
1953-1958, (M. Breuer
in cooperation with P.L. Nervi)

Free-hypars and tordos as architectural elements
Often architects applied the new techniques in small projects like entrance canopies and bell towers. Their modern appearance, sometimes frivolous, often contrasted with large adjacent rectangular building volumes.
The side contours of the entrance canopy at the UNESCO building in Paris are straight, coinciding with the rules of a hyperboidal (hypar) surface.

Bell tower of the Mary
College, 1954-1963,
(M. Breuer)

Bell tower Pius VI Church

At the bell tower of the Mary College in Bismarck, North Dakota, USA, a flat surface serves as a background for two ruled surfaces, placed against each other, out of which a cross has been cut. [2-12] The Pius VI Church in Zaventem, Belgium is located at a T-junction. Each of the four concrete slabs makes a 45° twist. The top of the tower is parallel to the through road and visually 'blocks' the linking road. At the base the tower opens up in four directions, leaving space for a canopy to be suspended between the slabs. It covers the entrance path.

Le Poème Électronique,
the Philips pavilion at the
World Fair of 1958,
Brussels, Belgium, designed
by Le Corbusier-Xenakis

'Le Poème Électronique' is a **free-hypar**. The hypars were assembled from concrete prefabricated elements. Each shell has been measured out on a banking of sand, after which it was divided into small elements by planks. The elements, cast one by one, were numbered and then transported to the building-site. On the outside the shells have been covered with water tight foil. They were assembled on a temporary wooden structure. Steel cables, applied to both sides of the shells, provided external reinforcement. Charles Jencks on the straight lines and distorted grids in this pavilion: 'We are accustomed to an orthogonal building resulting from these elements, so when we see them twisted the result looks like a building that has collapsed. In fact the hyperbolic paraboloid is a strong structural shape. Thus a double form of 'oxymoron' is produced: 'safe/unsafe', 'orthogonal/curved'.

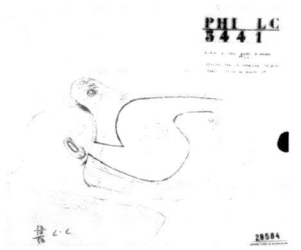

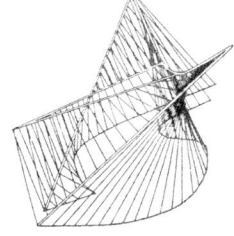

The ground plan as a stomach   *Perspective*   *Assembly Hall, Chandigarh, India*

The peaks in the roof of the 'Poème Électronique', opposite the entrance, are elements typical of the 'atom style' of the Fifties. They refer to the trails of ice-particles behind comets and the orbiting of sputniks, symbolising the expectation of technological progress. The narrowing of the entrance and exit connects up with accentuations in height. The ground plan looks like a cross-section of a 'stomach' where great numbers of visitors are supplied, processed and discharged. Prior to the Philips Pavilion, Xenakis in 1951 had designed the hyperboloidal shape on top of the Assembly Hall in Chandigarh, India. 2-13 It was based on that of a cooling tower.

  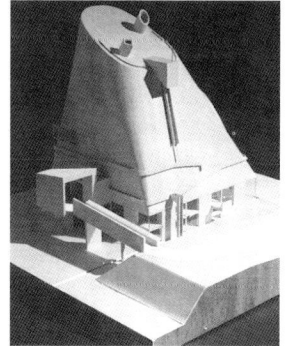

Le Corbusier made his first sketches for the church in Firminy in 1961; the construction was abandoned by the end of the Seventies. He regarded the conoid building shape as next in line to the sequence pyramid – cube – sphere. [2-14]

Study model, wire (rule) model

Wire model as a volume
with twisted surfaces

The final model,
Church in Firminy, France,
(Le Corbusier)

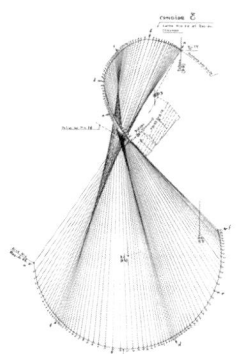

Polytope Beaubourg, Paris, France 1974-1975

The theme of conoidal shapes reappeared in the later designs of 'polytopes' by Xenakis, e.g. the 'Utopian project for 'cosmic' cities', 5 kilometres in height (1965) [2-15], the 'Polytope Beaubourg' in Paris, France and a pavilion at the Expo 1967 in Montreal, Canada.

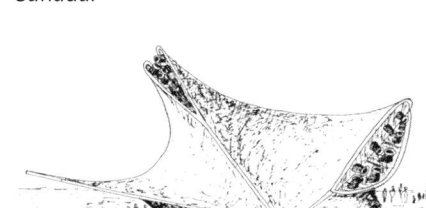 

Villes Cosmiques, 1965   *Polytope, Expo 1967, Montreal, Canada*

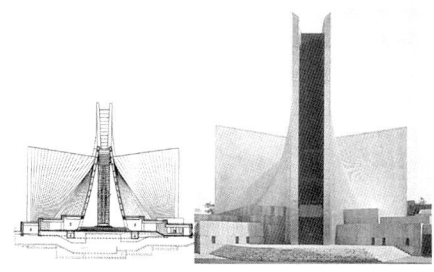

Saint Mary Cathedral,
Tokyo, Japan, 1961-1964,
(Kenzo Tange)

Saint Mary Cathedral,
San Francisco, USA, 1966-1971,
(P.L. Nervi, in cooperation with
P. Belluschi)

The walls, composed of eight hypars, twist from a kite-shaped ground plan up to a crucifix of light. In the interior the concrete of the walls remains visible; the outsides of the walls are dressed with stainless steel. Shape and function are one: place to gather, the internal space of the nave, soars up into an icon of faith: the cross of light. Two different figures are flowingly connected (with 'rule morphing'), and so are the meanings of these figures. The pylon-like vertical ends, that are reminiscent of both Torii fences and the vertical accentuations in Gothic cathedrals, miraculously turn into walls and roof. Strikingly identical to the design of Kenzo Tange is the Saint Mary Church in San Francisco, USA, designed by Nervi and Belluchi. This building has a more accentuated roof profile than Tange's cathedral.

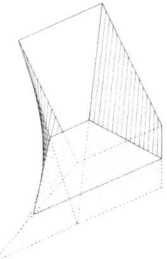

San Francisco Church, Muskegon, Michigan, USA 1961-1967 (Marcel Breuer, in cooperation with H. Beckhard)

In the San Francisco Church in Muskegon in a different way again, atechnical image an assymmetry were combined.

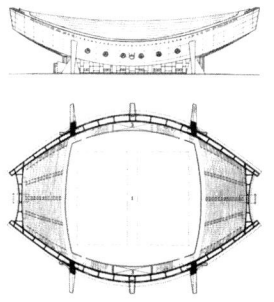

Sports Hall, Takamatsu, Japan, 1964 (Kenzo Tange)

For this sports hall the hypar-shaped floor is made of steel cables carrying concrete slabs.

Free-hypars and tordos as roofs

In the scarcity shortly after World War II, hyperbolic vaults had the advantage that they could be built with a relatively small amount of material. The shortage made building materials expensive, while labour in those days was cheap. By the end of the sixties, however, the situation was reversed: in particular the structural characteristics led to the use of hypars in, for instance, utilitarian roof structures.

A typical use of hypar roofs is the 'forest-like shelter' for a warehouse, market place or public transport junction. It combines protection from the sun and rain, with good ventilation. The recurrence of a characteristic element links together the variety of activities that takes place at various levels. Felix Candela designed many varieties of fields of umbrella shells. Together with Enrique de la Mora, he also designed churches with hyperbolic roofs, of which the Church of Nossa Senora de la Soledad in Coyoacan (Mexico, 1956) and the Church of San Vicente de Paul in Mexico City (Mexico, 1960) are best known. 2-16

Rio's Warehouse, Linda Vista,
  D.F. Mexico, 1954,
  (F. Candela)

Nossa Senora de la Soledad
  Church, Coyoacan,
  Mexico, 1956,
  (F. Candela and E. de la Mora)

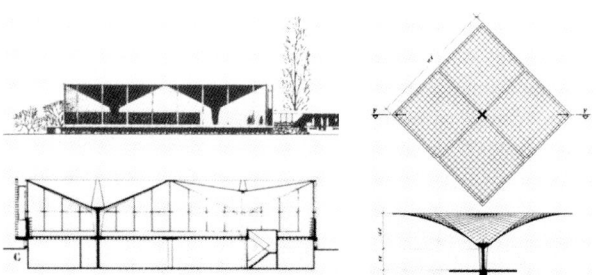

Hunter College, Bronx Campus, New York, USA, 1955-1959,
(M. Breuer, in cooperation with R.F. Gatje)

The roof of the Bronx Campus of Hunter College in New York, USA consists of four tordos. A similar structure was applied for the roof over the Public Water Supply Company Beerenplaat in Rotterdam, NL, 1959 (see Chapter 1).

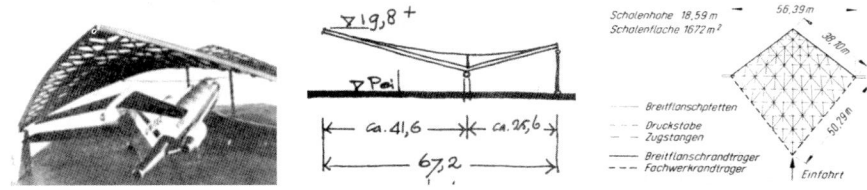

Saint Paul Airport, Hangar

United Airlines, Minneapolis,

Minnesota, USA, 1969

(Miller Dunwiddie Inc.)

LARGE ROOF STRUCTURES

The kite-shaped ground plan (sides 50.3 and 38.1 m) has a free span of 56.4 m; the free height is 19.8 m. Two points of the roof rest on reinforced concrete pillars. The steel truss girders covered with sheets of corrugated steel, act like a space frame, in contrast to vaults of which the roof skin is a membrane. [2-17]

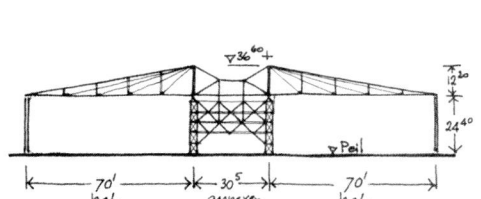

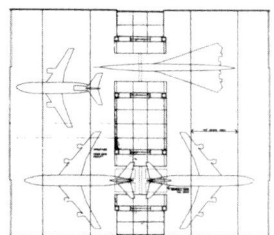

International Airport, Hangar American Airlines, San Francisco California, USA 1971
(Conklin & Rossant)

These halls can easily be expanded sideways. Their roofs consist of steel truss girders that hang from a steel structure. On either side truss girders form cantilevered hypar-shaped roofs that protrude 70 metres. Each hypar covers 17 x 70 metres. The halls are big enough to contain four Jumbo-Jets. [2-18]

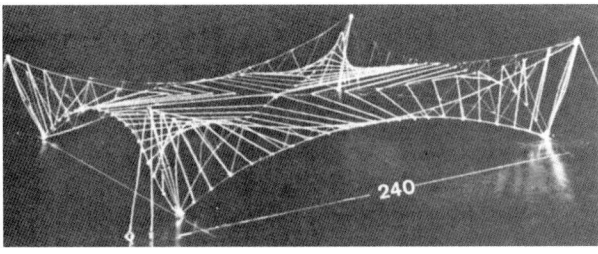
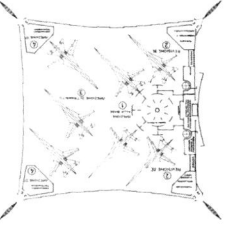

Airport Fiumicino, Hangar, Rome, Italy, not realized, 1967 (M. Paolini)

Pylons, assembled from steel tubes, stand at the corners of the above hangar. Along the sides and arranged diagonally are cable girders, composed of an upper and a lower cable, mutually connected by diagonals. The skin of the roof lies on secondary girders. Parts of the roof are ruled surfaces, probably conoids. The free height is 25 m. [2-19]

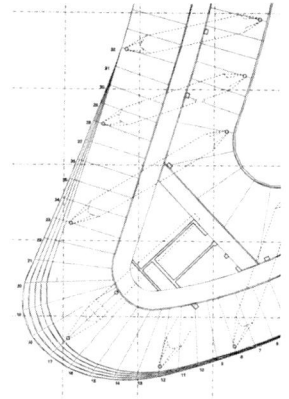

ORTHO-CONOID AND FREE-CONOID FRAGMENTS

Provinciehuis Zuid-Holland,
Den Haag, NL, 1996
(KPF, in cooperation with
LIAG-architects)

For a long time now, concrete and steel twisted façades have been feasible. Although to date no twisted glass was available, faceting with flat glass sheets was a good option. Twisted façades are still difficult to produce and hence expensive. Therefore they are firstly applied as prominent but small features. A twisted finishing of stone also is expensive and therefore only used in small quantities. Improving the skill of production techniques and geometry will increase the number and size of applications.

American Center, Paris, France, 1988-1994 (Frank Gehry)

In the Deconstructivist American Center in Paris variations are made on the usual laws of harmony in building geometry. In the upper part of the façade limestone plates are placed. It has been done gracefully: the façade attracts attention with its beautiful, firmly permed curls. The windows are flat. It is hard to ascertain whether the surface of the curved shape above the entrance is conical or conoid. The elements are defined and produced with CAD-CAM.

The windows in the twisted brickwork façade of the Provinciehuis in Den Haag, are spread irregularly over the façade, in order to obtain a peaceful image. All windows differ in size and slope. By positioning inner walls irregularly, under varying angles with the façade, variation in window frames sizes have been minimised. In keeping with this procedure it was not possible to align the window frames vertically.

MULTISTOREY FREE-RULERS AND MIXERS

Free-rulers are buildings with twisted façades, of which the rules rotate in two directions simultaneously. When rules do not rotate in parallel surfaces, they will not connect with straight lines to both floors and columns in an orthogonal building structure.
Mixers combine different types of curved and double-curved surfaces in one building.

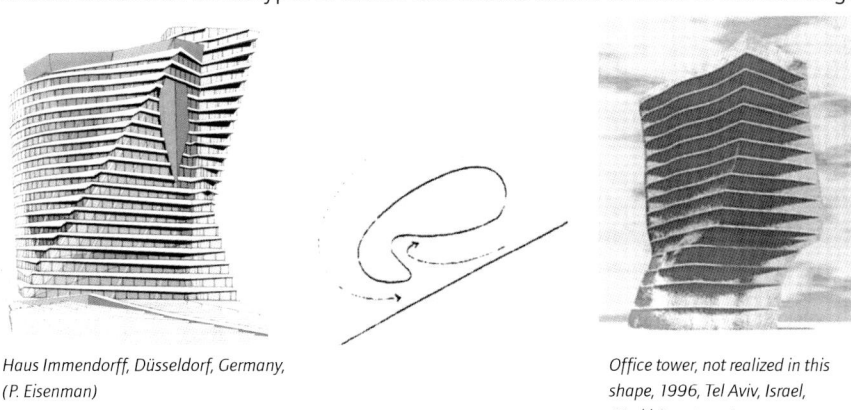

Haus Immendorff, Düsseldorf, Germany,
(P. Eisenman)

Office tower, not realized in this
shape, 1996, Tel Aviv, Israel,
(Yaski & partners)

The home and studio for the painter Immendorff is six storeys high and contains a
pub, a bar, a studio and office space, adding up to 1,245 m². Its shape is inspired by
soliton waves, which for example give non-linear reactions as a result of abrupt
changes in depth in water. Due to continuous changes, singular water shapes arise,
running and rolling back again alternately on their way through the water. Here two
waves curl through each other. The twisting of the façades is so slight that the glass
need not be transformed; faceting the horizontal strips with planar sheets of approximately 0.5 metre height would hardly be noticed.

The shape of the office tower by Yaski & partners, suggests that it is located at the sea
or on a windy plane and that like a stone, it has eroded. The dominant wind or stream
direction has become clear since one side of the building seems to have offered resistance. Some stubborn parts of the volume have persisted. The façade on the right may
be twisted. It is not clear what kind of surfaces the ones on the left are.

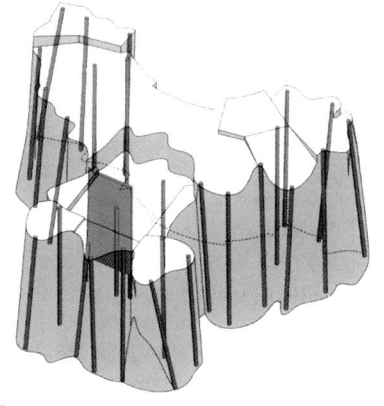

3

Der neue Zollhof, Düsseldorf,
Germany, 1994-1999,
(Frank Gehry)

1 Flat windows in rectangular
encasings pierce the façades

2 Structural concept diagram

3 Bird-eye view

The housing and office complex Der Neue Zollhof is located alongside a harbour. It is divided into three buildings, each of which has a different geometry and finish (white plaster, stainless steel, bricks). By bevelling the top of the volumes, the curved façades seem even more varied. With the white plaster and the brickwork, the outer buildings connect up with the materials of the buildings on either side of the complex. As the story goes, Gehry dreamt of making the curved brick façade with the sinuous lines of square windows look like the spotted back of a deer. In contrast, the stainless steel cladding of the middle building was to connect up with the harbour by using the shiny scales on the sides of a moving carp as a metaphor. The structural diagram of this building shows twisted outside walls. They are built with prefabricated concrete elements, almost all of which are different.

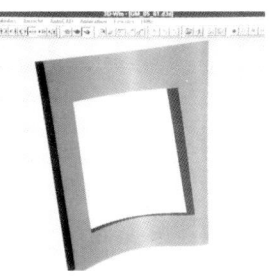

Their polystyrene molds were produced with CAD-CAM and recycled after use. Flat windows in rectangular encasings pierce the façades. 2-20

'Fred and Ginger',
office building Nationale
Nederlanden, 1992-1996,
Prague, Czech Republic,
(Frank Gehry)

The geometry of the works by the American architect Frank Gehry often is complex. Similar to the design process, were shapes evolve through an interaction between scale-models and computer modelling, the building process combines new industrial techniques with extensive handwork. The nickname 'Fred and Ginger', of the Nationale Nederlanden office building in Prague, Czech Republic, refers to the dancing couple Fred Astaire and Ginger Rogers. It's inspiration came from the two elegantly curved intimate volumes in the façade. The transparent one resembles a tailored ballroom gown; it is facetted with flat sheets of glass. A practical reason to constrict the volume and produce it in glass, was the neighbours' wish to maintain their view on the historic buildings across the river.

Ginger consists of two layers of steel-supported glass curtain wall. The interior layer, the underskirt, is the actual wall of the building, while the outer layer acts as a screen for the office spaces underneath. Ginger's vertical steel T-members curve in two directions and also twist.

Fred is formed from precast concrete panels. To cast each of the façade panels – all of which are different – the computer sorted the pane geometries into five or six categories based on their surface curvature. Each group was cast from the same mold, which was modified slightly after each pour for the next unique shape. Rectangular flat window frames protrude at varying distances from the plastering over the concrete elements. Thus, cheap opening windows could be used.

Business centre, not realized, Berlin, Germany 1996, (Philip Johnson)

The scale of this project can be deduced from the tiny human figures next to the 15-40m high buildings. It is not clear whether twisted or unrollable surfaces were considered. If it is a cardboard model, it will be the latter. The difference in surface type will hardly be visible. These buildings are expensive as they show little repetition in elements. 2-21

MULTI-STOREY TORDOS

Tordos connect with their straight lines to an orthogonal grid that usually corresponds with the walls and floors. They are hypars of which the upright rules are always in parallel vertical surfaces, and the lying ones are horizontal. They are easy to define because the horizontal straight lines have a constant height, e.g. a parapet edge or a connection to the floor structure. The upright rules connect to columns or walls.

The many canyon-like cuttings of the Airport Hotel, Schiphol, NL were designed to allow light and air to enter the hotel rooms. The spatial effects in the interior were supposed to neutralise the guests' jetlag and to entertain them. The columns would obtain varying inclinations and spacings in order to avoid having them protrude into a canyon. The building is called a **tordo**, assuming the irregular grid in the buildings does not intervene with the connecting of parallel walls and floors to the hypar-shaped façades.

Airport Hotel, Schiphol, NL (project), 1991 (Winy Maas and Floris Alkemade)

Bird's eye view   *View from above*
Building complex, Amsterdam, NL, not realized, 1998, architect: Fenna Haakma Wagenaar

The building unit encloses an 'orthogonally twisted' urban square (110 x 300 metres) with various functions allocated to the area below. It is flanked by an office building with a 100 metres high and 110 metres wide façade that is also 'orthogonally twisted': a tordo. The twisting of the inner façade improved the acoustics in the atrium.

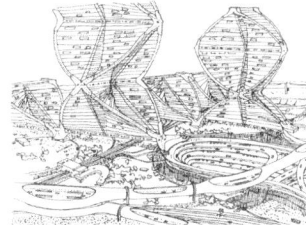 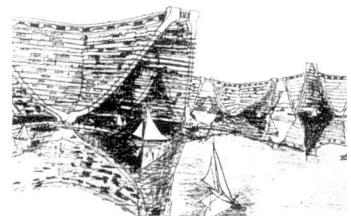 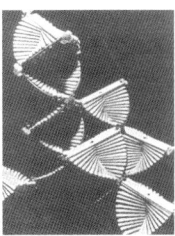

Helix City, plan for Tokyo, Japan,
1961 (N. Kurokawa)

TWISTERS

Rotation models are built up by repeating a ground plan with rotation around an axis on the upper floors. They feature a great recurrence of elements. Therefore, the cost price per part is relatively low. With the rotation axis centred between parallel façades, repetition also occurs within the same floor. The models in the plan 'Helix City' (1961), later appeared regularly and in various dimensions in works of art and building designs.

As mentioned before (in 'Twisting and Urban Planning', Chapter 1), the Japanese architect Noriaki Kurokawa designed a visionary project for Tokyo with twisters. He made many variations on the theme: single twisters with a central cylinder-shaped core, double-mirrored 90° twisters and twisters with additional stabilizing walls.

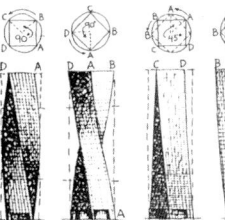 

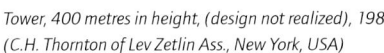

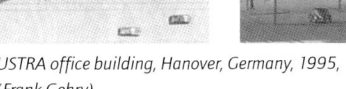

Tower, 400 metres in height, (design not realized), 1980,
(C.H. Thornton of Lev Zetlin Ass., New York, USA)

USTRA office building, Hanover, Germany, 1995,
(Frank Gehry)

Taking the tallest and most efficient structures in the world, guyed broadcasting towers, as an inspiration for buildings in the super tall range, Charles H. Thornton, of Lev Zetlin Associates in New York, designed a twisted tower with architect Harry Weese. In their design the corner columns imitate the action of guy lines, pulling the tower back to the vertical when it tries to sway in any direction. This way the guys need no anchoring. The ground plans of this twister (400 metres in height) rotate 45° around a vertical axis. The side contours are helical. In a subsequent design the floor layout was changed: the top was reduced in size, to decrease windage.

This twister designed by Frank Gehry has the vertical rotation axis at one of its corners. All four façades are different: two complementary surfaces have the rotation axis as one of their sides; the other two have the rotation axis outside the surface.

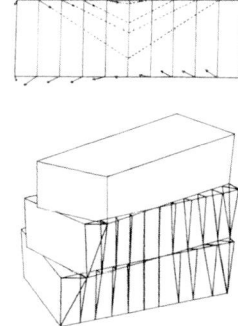

This tower designed by S.L. de Bever, Amsterdam, NL makes a 70° twist. The 'contrary' inclining position of the columns and the bevelled top are distinctive. The inclined columns introduce compensation for the twisting forces that arise by rotating the ground plan. The top is bevelled merely for aesthetic reasons. The façades are facetted with flat glass panels. 2-22

Tower, 200 metres in height, Rotterdam, NL, 1991

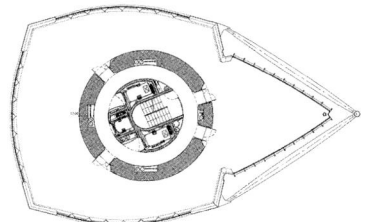

'Turning torso', Floor plan

This 186 metre high appartment building tower is to be constructed in Malmö, Finland. The number of appartments per floor varies. The open spaces in-between the segments will be used for communal activities, e.g. sport, leasure, restaurant, bar. 2-23

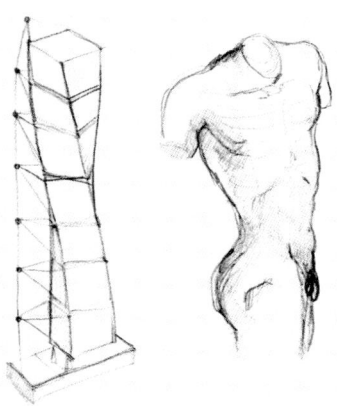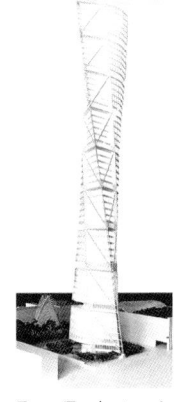

Drawing and model , 1991 (Santiago Calatrava)   *Entrance view*   *Tower 'Turning torso', Malmö, Finland, 2000 (Santiago Calatrava)*

Concrete sculpture at Zeeburg,
Amsterdam, the Netherlands,
(Jeroen Henneman)

Jeroen Henneman's tall sculpture, with its monolithic appearance resembles a high-rise building. One of the bridge pillars rises up to approximately 15 metres above the bridge deck. The oblong pillar twists 90°, so that the upper side takes on the direction of the road. It warns car drivers that the slip lane ends at the foot of the sculpture and the bridge will physically narrow there. After a few years the object was moved to the other side of the bridge. It still marks the crossing of the waterway.

ROTO-TWISTERS

These models feature a repetition of twisted elements within one horizontal level. They have no repetition along the rotation axis, unless the elements are repeated at a different height in a reversed or identical shape. If elements also are repeated in a vertical direction, we have a twister.

Nuclear Reactor in Rehouot, Israel, 1958

In the reactor, designed by Philip Johnson in collaboration with G. Liv of Lev Zetlin Architects, hypars are combined to make a facetted rotational surface. The modern cut gem-like appearance combined here with advanced industry.

Objects like vases are not just receptacles for flowers, but also expressions of aesthetic or philosophical views. Clay, 'par excellence', lends itself to investigate shape. It can easily be elongated and compressed. The contours of these 90° twisted vases are straight and not helical, like those of a twister. The sides are hypars. Ceramist Jan van der Vaart envisioned transforming his designs into buildings.

Cast vases, 1975

(J. van der Vaart, NL)

The square plan of the Cymbalista synagogue flows into a circular roof. From the corners of the square, and the mids of its sides, straight lines run to the circle. If the lines in-between are straight too, the façades will be conoids. The walls are facetted with pink stones.

Cymbalista synagoge,

Tel Aviv, Israel, 1998

(Mario Botta)

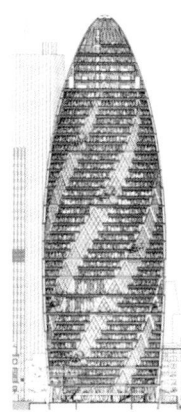

Office Swiss Re, London, United Kingdom, 1999 (Foster and Partners)

The spherical office tower (180 metres in height) of Swiss Re will have forty storeys. Each floor has a different diameter. By closing off the spaces between the building wings with glass, the surface of the expensive curtain wall is minimized. Because of the twisting, the spaces between the office wings form a spiral. They are segmented with floors into high atriums. The varying orientation results in wind pressure differences, which will be used for ventilation. The building elements are only repeated at the same layer, unless they also appear upside down elsewhere. The exterior is facetted with flat triangular glass sheets.

03

ASPECTS OF FORM

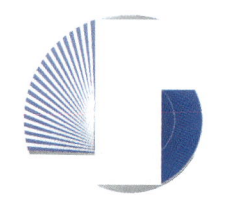  

The use of specific curves or the use of a particular technique that gener-
ates a particular kind of shape, of which the connotations are experi-
enced collectively, is typical of Western culture. For example the applica-
tion of circles or segments thereof, reniform shapes or sections of wing
profiles (Nurbs, Nacra, etc.), can be dated accurately to within two or
three years. In Western civilisation the individual character of the archi-
tect's work manifests itself in the choice of standard shapes that are
assembled into a whole, and hardly ever by individual associative or lyri-
cal line effects. In most cases, curves and the use of techniques that gen-
erate them, have specific symbolic values.

The highly individually coloured meaning of a curve is hard to describe,
due to the great number of parameters. The description of a 3D curve is
very complex: it changes shape, depending on the viewpoint. Each part of
the line may change from concave to convex, or vice versa. Thus, the asso-
ciations between the segments and the whole will also change. They vary
from emotions to technical notions like acceleration, laws of gravity or air
resistance. Associations may appeal to someone, or they may not. The
impact of the experience, may, in the course of time, vary in intensity,
(wearing off faster for one person than another).

In this chapter, a number of aspects observed during the research into
twisted shapes, are reflected upon.

Case-study 'CAD on a roof'

When passing through the surface of transition, the concave ridge line changes to convec and vice versa

1

2

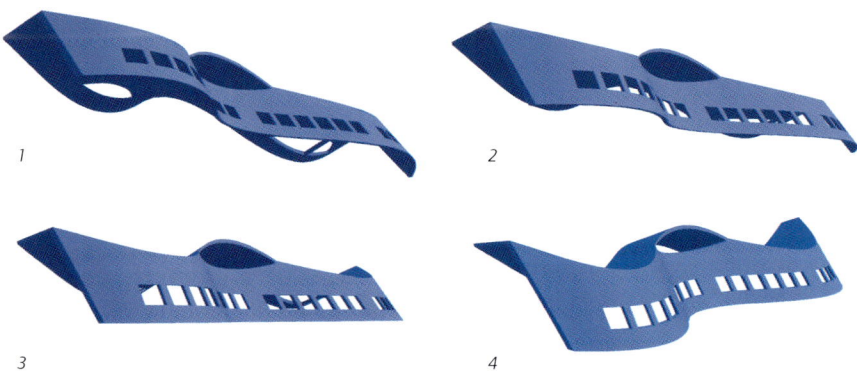

3

4

Because every now and then straight lines appear, e.g. by crossing through the transition surfaces, the image of this geometrically complex shape will provide a quieter image.

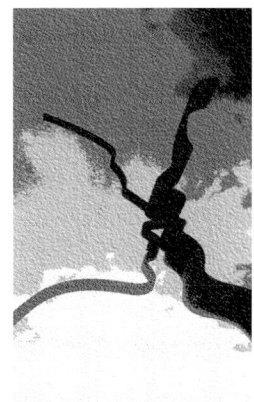

SURFACE OF TRANSITION

Sculptures do not have to fulfill the same functional and technical demands as buildings, but their visual appearance has to meet higher requirements. Each composition contains spatial effects that lead up to a visual or functional climax. Some effects are best experienced from certain positions to which the following terms are applied:

- A **focal point** is a position from which the effect of a certain view functions at its optimum, e.g. an axis, leading straight to or from the object.
- A **focal line** is a line along which the effect is experienced at its best. It may coincide with an axis, but not necessarily. This line may also be curved.
- A **focal surface** is a plane in which an optimally visual or spatial effect occurs in all directions. This will often be a horizontal surface, in which the position of the eye is often easily changed, e.g. when walking or driving. The focal surface may also be transformed three-dimensionally.

The point from which one views is called the **viewpoint**; the spot on which the sight is focussed, is called the **viewing point**. With the computer these parameters can easily be varied, whenever one wants to study some part of a building or create a different image.

The pictures on the facing page show the roof of one of the building blocks of the case-study, 'CAD on a roof'. The ridge line is singly curved. The flat plane in which the ridge lies is called a **transition surface**, because when the viewpoint crosses it, (e.g. while walking towards the building), the ridge line flowingly transforms from a concave – via a straight – into a convex line and vice versa. The transition surface is also a focal surface here, because a planned visual effect is experienced:

1   First, the ridgeline consists of two convex lines, on either side of the roof extension.
2   When the viewpoint is in the transition surface, the ridge is perceived as a straight line, only interrupted by the roof extension.
3   Subsequently, the ridgeline is an assembly of two concave parts and one convex part. The roof gutter also lies in a horizontal flat surface, at the bottom of the roof. Like the ridge line, the gutter changes into a straight line for a fleeting moment.
4   Thus the concave line and the two convex lines blend.

The sculpture 'The Kiss' by Jeroen Henneman stands at the entrance of the KBB head office in Amsterdam. It consists of two different singly curved lines, that stand out against the sky. When looking at them, their curvatures change with the position of the beholder. Only when seen from the public road, can the curves be recognised as the contours of faces. When viewed from the beginning of the entrance path, the lines seem to be kissing one another

CURVES AND THEIR ASSOCIATIONS WITH GENDER

Strikingly, connotations of curves are usually reduced to naturalistic notions: lines are compared with parts of the human body, an animal, a plant or a notion from life, e.g. protection. Straight and flat are often considered to be hard and masculine; curved in shape (concave or convex) is regarded as soft and feminine. This characterization is arbitrary. It is an interpretation consensus, which exemplifies the primary stage of development of a scientific connotation system. The mathematical description of geometry is very advanced. The associative effect of curves, however, can hardly be described in a scientific way.

It is remarkable that computer language in its coding, as the seed of a new era, originates from the binary system, represented by the dash and the dot, the much used archetypes of male and female, respectively. This description is arbitrary: it is hard to find a real straight line on a man's body; it can also be described by curved lines. It may be possible to distinguish the shaping of the curves of men from those of women, but curved they are! As a figurative typification of the genitals, the straight line and the circle depend greatly on the point from which 'the works' are viewed. The female pudendum looks more like a line than a circle. The male organ is almost always a curve but, with a little good will, becomes straight. However, if seen directly from the front, it again becomes a little circle. Apparently, the archetypical meanings are obtained in a prime time in life in which the objective or the action is reflected, rather than the actual shape. So, the dash is a reflection of the linear and reversible movement, or the action of entering, and the circle is an opening or widening. The circle thus symbolizes a centering sign. Most definitely the symbol for a female is always a little circle, (a figure across the linear movement), never a cylinder. Therefore, the line and the circle are intrinsic references and do not reflect the outer characteristics of the figure. The archetypes, the dash for the man and the dot for the woman, have been stretched during their active periods: the dash is extended maximally, the dot grows to be a circle.

The opening is born from a dot. Will the dot, the underlying basic element in a dash, when expanded, be blown up to a ball, a disc, a circle or be multiplied to a line? In other words: is a circle the same as a circular line of three points or is it an enlarged point?

1

2

THE SMALLEST TWISTED SURFACE

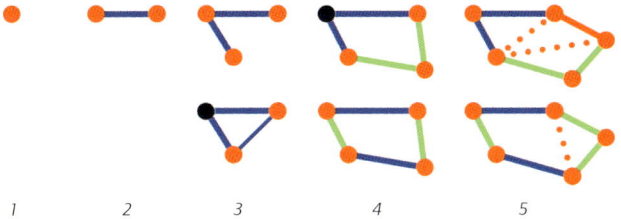

1   2   3   4   5

The façade of 'Superior Tribunal da Justice', Brasilia
(Architect: Oscar Niemeyer ,
façade design: Marianne Peretti)

1 *Read from left to right:*
A thriving power, joyously
started and gently, but
resolutely brought to a halt
from the centre.
Passion brought to peace.

2 *A mirrored print of the façade*
also read from left to right:
A restraining effect, shrinking,
emphatically brought to a
standstill from the centre.
The thick concrete slab on
the right whips up those
on the right side

The sequence illustrates how, by adding one point to the starting point each time, space is built up from nothing:

1   A point has no dimension.
2   The minimum line consists of two points, the second point introduces a direction and results, together with the starting point, in the first dimension. The line has no thickness, only a length.
3   When three points are not aligned, they form the minimally buckled line (a curve?). These three points determine a flat surface, in the second dimension. Can it be a curve and a flat surface at the same time?
4   When four points do not lie in a flat surface, they define a three-dimensional plane and a volume simultaneously. The one point that lies outside the surface of the other three points, can be regarded as part of a curve. The plane may also be regarded as a surface of revolution, composed by revolving a curve around its ends. When the green lines are not in one flat surface and do not intersect, then this is the smallest possible twisted surface. The four points may also be described as two non-intersecting straight lines.
5   By adding a fifth point, many more lines or volumes appear.

A mathematician will solve the problem of plural reading of the set of points by simply stating that one sees what one wants to see.

READING VECTOR

The Superior Tribunal da Justice in Brasilia (architect Oscar Niemeyer) was completed in 1995. Marianne Peretti designed a concrete **open-frame girder** (60 x 11 metres) (this is a plank-shaped beam on its side, with large holes) for this building. Instead of the usual rectangular or round holes, she designed perforations with varying contours.

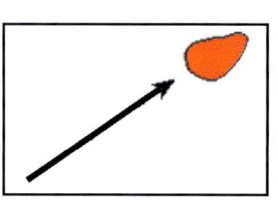 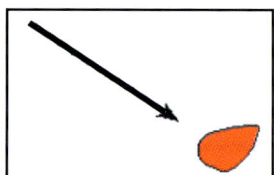 

Reading vector over diagonals

Every one of these evokes its own associations, and a strong interaction between the lines occurs. In the mirrored picture the lines have a totally different meaning. Here, it can be seen very clearly that the Western preference for left to right reading results in specific associations.

The Western preference is not only to read from left to right, but also from top to bottom. After 'reading' the picture, an overall appreciation takes place, in which accents in the image also play a major role. Within a 2D image, in addition to the vertical and horizontal vectors, diagonal ones also arise, for example by positioning the text at the base and then adding colour accents in the corners, or literally adding diagonal lines. This may result in strong diagonals from the upper left to the lower right, or from the lower left to the upper right corners. Ending the reading of an image with an upward movement is usually considered optimistic and progressive (the positive vector). Ending in a downward direction, from the upper left to the lower right, is experienced as collapse, a disillusionment (the negative vector). A slanting position of a twisted façade, or the swaying away of a corner, may evoke a similar diagonal line in the façade. Perspective distortion may amplify this.

When taking a photograph, the image of a 3D building is reduced to a 2D picture. Particularly when façade surfaces are not at right angles to the viewer, and this is certainly the case with curved or inclined surfaces, a distortion may be caused because the stereometric experience is suppressed. With a twisting volume, it is often difficult to perceive in what direction the reading vector runs: is the main accent the part of the façade which falls backwards, or is it the forward leaning part? When twisting, in what direction does the main vector point? Does the roof line point downwards, weak and tired, or in contrast upwards, with a desire to reach out into the distance? If a line remains erect in the centre of the façade, is it neutral and without energy, or is it in contrast standing tall and proud? The degree of twist is important. The connotation will vary from a weak, faint gesture of turning away from reality to a constricting or even strangling torque.

Whether or not the Coreolis forces, that make whirlpools turn clockwise and climbing plants grow anti-clockwise in the Northern Hemisphere, influence the associative effects for Northern people watching a twisted tower, is not clear (as yet).

When looking at a twisted tower, as one side of the building sways out of sight, the other side immediately appears. This leads to continuous dynamics in the image,

where the attention is drawn to that part which fades away or to the part that appears. Within these dynamics, taking bites out of the upper and lower sides of the wings can create additional points of attention. Also the application of different façade finishes may cause accents, whereby the turning away of one side is no longer equally compensated by the appearance of the other. Changing light will also vary the accentuation on either surface. For instance, the curtain wall reflects the sunlight brightest, while the horizontal concrete panelling of the other façade may emerge stronger in the dark. Sometimes a vertical accent will dominate; on other occasions a horizontal one. Within each wing a reversal may happen, due to the perspective effect of twisting. At times the horizontal paths will seem to be almost vertical.

Arms counteract the movement of legs

In short, when many parameters are used to describe a shape, the complexity increases. A rich and dynamic image appears, but it is difficult to establish the essential associative meaning. In such complex matters coincidence will play a great part. Depending on the viewing point, a tower might look elegant, haughty, even arrogant, or flow smoothly and be desirous in appearance. The eventual choice is subjective. A number of preferred viewpoints, representing the corporate image, will soon be evident.

ACTION LINES

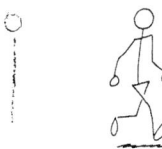    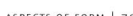 

The posture of cartoon characters in action is typified by a rapid intial line: the **action line**. The speed must be retained in the final sketch. After drawing the action line a thread figure is sketched, which develops a body by the addition of oval and rod-like shapes. In a walking movement the position of the cartoon figure is very important. A walking figure usually has one foot on the ground. When walking faster, the body will lean further forward. Running figures are almost always drawn with both feet slightly off the ground. A shadow on the ground clarifies this. When sprinting at top speed, the cartoon figure is often drawn in an almost horizontal position.

In many cases not the moment of action is drawn, but the situation immediately afterwards, with its explicit effects

The correct posture and the correct moment of action determine the success of the picture. The variations in the curves of the action lines tell an entire story

The combined action of various bodies also evokes an interaction of their action lines.

Architecture is mostly concerned with 'reading' and 'experiencing' 3D shapes. The action line of a building changes by moving the viewpoint. The action line in one sight may disappear in another or become secondary with regard to others that appear. Because of this, associations evoked by the shape of a building, will change when walking around the building, approaching it or walking through it. The sequences of views of buildings and comic strip pictures have similarities: in both cases images connect in a logical order whereby sudden changes of accent can be enacted. 3-1

CONTOURS VARYING IN SHAPE

Oscar Niemeyer drew the figure of a woman as a landscape. Her hair represents the sea, her skin is the beach, shells form a necklace and dunes are her head. Thus he merged the aspects of the life he loves into a new image

The buildings of the Brazilian architect Oscar Niemeyer are fascinating study objects. He reduces them to compositions of a limited number of geometrical shapes, in which one is very much aware of the contours. For the parliament building in Brasilia he applied a shell shape. The inclined sides are at a sharp angle with the horizontal roof plate. It looks relatively light, as the image of the flow of gravitational forces is secondary: from nearby no horizontal surfaces or supports are detectable. The eye does not see this building isometrically with the contours meeting at angles, but in perspective, with freely curved contours that merge flowingly.

ASSOCIATIONS AND SCALE

Oscar Niemeyer drew the figure of a woman as a landscape. Her hair represents sea waves, her skin is the beach, shells form a necklace and dunes are her head. Thus he merged the aspects of the life he loves into a new image.

Each segment of a curve can evoke its own association. The segments, differing in scale, flowingly blend together and as a whole they evoke another. In fact, a shape only acquires scale in combination with other (mostly naturalistic) objects. The intensity of every segment-association depends on the mutual proportions of the segments, their thickness, their colour etcetera.

I reach for time

and know not where to turn

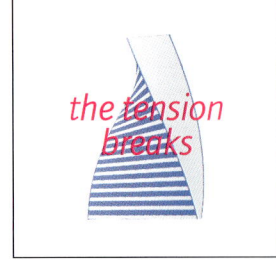
the tension breaks

and I remember

strips of turmoil and sensation

stretched out to the water-edge

what in vain I bring about

every line draws

its individual track in the landscape

on which many mouths suck

suppose I were to inhale you

and then must wait till nightfall

she rises from the cold ground

into the air and becomes visible

embrace me

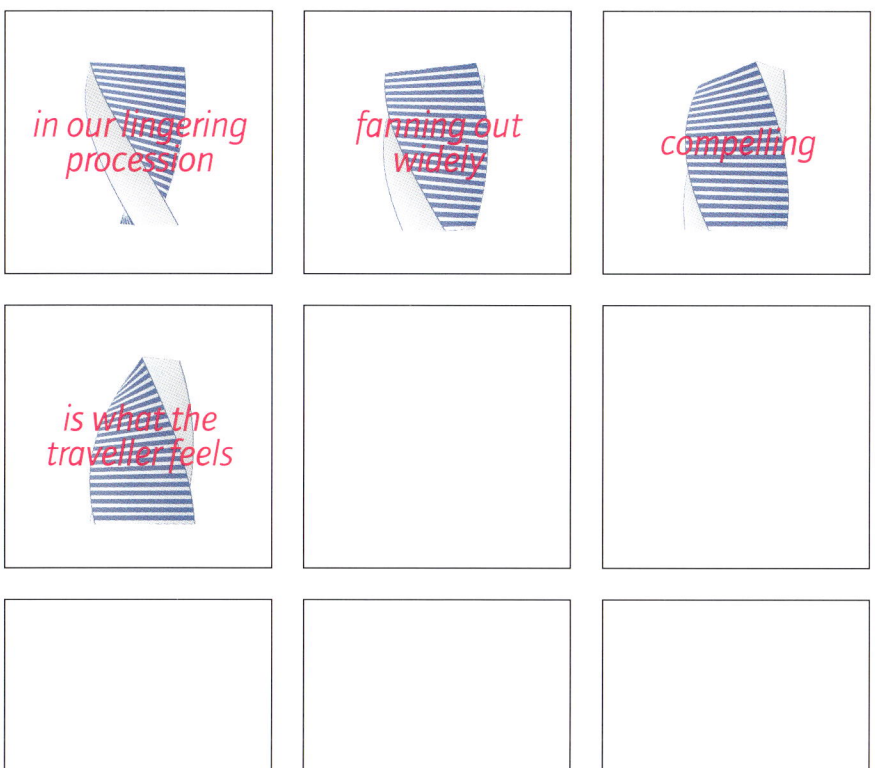

The lyrical experience when walking around a building

When walking around a building, a sequence of aspects can be distinguished, each reflecting a characteristic image. Thus a 'comic strip' emerges, composed of a series of various associations. This particularly holds true for buildings with curves. Although a general experience may prevail, everyone experiences the building differently. It is interesting to try and put the sequence of blending associations into words. It has often been said that it is annoying when an explanation is given with an image. A strong image, however, has so many interesting aspects that text is capable of describing a few images. Enough 'space' will be left for personal interpretation. The experience can probably best be compared with poetry or music. They too are subject to multiple interpretation.

Hanneke van Gent often has her abstract paintings accompanied by text. They provide her work with an interesting enrichment because, on the one hand, they are recognizable in the image and, and on the other, they add an idea. Therefore, she was asked to provide text to accompany the series of images of the author's tower model 'Twister 1'(described in chapter 4.2.4). The series is introduced with the view from above - a bird's eye view. She provided the following text:

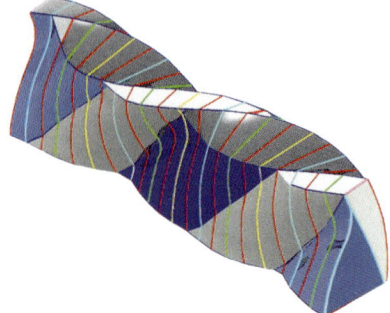 

SEQUENTOGRAM AND SEQUENTOVOL(UME)

In this project an interesting phenomenon was discovered: the sequence of images can be joined into one picture. If one walks around a building taking photographs at regular intervals, they can later be stacked on top of each other to form an overall picture. In a building with vertical sides, such a vertical assembly produces a 'staccato' image from which it is not easy to draw conclusions. In a building with slanting sides, the sights can be chosen in such a way that a linked image can be produced, with flowing transitions between the parts. This image repeats the character of the surface progress, in this case: twisting. In one overall picture, a **sequentogram**, all façades can be viewed. It reflects the building's form characteristic.

There are parallels with the work of the artist Jan Dibbets. He photographed the landscape around him from one viewpoint, with a constant angular deflection between the camera positions and assembled circular compositions of the photographs. Their message is not very clear, but they are beautiful. At least they represent a geometrical quality of the panorama, the convex shape of the earth. The effect of architectural shapes can also be described in this way, because the movements underneath, alongside or around a building can be established in a 2D image. The adjoining illustration shows how the sights of the tower 'Tordo 1' have been placed on top of each other (chapter 4). The twisting of the volume is clearly visible in the new 2D overall picture.

The sequence of contours can also be assembled to produce a 3D model. Such a **sequentovol(ume)** is an integral of visual appreciation of the contour effects, when moving around the object. The other way around it should also be possible to make a differential, which restores the essence of the shape to, for instance, only a twist. This idea, however, has not yet been further developed. The contours of the views of 'Twister 1' have been placed in a row and were subsequently morphed into a sequentovol. Twisting as a fundamental transformation process can be recognized in the volume.

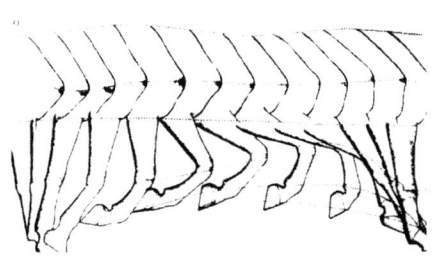

SEQUENCES IN ARCHITECTURE

The eye does not see an instantaneous phase, but the result of many motions, which is generally what artists aim to reproduce. Eadweard Muybridge did photographic studies on the attitudes of man and animals in motion, showing what actually happened. The illustration shows the movements of a running man, photographed by Thomas Eakins with the apparatus that Muybridge suggested. 3-2

Etienne-Jules Marey studied rhythms, movements, pulses and flows and their effects on form. He would connect points across snapshots, for instance on the legs of a horse, to describe a curvilinear continuity. Twenty years later the Futurists expanded on Muybridge's and Marey's work. 'We affirm that the world's magnificence has been enriched with a new beauty: the beauty of speed,' their 1909 Manifesto exulted. The paintings of Umberto Boccioni, Giacomo Bella, or Gino Severini, who concentrated on the analysis of speed in movement, were forecast in the photographs. Parallels are obvious in Marcel Duchamp's Nude Descending a Staircase and Kasimir Malevich's The Scissors Grinder. 3-3 The pictured limbs can be seen as a combination of line fragments. The succession of particular line fragments, resembles the repetition of lines in twisted surfaces. In a similar way as the painters tried to catch movement in a flat picture, a twisted façade as a whole may suggest it, and have the image supported in its parts by the sequence of seemingly temporary positions of a moving shape. This varying interpositioning of similar lines is characteristic of twisted surfaces.

SCALING OF ELEMENTS AND HUMOUR IN ARCHITECTURE

In addition to shifting and rotating, it is easy to scale elements when using a computer. It is an ancient manipulation technique, in architecture as well as in humour in general. The idea is to get a message across. The degree of scaling determines the effect. Thus, an element of a building is allocated a place along with the others: from ingeniously minuscule, via pathetically small etc. to impressive, monumental, frightningly large or grotesque. A series describing the effect of the degree of scaling, can be produced. Each element has a scale, usually related to the size of the observer or of surrounding objects. A deviation from the usual dimension is indicated by providing the object with an adjacent term on the scale (e.g. 'heavy') or, if the standard measure has to be retained, by adding a tendency on the scale series (e.g. 'small' or 'large', sometimes reinforced by a normative notion e.g.

Jesse Godley running, 1884
(Thomas Eakins)

Nude Descending a Staircase,
No. 2, 1912

Oscillations of the front limb of
the horse galloping
(E.-J. Marey)

'too'. Repetition intensifies the effect. Large differences compared to normal result in absurd image associations: 'beetle crushers' instead of shoes.

Exaggeration is part of humour, like the bow tie of the clown, enlarged to the size of a pillowcase. The selective attention to defects of the human body, strange habits or the limitations of human existence, and emphasizing these by contrasts, makes a caricature of reality. The short, fat man with his tall, skinny companion, or the bald head emphasized by a few strands of hair at the sides. It's like looking in a distorting mirror at the fair. And they always laugh, even for a third time: at the unexpected, high-pitched, squeaky voice coming from the tall man or a loud shout in someone's ear when a whisper is expected.

Laughing is often a reaction to the fact that an unfortunate situation did not happen to oneself, a venting of emotions when danger is over.

Elements are taken out of context by the reversal of their meanings, the creation of unusual combinations or the strong emphasis on fragments. By changing the characteristics of objects, an estranging surrealistic effect occurs, like the flower on a clown's small waistcoat that sprays water in one's face when one wants to smell it. It is also strange that there is no pain, in spite of the absurdly large size of the hammer with which the clown anaesthetizes his friends. Melancholy becomes dominant and time is stretched when the clown's huge painted mouth laughs constantly while one eye is weeping. Social relations are put into perspective because the clown always laughs last. The clown's broom and the carpet-beater of Koot & Bie (Dutch comedians) symbolize the underdog.

The same effects are used in architecture, often because of social and financial interest and with a serious undercurrent:

- scaling of elements, or of the whole, with regard to the observer
- unexpected combinations of notions or objects
- taking elements out of context, e.g. by the reversal of meanings
- timing and rhythm, which intensify an effect until it becomes ridiculous or inescapable

THE SUCCESSION OF ARCHITECTURAL STYLES

In the Post Modernist design style at the end of the seventies and the beginning of the eighties, references to a noble and refined foregone lifestyle were used on a large scale by placing classicistic elements in a modern building. The interrelation and choice of the positioning were often 'haughty' and 'cynical' with regard to the original purpose and location of the parts. As if the architect had to make up for referring to old styles by treating them in a disparaging manner.

All the aforementioned manipulations of 'scaling' have been used in buildings: torsos became too big and too dominant, or too small and placed in a belittling manner as if inferior. Classical elements were abstracted to simple geometric shapes, brightly coloured or excessively enlarged, to provide them with a value that authentic elements had, due to their refined profiling or sincere intrinsic meaning, as in a temple. The virtuosity of manipulating classical and modern elements has been a summarizing, final clever feat, an evaluation of designs of old. All style-elements were put together for one last time: the deliberate avoidance of style purity became the norm. This virtuosity could only be thanks to a general consensus on what architecture is supposed to look like. In spite of a generally proclaimed apparent lack of direction, there is a fascinating subdued unanimity about what architecture is, an immediate agreement on what is too sharp, what too long, or what too green in architectural composition.

Post Modernism also tried to bring the good elements of each style together and breathe new life into each one of them. Ornaments, which had been declared unwanted by Modernists, returned, among other things, by using Modernist fragments as ornaments. A contradiction like this was the style trademark of Post-Modernism.

After this cacophony of styles, in the eighties Deconstructivism came along: a quest for a new way of designing, even more recklessly trying to disturb old conventions. The building seemed to fall apart: beams shot at random through windows, floor plates lay at sixes and sevens, almost literally portraying the demolition of the traditional building. Seemingly torn-apart structures became a characteristic ornamental feature. By destroying conventions architects tried to create new spaces and a new type of building by looking for a literal shape similarity, or rather a co-existence, to fit the disorganization, the unorganized violence in society. Chaos opposite coordination.

The architectural theories obtained a scientific touch by referring to pictures illustrating chaos-theory. 3-4 The overlapping plates and volumes of the Deconstructivists and the almost literally executed 'exploded views', inspired the study of tectonics (landslides or layered displacements). An archetypical portrayal of movement, not so much a flowing but rather an uplifting and breaking force, was introduced in building shapes. Its portrayal still leant heavily on straight lines: flat surfaces and singly curved lines and surfaces. This simplification was a result of the limited possibilities to build 2D shapes as in current industrial production.

Just like Het Nieuwe Bouwen in the twenties and thirties designs with their 'floating' flat surfaces, beams and wires had associations with the somewhat earlier double-decker planes, in the seventies reminders of space travel became fashionable. Front and rear, below and above, horizontal and vertical now increasingly become of equal importance, as architects are experimenting on the computer screen, where objects can weightlessly tumble around.

The development of the computer in the eighties allowed architects to visualize these images. Recently, with the new software, 'morphing' and 'extruding' has become fashionable. By 'morphing' shapes, instead of combining and contrasting them, flowing transitions are simulated. Einstein's theory of relativity comes in as an inspiration, without experiencing the lack of intrinsic logic in the designing process as a hindrance. Again, the possibilities offered by technology are declared an extreme actuality. However, the selection from the newly offered options in CAD is, for the time being, determined by the limited degree to which architects are able to cope with them.

Research is done into building notions like growth and movement with a few shape manipulations, e.g. stretching, morphing, sometimes with a twist. Nature plays a great part in the attribution of associations to free curves, and the comparison with internal human organs inspires design and function of building parts. The theory of architecture as a transition between man and machine is related to this. It must find its shape yet.

With the widespread introduction of the computer, the notion 'virtual reality' became fashionable. The shapes currently credited to the use of the computer, could also, within acceptable tolerances, be defined with conventional drawing techniques. In the architectural designing practice, the computer is primarily used for the visualization of 3D shapes, particularly in presentations. This is of great importance to mini-

mize building risks and to gain insight in the possibilities. As to the use of curves in architecture, compared to shipbuilding, car and aircraft industry, designing in architecture is still backward.

The abstract shape replaced by a natural one, the image of static support replaced by that of movement

CLASSICAL AND MODERN SHAPE LANGUAGE

Marble columns used to have a 'ream' (widening) at approximately one-third of their height. The cylinder with its clinically exact dimensioning and sterile character, an 'unearthly' geometrical shape, has obtained reference to a sensory experienced world by curved tapering. The narrowing upwards from the ream, introduced human observation of distance, with its suggestion of perspective. Beneath the ream, the columns narrowed. As the spectator stood at the base and visually followed the widening up to the ream, high above, the image of a direct physical reaction may have been evoked, not unlike widening of the chest when taking a deep breath. In trees, the downward swelling of the trunk reflects the effects by the laws of forces, e.g. of gravity and wind. But in columns the force of gravity seemed to flow upward, giving the column, as well as the spectator, a sense of lightness. The abstract shape became worldly. By adding curvatures, the cylinder became laden with associations.

The Ereichtheion of the Acropolis in Athens shows a replacement of the proudly erect columns, usually assumed male, by 'dancing priestesses of Artemis'. An abstract shape has been replaced by a natural one. Movement took the place of static support. In the picture the two dancers on the left stand on their right leg while their left is at rest. For the two dancers on the right it is exactly the other way around. A visually rotating effect is introduced by bending the leg in a special way. The pleats of the garment are like the cannelures of the classic Greek pillar. In their turn being shaped as reversals of cylinder segments, they remind of the bark of trees. By placing their statues upon 'a step too high for humans to take', the priestesses got to stand on a pedestal. The beholder literally looked up to them and was forced to stay at a respectful distance. By modelling the dancers on an enlarged scale, the beholder was made small. Thus, the priestesses may be regarded as adults, in a world they protect and in which the beholder had become a child again.

The game of reflection and complementarity, repetition, rhythm and meaning reversal, is an ancient design tool. The point is not to copy, but to be inspired.

04

CAD AND GEOMETRY

Circles, ellipses or complex irregular figures can be drawn as if they were floating in the air, inclined and partly continuing underground. By lines they may be connected to other, mathematically determined figures. This is fine when designing or calculating, but does not relate very well to the physicality of building activities, often under difficult weather conditions.

Nowadays hardly any designer, draftsman or craftsman still works with analytical geometry, or remembers the difference between descriptions like 'hyperboloid' and 'parabolic hyperboloid'. Nor does he remember how to handle mathematical formulae. It is not practical to refer to complex shapes, when defining a building.

Dimensioning complex distorted surfaces has become easy with computers, far easier than in the days when geometrical calculations were necessary. Therefore, in this study the shapes were classified in a new manner, one that fits the notions the building industry is familiar with. The shapes were 'computerized', e.g. arranged according to a scheme that is based on the basic elements (a straight or curved line) and elementary manipulations for computer drawing (shift and rotation). The parameters are described figuratively. The diagram serves to provide insight in the geometry and facilitate the realization of the depicted shapes, for draftsman, designer and producer alike.

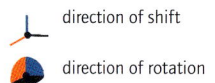

LINE SURFACE		OF STRAIGHT LINES	OF CURVED LINES
translation surface		single	curved surface
twisted surface		ruled surface	curve surface
rotation surface		cone	boloid sphere

direction of shift

direction of rotation

SHAPE DESCRIPTION

Classification scheme
based on shift and rotate

A NEW SCHEME FOR LINE SURFACES
The diagram starts from **line surfaces**. A line surface is a new name for a surface, composed of adjacent equal lines (**base lines**). In line surfaces, the base lines may be straight or curved, or a combination of both. Distinctions within the line surfaces are **shifted surfaces** (caused by parallel shifts), **twisted surfaces** (with a shift and rotation) and **surfaces of revolution**. Twisted surfaces are divided into **ruled surfaces**, composed of straight base lines (rules) and **curve surfaces**, composed of singly curved base lines. Singly curved lines will be referred to in this research, as **curves**.
Also double curved lines can be shifted and rotated. Their description partly overlaps that of surfaces composed of curves. Three-dimensionally curved lines are left aside.
- In the diagram a rule coincides with the x-axis; a curve lies in the xy-surface.
- The rotation of a rule around its own length is not visible. Therefore, the number of rotation directions in the figurative depicting of rule manipulations, was restricted to two.
- The trajectory of movement in this diagram is a straight line.
- Rotation point and turning direction, as a combination, are represented by a red dot and circle segment, application point and displacement direction by a black dot and vector. Only the combinations of direction components that result in a curved surface, are indicated.

CONVENTIONAL AND NEW NOTIONS
In the course of time, vaulted structures have been classified in many ways.
A few examples:
- Associative characteristics, e.g. domed vault, barrel vault, pavilion roof
- Geometrical description in analytical geometry, e.g. ruled surfaces, hyperbolic parabolas (or hypars), boloids, conoids, synclastic and anticlastic surfaces etc.
- Description when drawing with the computer, e.g. offsets or morphed figures
The (hypar)parabolic shape was of great structural importance when making vaults. Nowadays twisted surfaces in architecture hardly function as a shell structure, and mainly are used in façades of buildings with an orthogonal superstructure. Therefore descriptions that connected to calculating the structure have lost importance. In practice, differently classified notions now are used interchangeably.

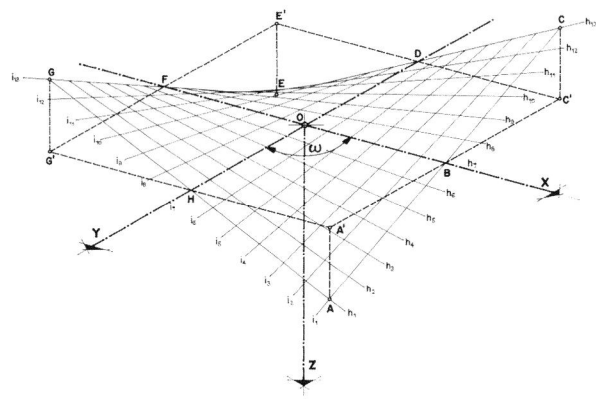

A ruled surface is generally known as a surface composed of straight lines, where each straight line does not run parallel to its adjacent lines, nor intersects them in one point. Webster's New twentieth Century Dictionary of the English Language, unabridged, second edition 1997, describes notions connected to twisting of a surface as follows:

- Conoid (Greek: kōnoeidês, cone-shaped) in geometry: a solid formed by the revolution of a conic section about its axis. If the conic section is a parabola, the resulting solid is a parabolic conoid, or paraboloid; if a hyperbola, the solid is a hyperbolic conoid, or hyperboloid: if an ellipse, an elliptic conoid, a spheroid, or an ellipsoid
- Hypar: hyperbolic shell (in combination with shell)
- Hyperbola: (Greek: hyperbolê, a throwing beyond, excess, from hyperballein, to throw beyond; hyper, over, beyond, and ballein, to throw) a curve formed by the section of a cone cut by a plane that makes a greater angle with the base than the side of the cone makes; (fig. hyperbolê) exaggeration for effect, not to be taken literally: this story is as old as time; exceeding the truth
- Parabola (LL = Late/Low Latin) (from Greek: parabolê, so called from its axis being parallel to the side of the cone; para, beside, and ballein, to throw): in geometry, a plane curve, the path, or locus, of a moving point that remains equally distant from a fixed point (focus) and from a fixed straight line (directrix); a curve formed by the intersection of a cone with a plane parallel to its side
- Generatrice (Latin: (feminine) of generator, a producer, generator, from generare, to produce, generate): a point, line, or plane whose motion generates a line, plane, figure, or solid
- Directrix: in geometry, a fixed line that serves as a guide in drawing a curve or surface
- Helix (Latin: helix, a kind of ivy, a spiral (Greek: helix (-ikos), a spiral, anything of a spiral shape, from helissein, to turn round): any spiral, either lying in a single plane or, especially, moving around a cone, cylinder, etc., as the thread of a screw. In architecture, an ornamental spiral, as a volute on a Corinthian or Ionic capital. In mathematics, a line so curved around a right circular cylinder that it would become a straight line if the cylinder were unfolded into a plane

Conventional drawing in which a directrice moves along a generatrice

NEW NAMES FOR SURFACES

In the following definitions old names have been rephrased and new names have been created, to provide a better connection with computer drawing, e.g. by manipulating lines and surfaces by shifting and rotating. Old notions that connect up to the new definitions are included too:

- Ruled surface is a surface formed by rotating and shifting a straight base line, whereby a component of the turning direction is at right angles to the displacement direction. With a curved displacement line, minimally one direction component of the rotation has to take the line outside the surface that runs through the base line and the curved displacement line
- Curve surface is formed by rotating and shifting a curved base line, whereby the lines are not in one surface or in parallel ones and where they do not intersect at the same point of their lines. (In the latter case a surface of revolution would be formed)
- Surface of revolution is formed by rotating the base line, around a point of application on the line or its produced part
- Track line is the line along which, when manipulating a base line, an extremity of the base line is moved
- Conoid: a surface, formed by the shift and rotation of a base line, where the shift line of the centre of rotation is straight or curved. The base lines are intersected by, at the most, one straight line.
- Helix: the line that is formed as a track line, when a line (whether or not regularly) is replaced along a straight axis, with at least a component of the rotation at right angles to this axis. The kind of curvature is called helical
- Hyperbolic paraboloid: a non-planar surface in which at any point are two intersecting straight lines

Shapes with a 'free-geometry' are, with a view to their complexity, the next in line to curve-surfaces. The adjacent lines no longer are similar and rotated, but are different. They are often called blobs. 'Blob' is an old word. The notion only recently became fashionable when in 1988 the film The Blob was released, directed by Chuck Russell. It has been described as 'a quasi-camp horror remake about huge gelatinous mass gobbling up townspeople'. Webster's describes 'blob' as follows: (Provincial English, from Scottish bleb, bleib, blab, a bubble).)[1] a drop or lump of something viscid or thick; a bubble; a blister.)[2] a small mass or splash of colour.

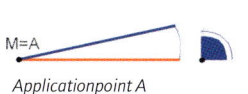

Applicationpoint A

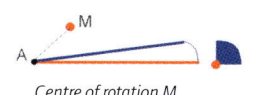

*Centre of rotation M
on rotational axis*

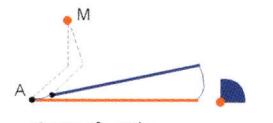

*Centre of rotation
not rototional axis*

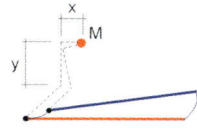

SURFACES COMPOSED OF STRAIGHT LINES

LINE MANIPLULATION

In these drawings, the starting rule is red; the blue rule results from shifting and rotating. The determining factors for the rotation are:

- The **point of application A** of the rule (the black dot). To simplify the description and the graphic notation, it was placed at one of the ends of the line. It may also be placed somewhere else (upon or next to the base line).
- The **centre of rotation M** (the red dot). This is the point relative to which the application point is moved. It may be a fixed point, but it can also shift along a (possibly curved) line. If the centre of rotation coincides with the application point, only the black dot is drawn.
- The **arm**. This is the distance between the point of application and the centre of rotation.
- The direction and amount of rotation.

Examples

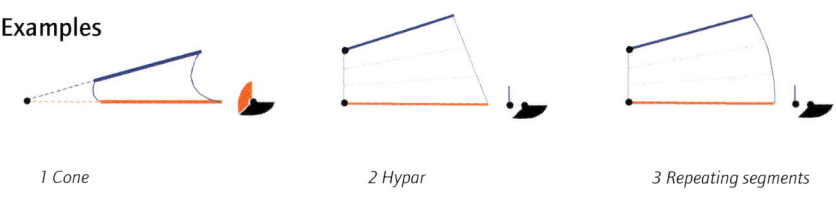
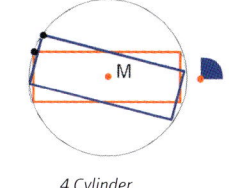

1 Cone   *2 Hypar*   *3 Repeating segments*   *4 Cylinder*

1   When the rotation and displacement are chosen in such a way that all lines intersect in the same point, then a cone is formed.
2   With a linear shift of the application point and a varying rotational angle and rule length, a straight track line may occur. Such a surface with rules in two directions is called a hypar.
3   When the centre of rotation is moved at right angles to the rotating direction, a helix-shaped track line is formed.
4   The point of application may be adjacent to the line, e.g. in a building ground plan. The corners of the plan then move at a constant distance around the centre of rotation. With the torsion axis chosen at right angles with the floorplan, the sidelines of a building are on a cylinder.

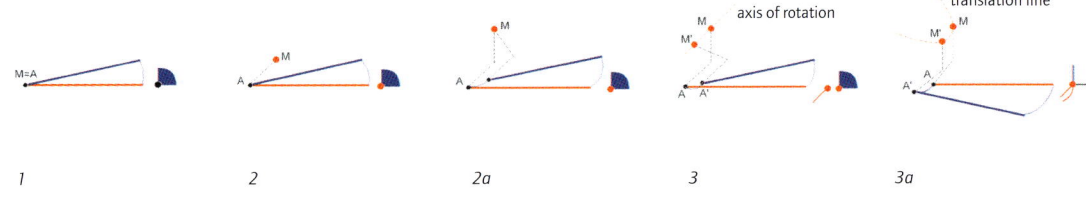

1 2 2a 3 3a

Adjacent centres of rotation

The shift, with a rotation, of a base line may be described as:

1   rotating around application point A, on the line or its produced part.
Here, the centre of rotation M coincides with application point A.
2   rotating around the fixed centre of rotation M, next to the line.
3   rotating around the centre of rotation M, which moves along a straight or curved line.

In the drawings a constant relation between the centre of rotation M and the rule is assumed.

The spatial distortion and displacements that occur when several rotational directions are combined, are sometimes complicated, particularly when they vary. Most buildings consist of simple geometrical shapes. Therefore, the transformation of a window frame or a façade (e.g. when rotating a ground plan), will usually be simple to draw with a computer.

Equal shiftings of the application point

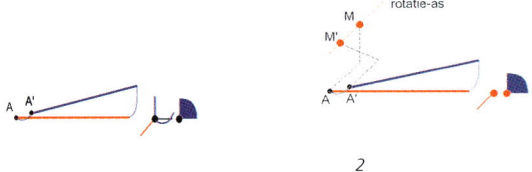

1 2

Various manipulations can result in the same shift, e.g.:

1   shift and rotation of the application point A itself.
2   rotation and shift of the centre of rotation M, that moves the application point A along.

First and second rotational axis

1   Here, the rotational axis is at right angles with the rotational direction. When there is only a rotation around the centre of rotation M, it will remain at the same position relative to the base line. The rotational axis offers insight into the geometry while reading the drawing. In addition it is important for production purposes.
2   When rotation is also performed around the point of application, a second rotational axis occurs.

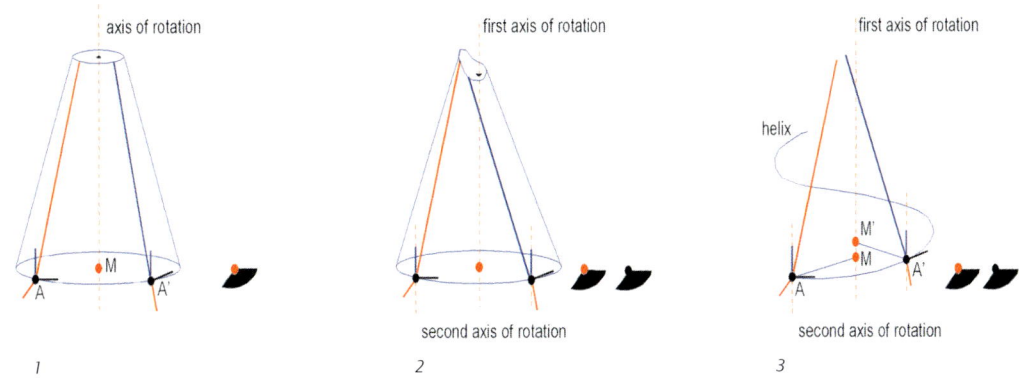

1   *2*   *3*

3   Here, a helix-shaped displacement line is formed by the linear shift of the centre of rotation M.

SURFACES OF REVOLUTION, COMPOSED OF RULES
A surface of revolution evolves from rotating a line around a centre of rotation. The first rotational direction component is the one around the vector of the rule.

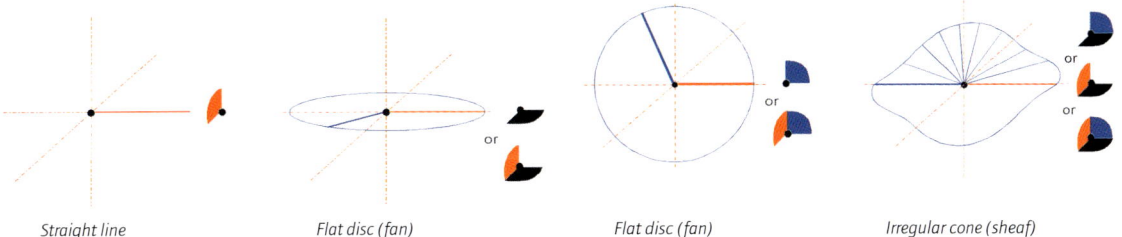

| Straight line | Flat disc (fan) | Flat disc (fan) | Irregular cone (sheaf) |

This rotation is not visible. With the rotational direction component parallel to the surface in which the rule turns, a flat disc, or 'fan', is formed. When a rotational direction component is neither parallel to the surface in which the straight line turns, nor at right angles to its own axis, a cone, or 'sheaf', is formed. By varying the degrees of the rotational direction components, an irregular cone is formed.

Rotation of rules around adjacent centre of rotation
The centre of rotation (the red dot), lies on the rotational axis. The application point (the black dot) may be adjacent to the rotational axis, at a varying distance. When this

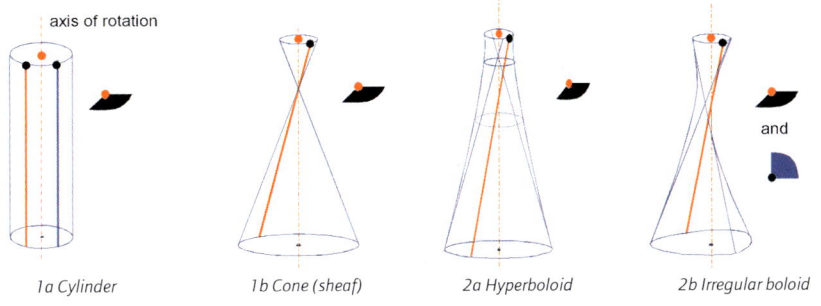

| 1a Cylinder | 1b Cone (sheaf) | 2a Hyperboloid | 2b Irregular boloid |

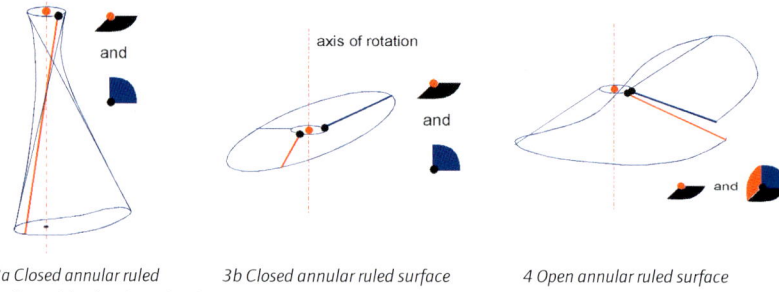

3a Closed annular ruled surface with rules through axis

3b Closed annular ruled surface

4 Open annular ruled surface

distance is constant and the shift of the application point in a surface is at right angles to the rotational axis, the shift line is a circle.

The twisted surfaces, of which the rules run through 360°, are called **annular ruled surfaces**. This is a new notion. When the straight line, after shift around the circle, connects to a straight line again, it is a **tight annular ruled surface**. As opposed to twisted surfaces, in surfaces of revolution the base lines (or their produced parts) run through one point, as with a cone. When this point is infinitely far, we have a cylinder. Cones and cylinders are not twisted, so they are not annular ruled surfaces.

Ruled surfaces with linear shift of application point

1   With a constant rotation, a curved sideline is formed.
2   This is a hyperbolic paraboloid (hypar) with a horizontal rotation of the base lines.

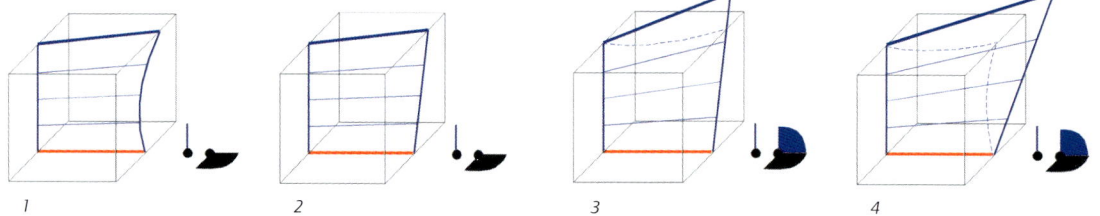

1

2

3

4

A hypar has straight lines in two directions. Of the above straight lines, only the sidelines of the surface have been drawn. The lengths of the straight lines and the degree of rotation vary. Should the length of the base lines remain equal, the result would be a helix-shaped curved sideline, according to the red dotted line.

3   Hypar with a rotation of the rails in two directions.
4   Hypar with mullions and transoms that are rotated in two directions. When cut off by parallel surfaces, this type of hypar is not immediately recognizable as a ruled surface in the intersecting lines.

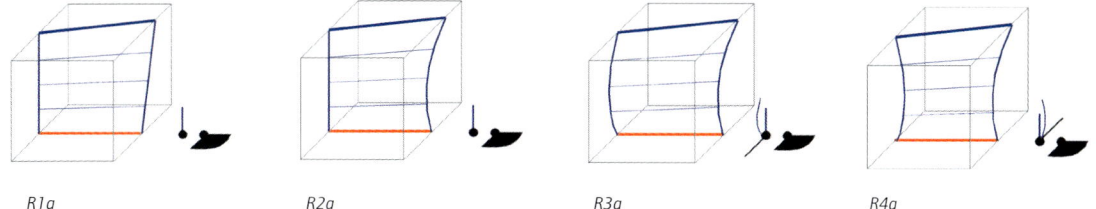

R1a   R2a   R3a   R4a

CLASSIFICATION DIAGRAM FOR RULED SURFACES

With the horizontal straight lines as rules, four base types of ruled surfaces occur, depending on the shape of the sidelines:

R1 Two straight sidelines.
R2 A straight and a convex sideline.
R3 A spherical and a concave sideline.
R4 Two convex sidelines.

The respective perceptions of concave and convex depend on the viewpoint.

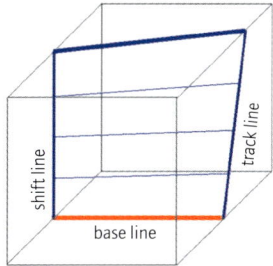

Comments:
- The ruled surfaces in this diagram are restricted to those with horizontal rules, and straight and/or curved sidelines.
- Because the rotation of a rule around its own axis is futile, its direction has not been included in the diagram.
- The diagram is based on straight and singly curved intersecting lines of cube surfaces with the twisted surface.
- Within a flat surface, all lines that run through one point may be either straight or curved. With a ruled surface that does not intersect itself, however, either one or two straight lines can be drawn through one point.

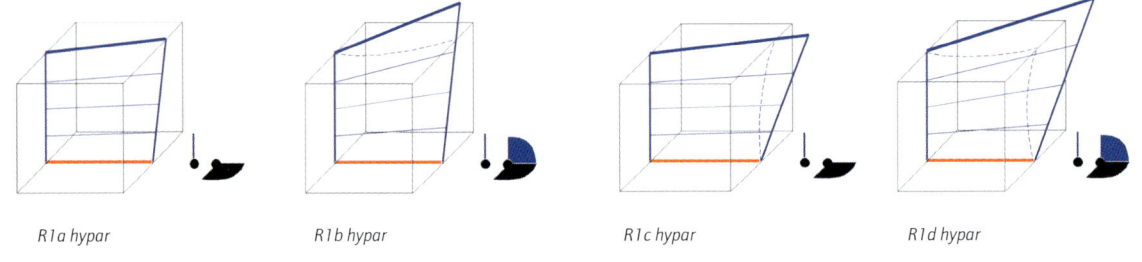

R1a hypar   R1b hypar   R1c hypar   R1d hypar

RULED SURFACES TYPES R 1, 2, 3 AND 4

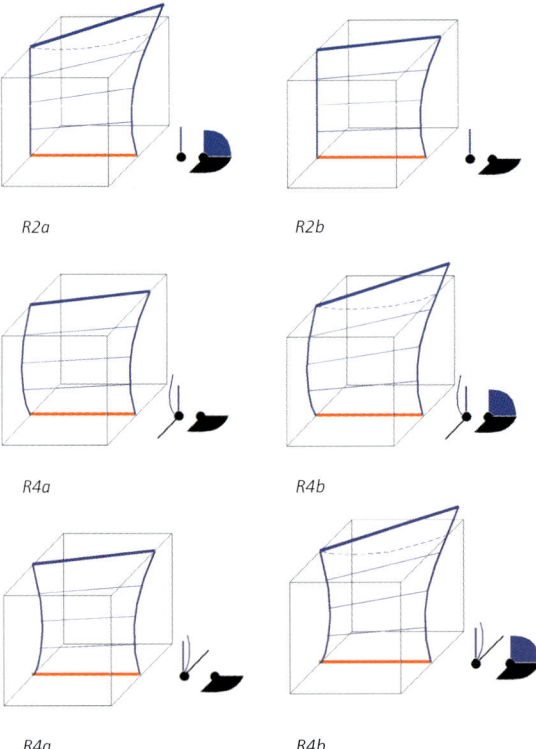

R2a   R2b

R4a   R4b

R4a   R4b

In the past decades, twisted hyperbolic vaults were built with concrete and wood. Before this project, twisted glass panels had not yet been developed. Some transparent hypar-shaped grid constructions were drawn to demonstrate architectural applications, e.g. roofs. Most of the examples feature a rotation of the rules in two directions. The series finishes with large roofs, suitable for public rooms, as they were often applied in factories, market halls and public transport junctions in the sixties and seventies, particularly in South America.

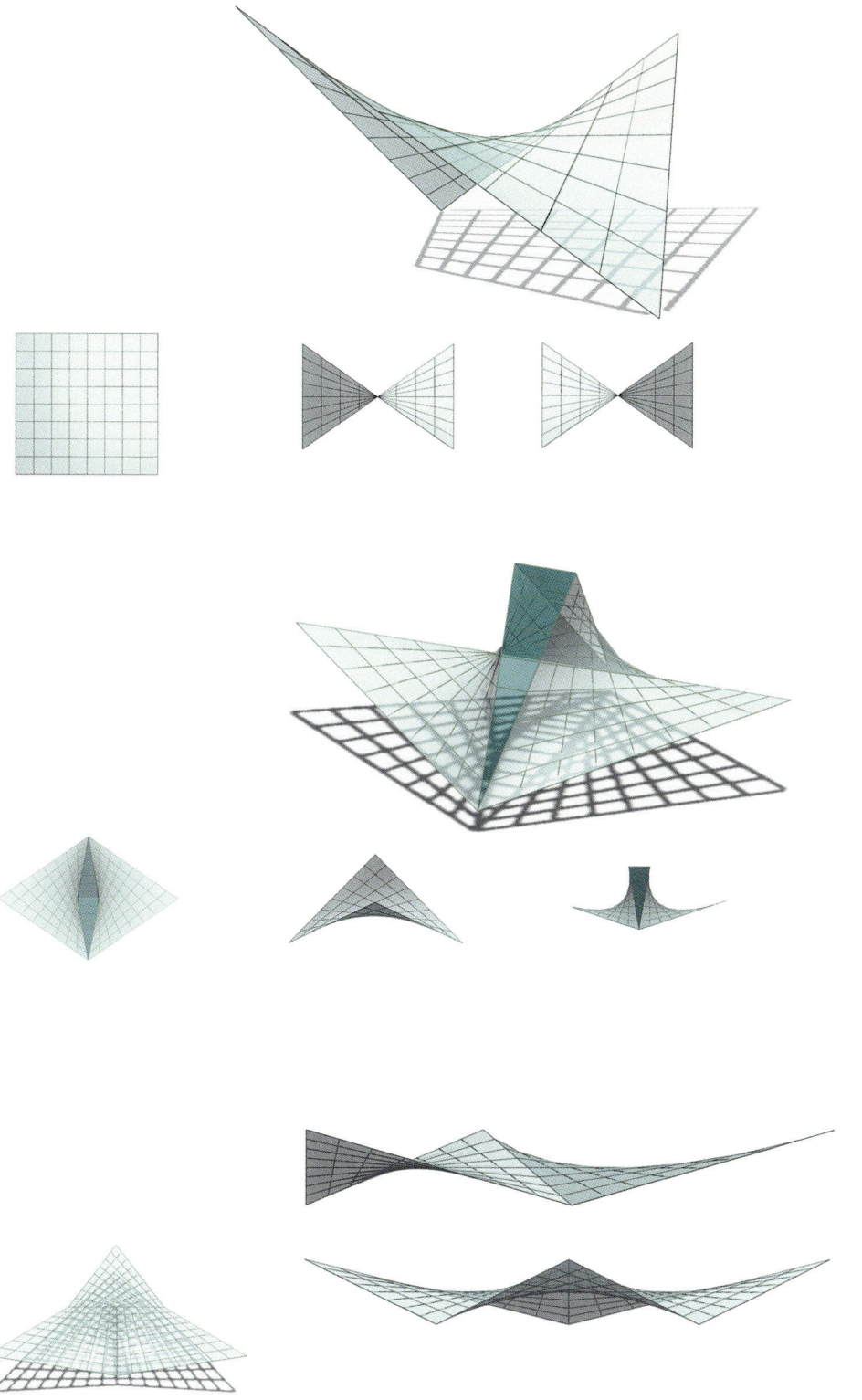

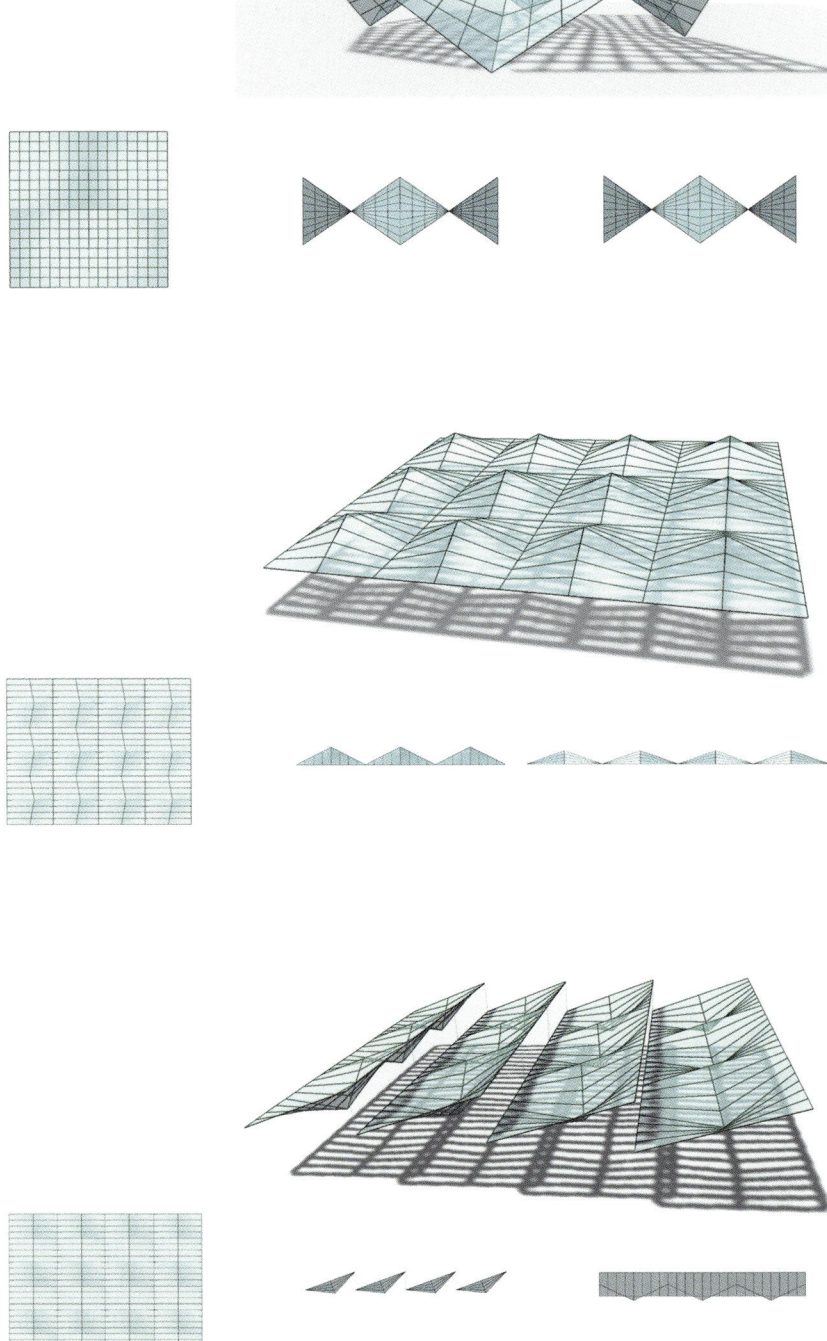

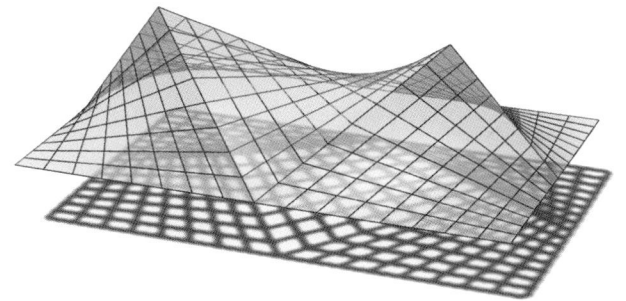

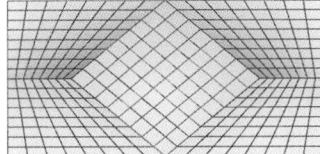 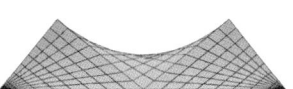 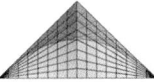

Particularly with a glass wall or roof, shadows offer interesting architectural opportunities.

The sunlight projects, through the grids of glazing bars and supporting structure, a spectacular pattern on the walls and floors of the interior.

One walks through the 3D object and its 2D projection.

The sequence of projected figures, which, in the course of the day blend together, can be compared to the image seen when flying over the building.

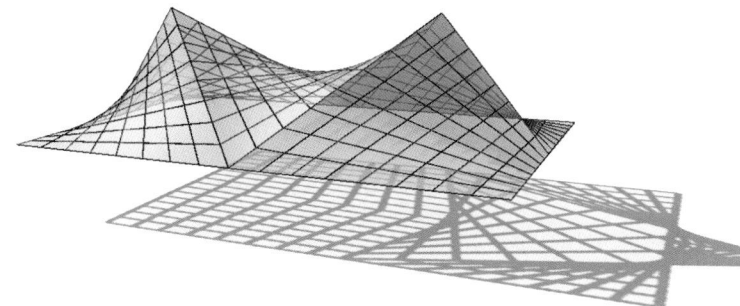

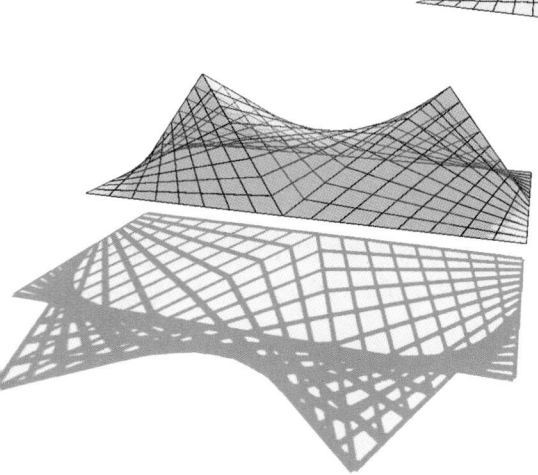

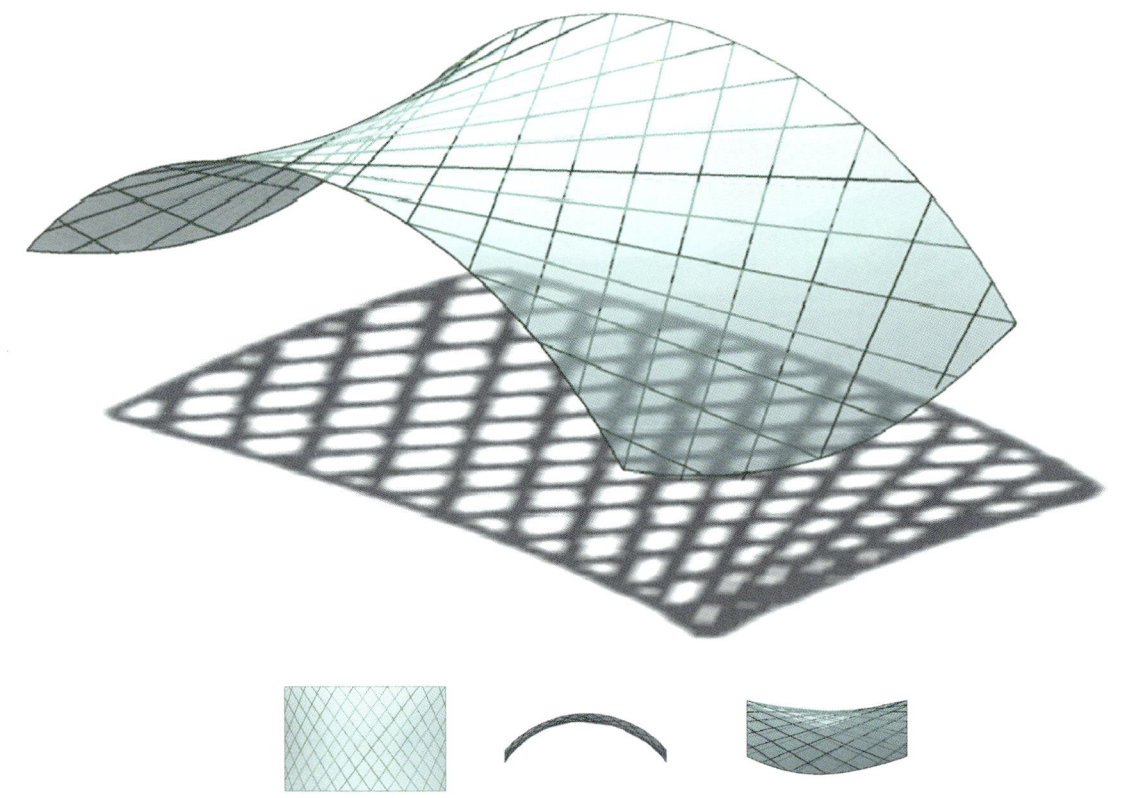

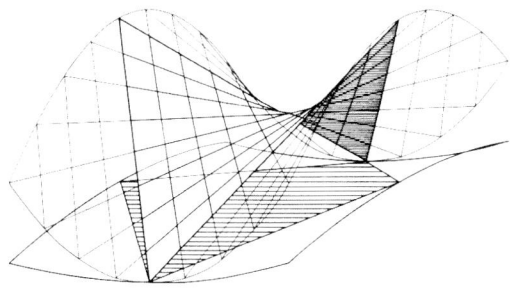

BOLOIDS

Hyperbolic paraboloids are hypars as well as boloids. They can be regarded as type R1 ruled surfaces (with rules in two directions in each point), but also as type R3 ruled surfaces (with two curved sides). Usually, in an R3 ruled surface, each point has only one rule, but a hyperboloid has two, due to symmetry. The above drawing shows equal borders in two parallel surfaces, with a double-symmetrical position of the rules. The second curved border was drawn shifting the first at right angles to the surface in which it lies.

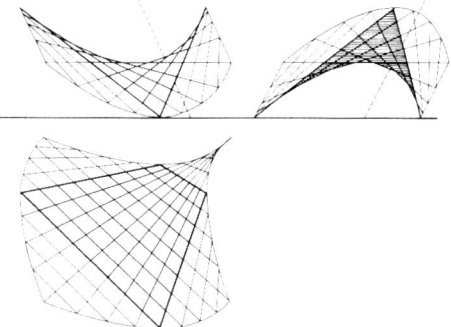

Geometry can also be more complex, with ellipses instead of circles. The above hyperbolic paraboloid was drawn with ellipses at the ends. They were mutually shifted sideways. [4-1]

SURFACES COMPOSED OF IDENTICAL CURVES

SURFACES OF REVOLUTION COMPOSED OF CURVES

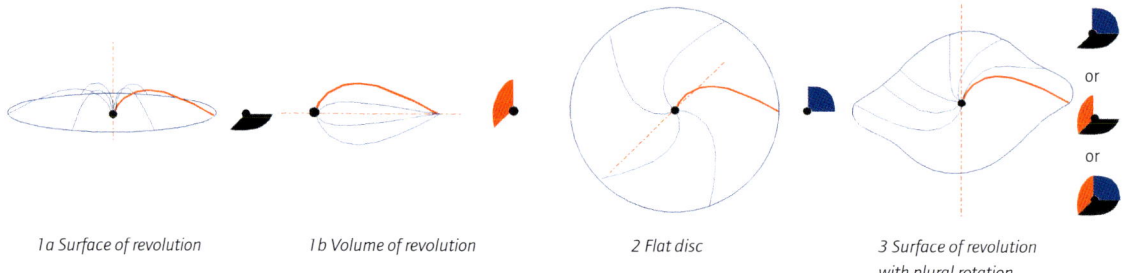

1a Surface of revolution   *1b Volume of revolution*   *2 Flat disc*   *3 Surface of revolution with plural rotation*

1 Surface/volume of revolution, e.g. dome shape and acorn shape. The rotational axis is in the surface of the curve and at right angles with the surface of the rotational direction. With a half circle as a base line, a sphere is formed.
2 Flat disc. The rotational axis is at right angles to the surface in which the curve lies.
3 Surface of revolution with plural rotation. This is not a twisted surface, because the intersection of the base line is not at the same spot on bot lines. It is a cone, composed of curves that rotate in more than one direction.

Surface of revolution in two directions   *Offsets in the surface of the trusses*

In this surface of revolution a series of twisted base lines was drawn. However, the curved lines cannot be materialized as identical trusses at every point, to support a glass surface of revolution.

By way of illustration, a curve surface was drawn with red base lines and straight shift lines. The curve surface in the glass roof, therefore, lies between red contours.

When the base lines would be changed into equal trusses, a blue line was drawn from each (red) base line by offsets, to indicate the lower side of the truss. The glass connection at 'a' and 'c' will be vertically below and above the truss and at 'b' horizontally adjacent. The angle of incidence of the glass will vary at the trusses.

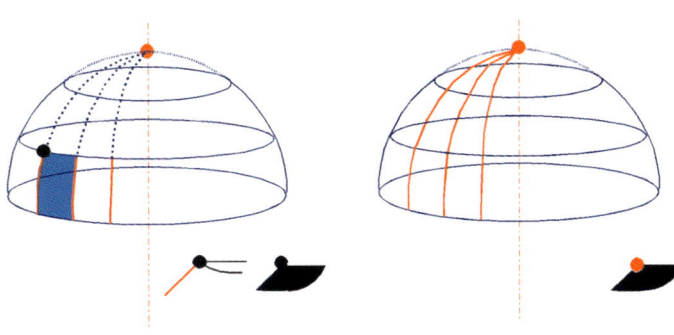

Surface of revolution, seems curve surface   *Surface of revolution*

Overlaps in the definitions

Sometimes, a surface of revolution has the appearance of a curve surface, for instance when the curve has an adjacent rotation centre. When a line can be drawn through the curve, that also runs through the (fixed) centre of rotation, then it is a surface of revolution.

Surfaces of revolution with adjacent centre of rotation

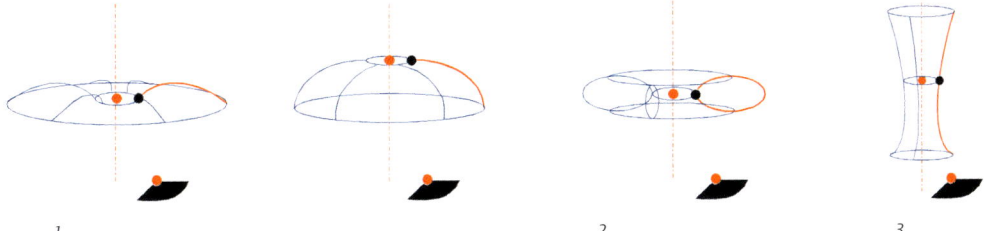

1   2   3

In a rotation surface, the centre of rotation and the application point do not necessarily coincide:

1 Dome with circle core. Depending on the position of the curve with regard to the point of application, a sphere or a spherical segment may be formed when the line has a constant curvature.
2 Ring, torus or doughnut. Here, an ellipse is shifted along a circle. The shift line (the circle) as well as the base line (the ellipse) can be chosen to be more complex, e.g. an assembly of straight and curved parts.
3 Hyperboloid. The point of application does not necessarily have to be at the end of the base line.

Identical surfaces with different base lines

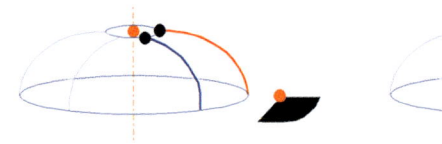 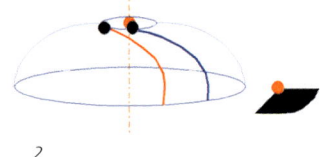 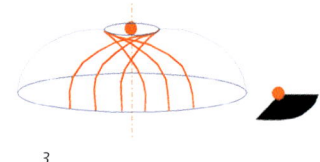

1   2   3

1   The base line is singly curved. It is the intersecting line of a flat surface and the surface of revolution.

2   The flat surfaces do not necessarily have to intersect the rotational axis.

3   Surfaces of revolution with only a rotation at right angles with the surface in which the line is, are mirror symmetrical. Therefore, the surface may also be composed of mirrored base lines.

Hyperboloids

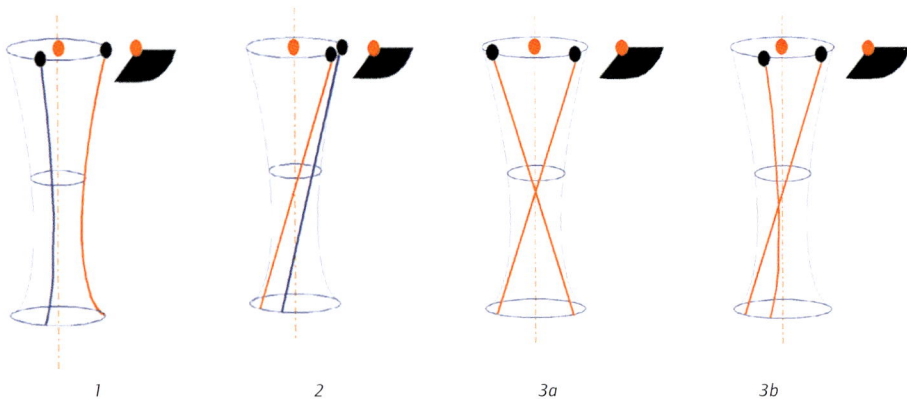

1   2   3a   3b

1   A hyperboloid may be regarded as a surface of revolution, composed of curved base lines, but also as a ruled surface, composed of straight lines. It evolves from a circle-shaped shift line of the application point. This occurs, for instance, with a rotation in one direction around a centre of rotation, when the base line does not intersect the rotational axis and is not in a surface that is at right angles with the rotation.

2   A hyperboloid is mirror symmetrical and has straight lines in two directions.
    This is an advantage for the materialization, because the shape may be composed
    of mirror symmetrical segments with straight sides.
3   With a hyperboloid a combination of recurrent straight and curved lines is possible.
    In concrete constructions straight edges for the molds and structural elements are
    often chosen, while the course of the reinforcement often follows a curved line.

CURVE SURFACES WITH ADJACENT CENTRE OF ROTATION

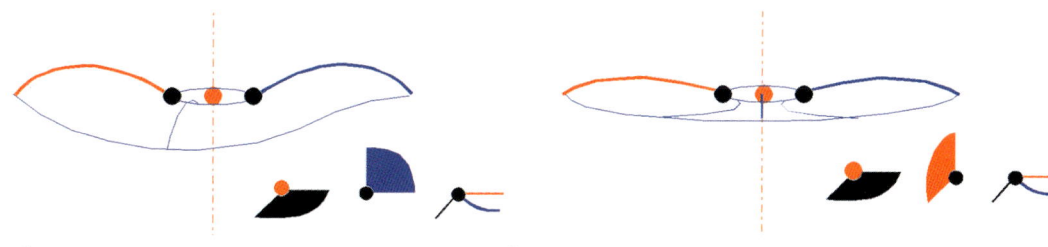

1   *2*

1   The curves turn within vertical surfaces. As opposed to surfaces of revolution,
    there is not one point on, or in the produced part of the base line where they all
    intersect. The surface has the shape of a fun fair train that is covered with an
    awning during its wavy ride.
2   Here, the surface in which the curve lies rotates from vertical to horizontal, and back.

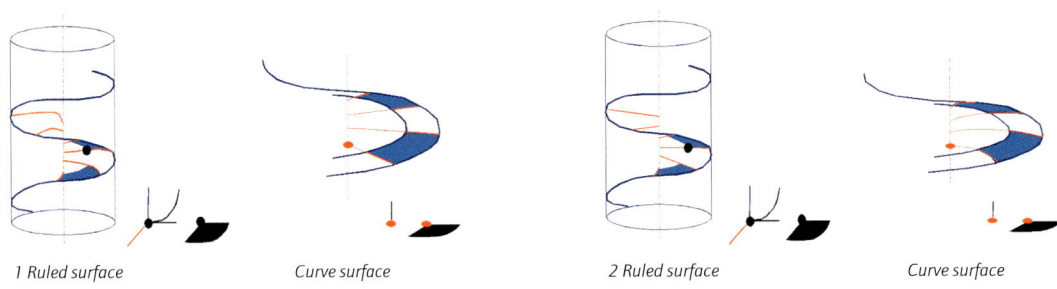

1 Ruled surface　　*Curve surface*　　*2 Ruled surface*　　*Curve surface*

Identical surfaces with different descriptions

With rotating models, the twisted surface often is a ruled as well as a curve surface; it is just a different intersecting line of a flat surface through the twisted surface that is repeated. The surface can be drawn in various ways:

1 Shifting the point of application of a straight or curved base line along a helix-shaped line and simultaneously rotating it.

2 Shifting and rotating a base line around a (possibly adjacent) centre of rotation.

Curve surfaces with linear shift of the application point

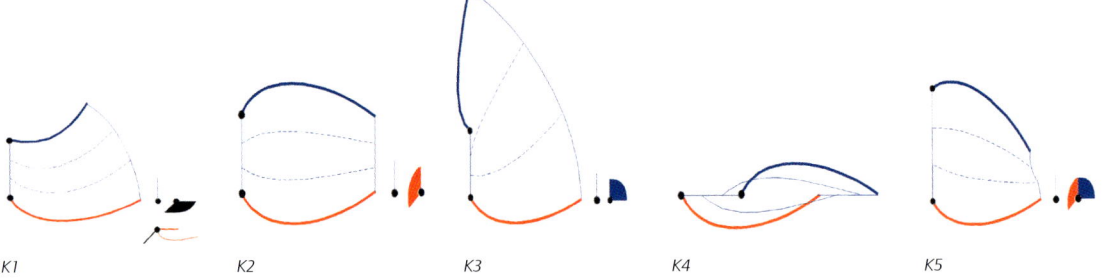

K1　　*K2*　　*K3*　　*K4*　　*K5*

When rotating at right angles with the displacement direction, repetition of segments may occur.

Curve surfaces with linear displacements are interesting, because the straight lines easily connect to adjacent flat or straight building parts. The straight lines offer a 'visual hold' within the unusual, often complex geometry of the curved lines and surfaces. By combination of mirrored and complementary surfaces, a repetition of building parts occurs.

The above types are shown in perspective in the following pages.

Perspectives

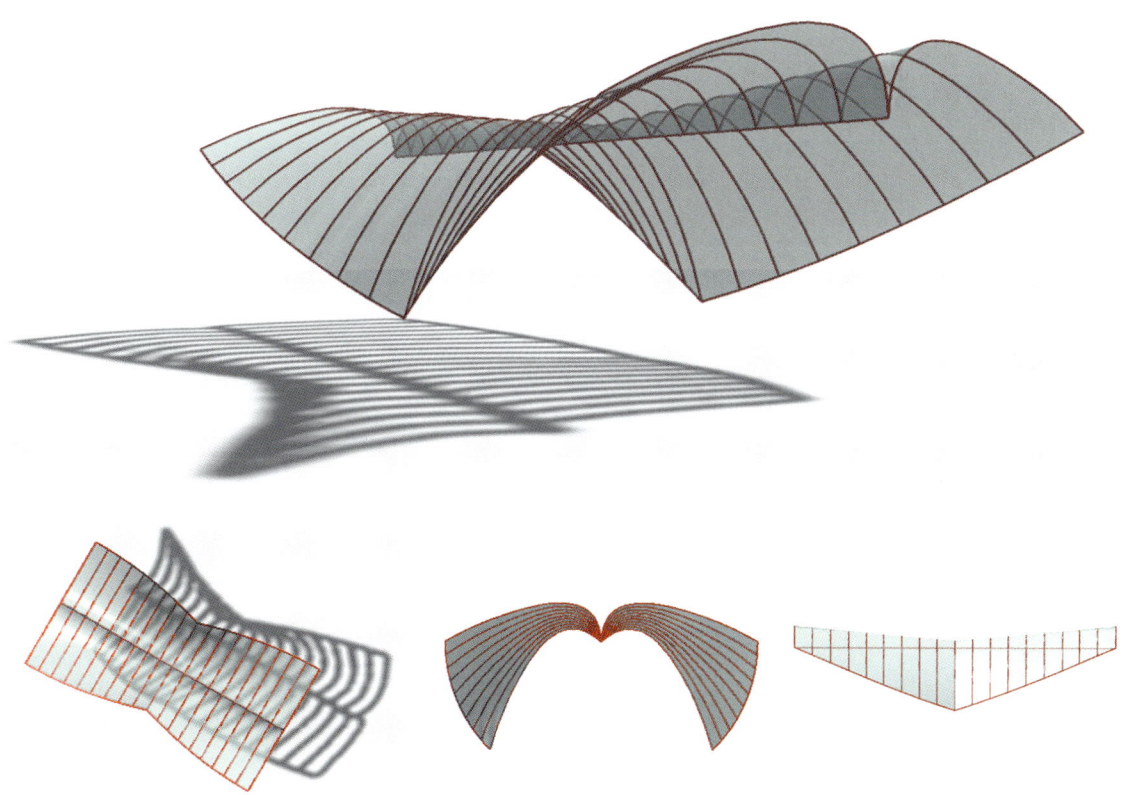

Curve surface type K1

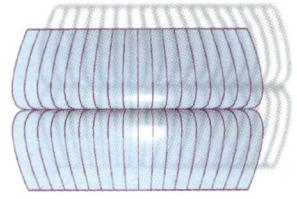

Curve surface type K2

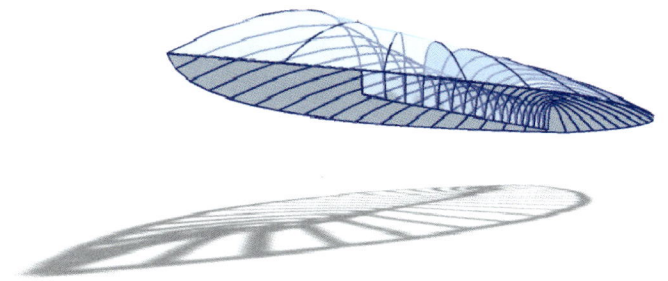

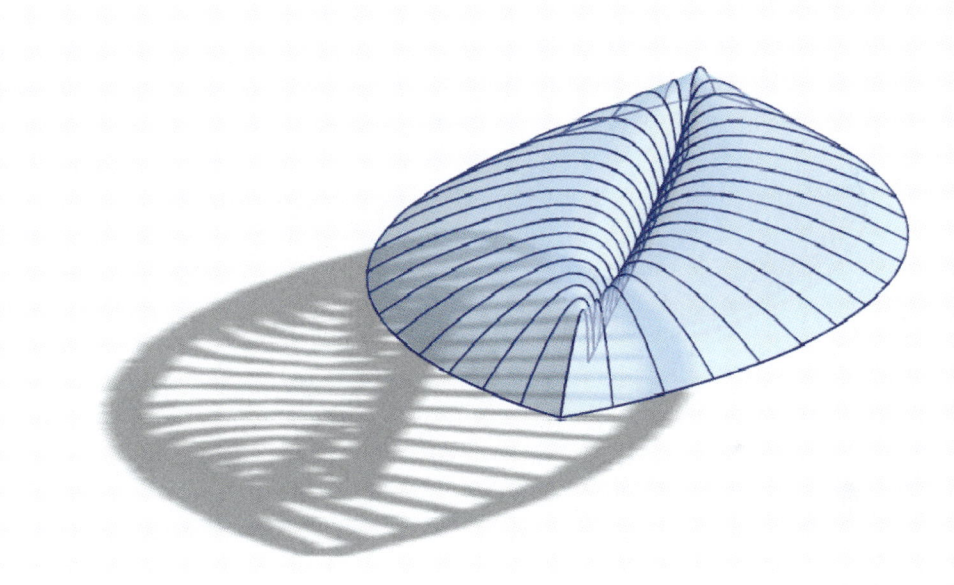

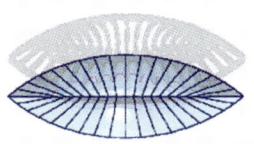

Curve surface type K3

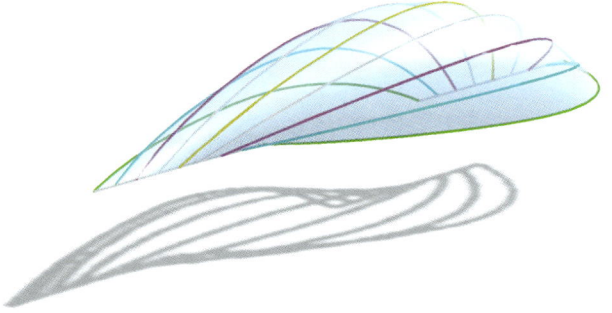

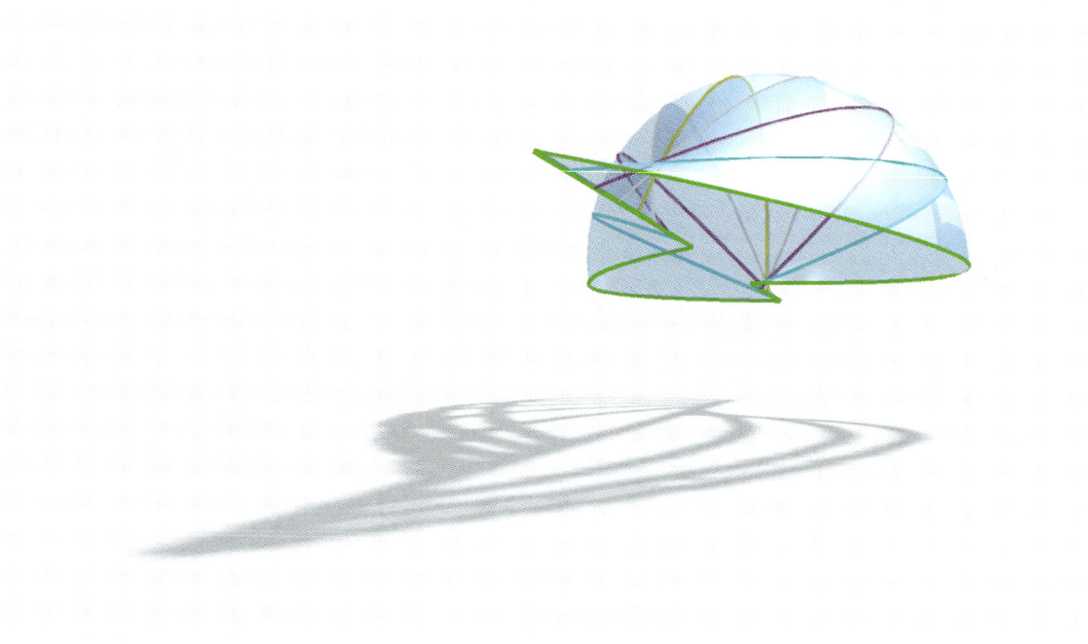

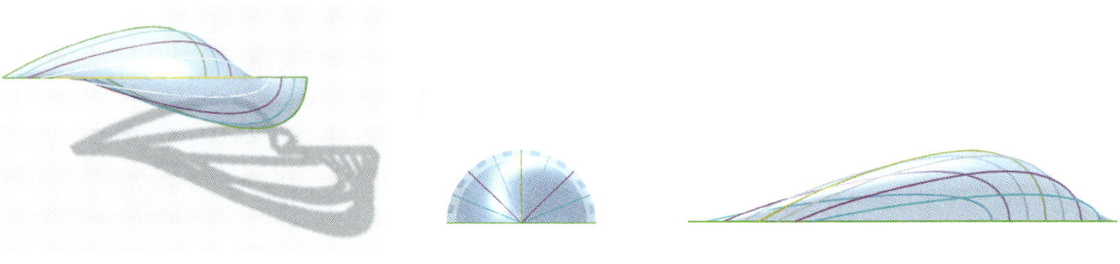

Curve surface type K4

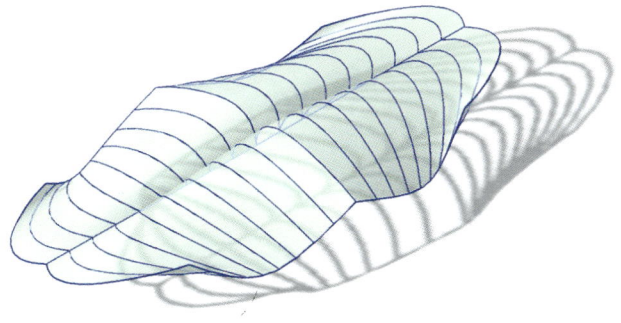

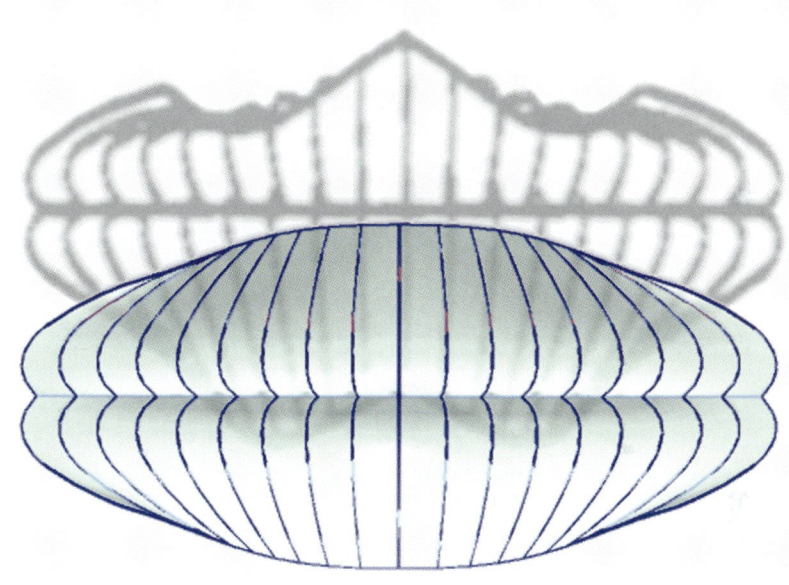

Curve surface type K5

05

MODEL RESEARCH

As an introduction to the development of twisted surfaces, the author designed a group of houses that integrally consists of 'uni-directionally freely curved surfaces'. They consist of 'rules' shifted along a free curve. Twisted surfaces are even more complex: rotation is added to the shift.

Realization of each of these steps in transforming, requires an integral innovation of the production process. Because of the broadness of the field in which developments are to take place, in the designs of both products and buildings, only a few geometrical parameters were varied. First 'tordos' were studied, that combine a superstructure similar to that of conventional rectangular buildings, with one or more relatively simple hypar-shaped façades. Subsequently models with a torsion axis were examined: 'twisters' that, by repetition of floors, feature large series of similar elements. One of the disadvantages of twisters is that the mullions in the façade are double-curved (in a helical shape). To solve the introduced problems, initially a high but only slightly twisted building was designed. The curving of the components was negligible. The loss of useful floor area could be disregarded due to the limited slope of the façades. Subsequently, models were designed with increasingly transformed parts and a decreasing repetition of components. The series was concluded with building designs composed of various surface types: combinations of strongly twisted surfaces with flat and cylindrical planes.

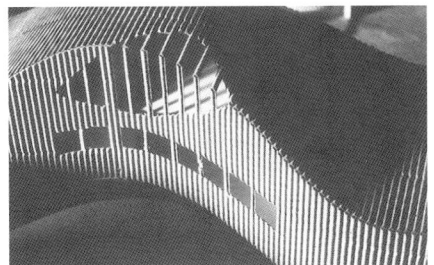

PRELIMINARY RESEARCH MODEL: SINGLE CURVED SURFACES

CASE-STUDY: 'CAD ON A ROOF'

Inspired by the many wonderful shapes that appear when a sheet of paper is folded along a curve, a building was designed. Just like the cardboard in the model, the roofs have a relief: blue corrugated steel plates are used for the finish. Surfaces in which the profile continues across the curved ridgeline, have not yet been applied in architecture. The shape has, however, been used in cardboard gift-wrappings and commercial packaging. In order to make the design look more harmonious and complete, a complementary model was added. [5-1]

Usually the council orders an urban-plan to be made. Subsequently a users target-group is determined and a developer appointed, who in his turn, will select an architect to produce a design. In this case it was the other way around. Therefore it became possible to find an optimum between shape, use and materialization, with less emphasis on economic aspects, and more time to develop components. A building block was designed with the help of a sheet of paper and the design was completed by adding a complementary building block. Hereafter industrial participants and an investor were selected. It wasn't until then that we went in search of a building site. Property developer and contractor SBB, Beverwijk, promised the Grondbedrijf in Rotterdam to realize the project, provided we would be allocated a location there. Eventually, no piece of land was allocated, because a higher building density than that of the designed model was required [5-2]

Introductory model research

A strong hull for catamarans and trimarans can be made by bending two plywood plates with curved edges and then glueing them together. This inspired investigating such sheet manipulations in architecture. If one folds a sterile piece of paper along curved lines, the effects of light and shadow can turn it into a landscape with softly flowing tones, laden with associations. 5-3

By applying cardboard instead of paper, the sheet's transformation options were restricted to single curved surfaces. This considerably simplified the definition process.

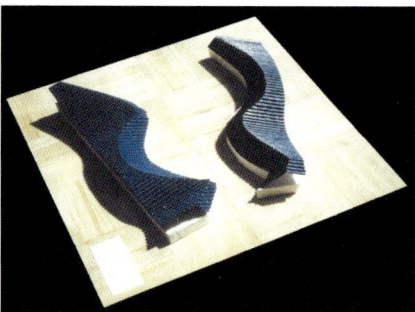

The model, based on a conventional row of terraced houses, combines strong and gentle curves. The roof corrugation runs across the ridge.

DRAWING BY COMPUTER

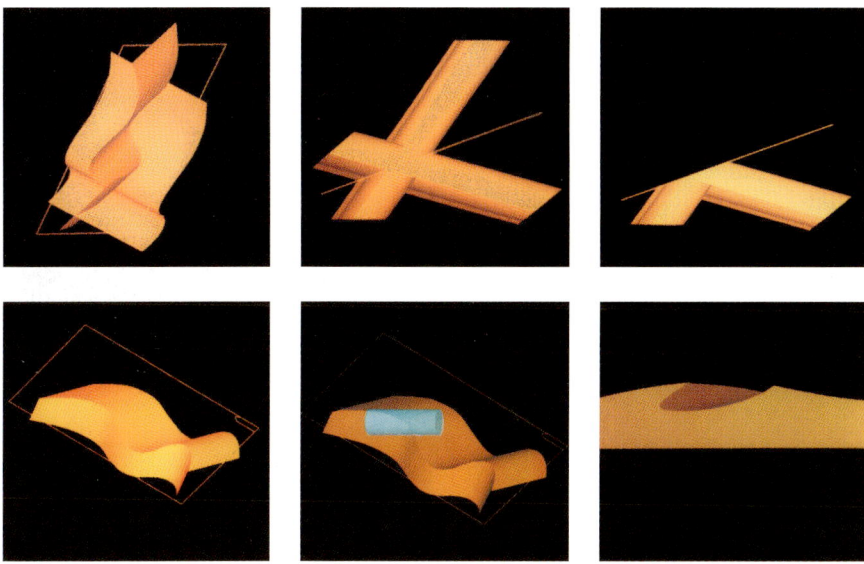

For a long time we tried to find the mathematical relationship between meeting angle (between the rules in both roofs at the ridge line), roof curvature and shape of the ridge line itself. This was difficult. When transforming a piece of cardboard, we observed that the folding line (ridge line) is in a flat plane, that also contains the bisectors of the intersecting rules. Their angles are constant. With these data four different combinations of two curved surfaces could be made, in which their curving directions were either equal or complementary. After this the search for a mathematical relation between curvature of the surface and folding line was abandoned. The cardboard building model was first drawn by hand and then, after determining the curvatures with small tolerances, by computer.

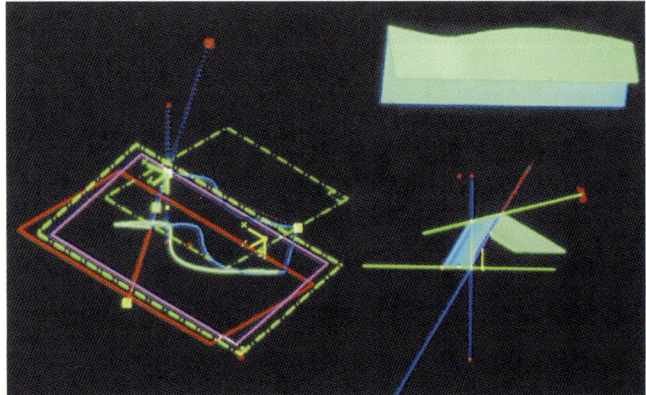

Examples of generated shapes

ASSOCIATIVE GEOMETRY

The overall image of the designed houses looks harmonious because the curvatures of lines and surfaces (e.g. ridges, roof edges and balcony balustrades), are interrelated. Finding the right curvature was a time-consuming job, as it also influenced the shape of the complementary houses. To simplify and accelerate the search, Robert Aish wrote associative geometry routines whereby parameters (positioning and curve of the ridge, as well as the position and angle of the rear and front façade) could be varied. Their effects on the model were displayed within seconds. 5·4 The complexity of design, however, made it difficult to quickly oversee implications of changes, not only aesthetically for curvature, but also functionally in façade elevations, floor plans and room heights. The associative geometry routine required considerable calculation power and slowed down drawing. Therefore, soon the decision was made to conclude the routine and fix the ridge line's shape.

When associative geometry routines are applied, all generated parts are geometrically interrelated. The resulting image obtains an ingenious harmony that is similar to that in 'art by engineers', like bridges. It also will occur in free-form shapes made by varying other parameters.

ARCHITECTURAL ASPECTS

The building blocks consist of four houses. The compact shape implies a small exterior surface compared to the floor surface. The costs accompanying the curving of surfaces are concentrated in the construction of the roofs and exterior walls. When applying curved surfaces, a concave and a convex wall have an equal outer surface, but a very different floor surface. An outward curving façade is more profitable. The models demonstrate many variations in the use of curved surfaces. Their different curvatures lead to high and low, deep and shallow, large and small houses. Their floor surface is larger than usual to compensate for the loss of space due to wall curvature. The sinuous fronts of the houses appear traditional with the brickwork and sloping roofs. In contrast the rear side has a flat curtain wall.

The geometry of the housing blocks is relatively simple.

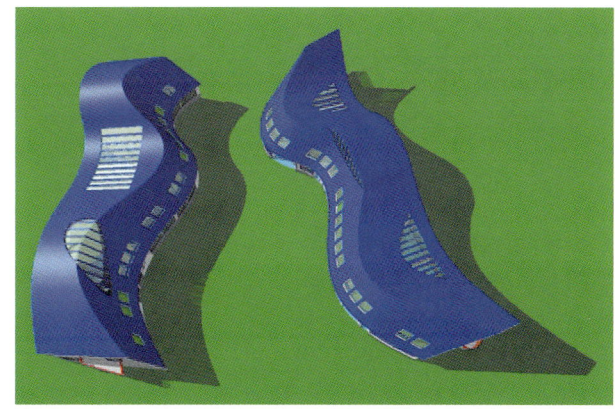

The rear façades incline at 15° and meet the 15° sloping sinuous roofs at right angles everywhere. This facilitates construction.

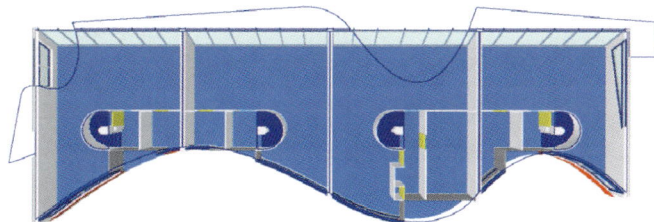

Each house has a different entrance, which is what many residents prefer. The cores of the houses (with stairs and sanitary unit) are in the centre zone. Due to the varying distances from façade to core, the houses have either a storage room or a garage next to the entrance.

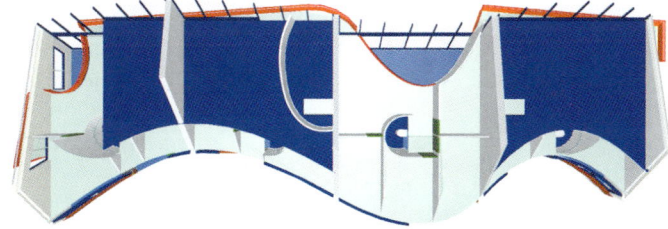

The skylight contours are determined by intersecting a horizontal surface with the sinuous roof, 2,400 mm above the first floor. The contours of the voids (open spaces) in the first floor are identical to those of the skylights. Therefore, all walls around the voids are equal in height. The skylights are easy to build, because their surrounding beams are in a flat surface. If there is no second floor, the walls connect to the roofs and above 2,400 mm are made aout of glass. Through this, and due to the large voids, the curved surfaces will be experienced as continuous elements throughout the houses.

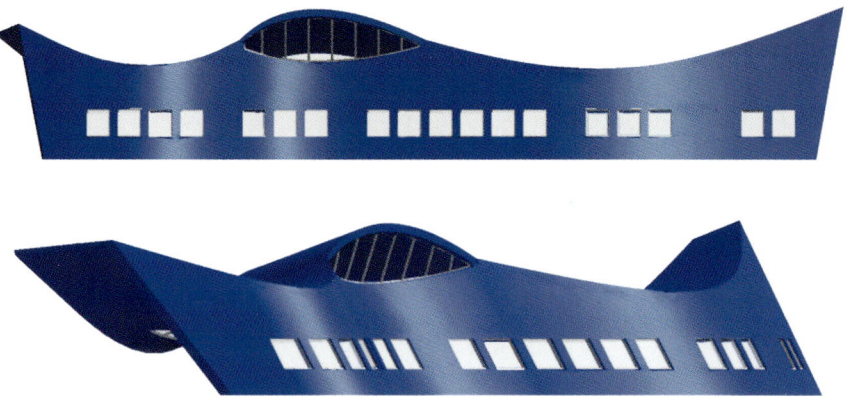

The skylights seem identical and rectangular when viewed straight on, but due to the curving of the roof, they all differ in curvature, size and corner-angles. This requires a different kind of detailing than an orthogonal design.

The roof is intersected by a cylinder to define the contours of a skylight. Due to the curvature of the roof, the hole acquires cutting edges that vary in width. Their tapering shapes evoke the image of speed changes.

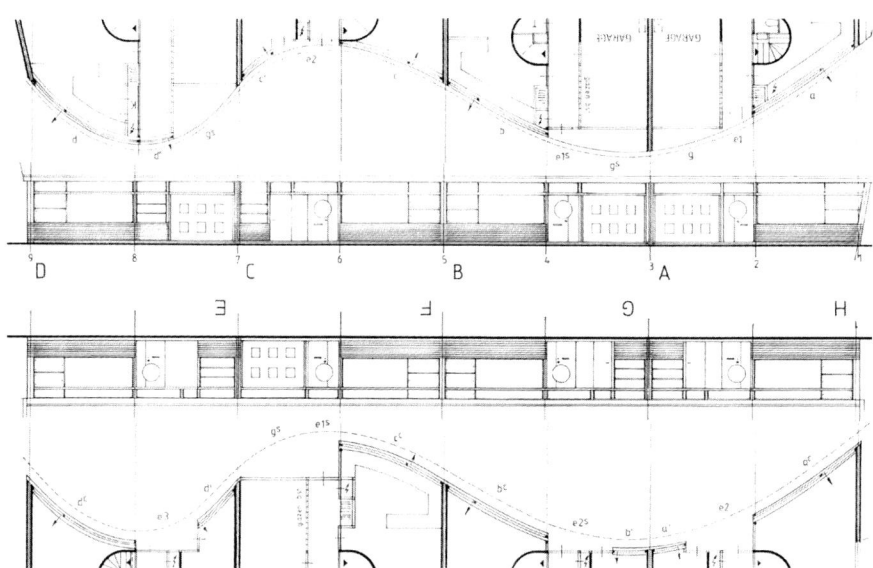

The reference plane is in the construction's centre. Therefore equally curved building parts, (e.g. window frames, glass sheets, lintels) can be applied to complementary and mirrored buildings. The details have been tuned to the implicit positioning exchange of interior and exterior.

Ground plans and front views of

houses ABCD

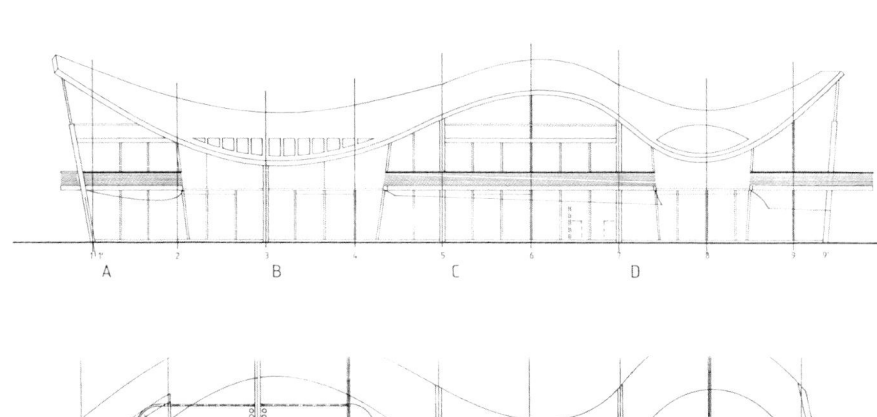

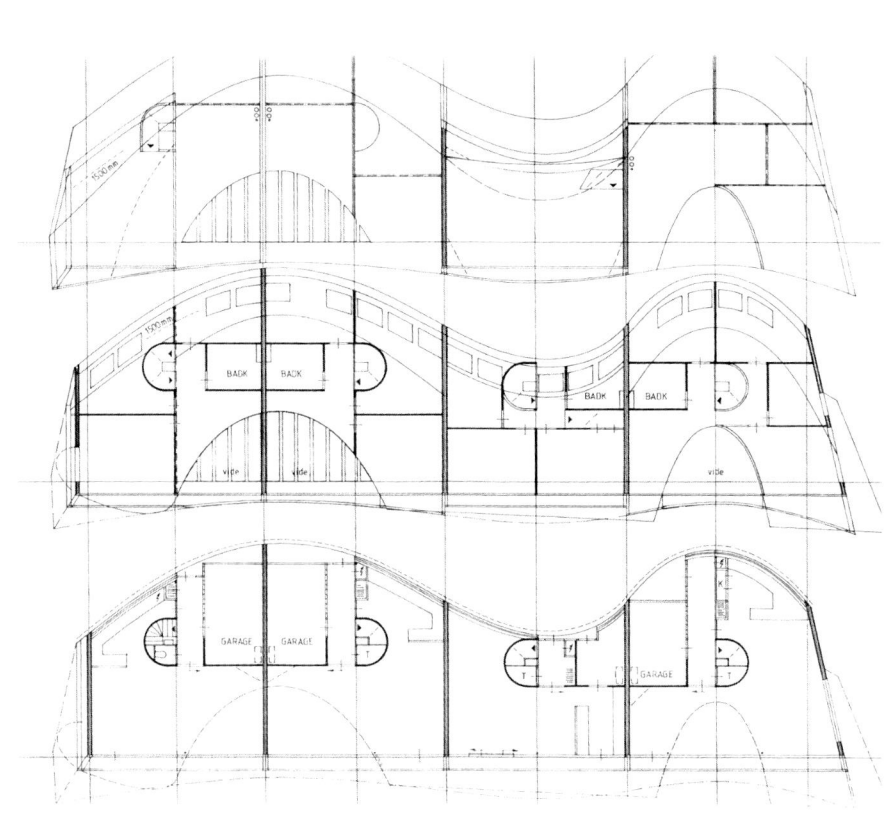

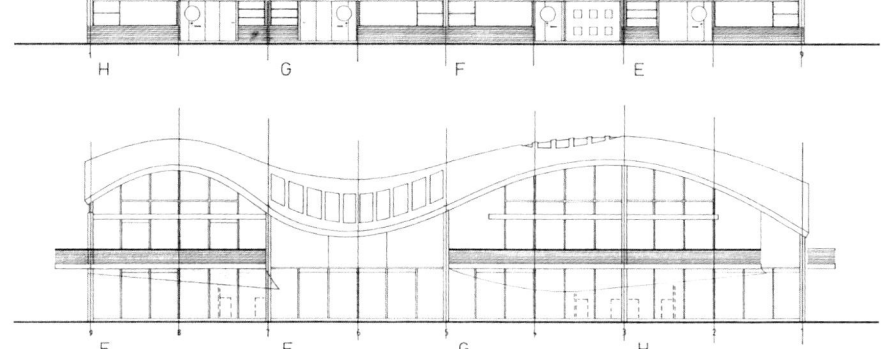

H G F E

E F G H

*Ground plans and front views of
houses EFGH*

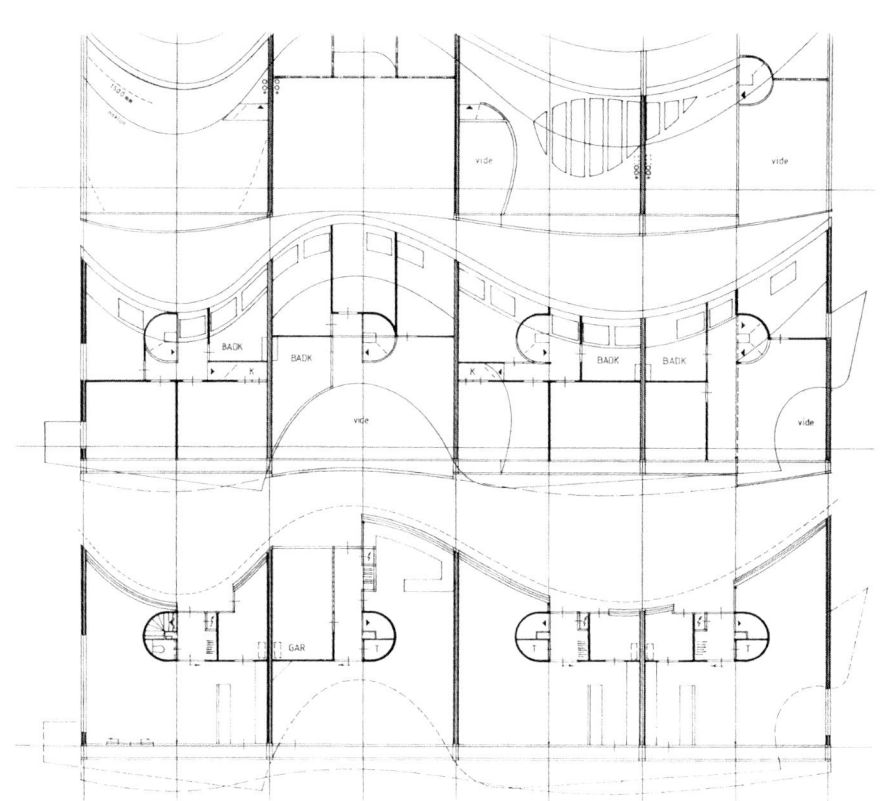

Sunlight produces ever-changing shadows on the sinuous roofs [5-7]

Repetition, mirroring, complementarity and matching

MODEL PHOTOS AND COMPUTER DRAWINGS

As in a musical composition the elements vary in rhythm: building walls indicate the main beat, while skylights provide the variations.

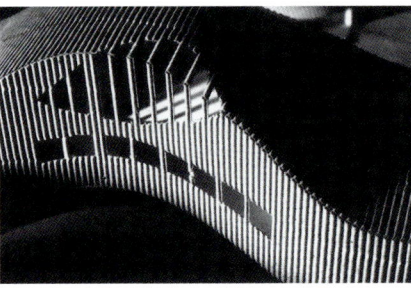
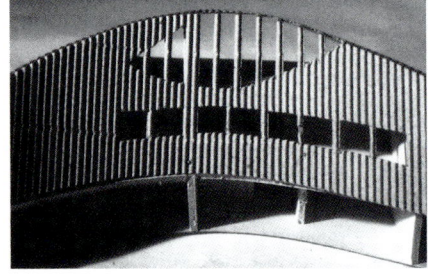

Floodlight

Rhythm in the façade

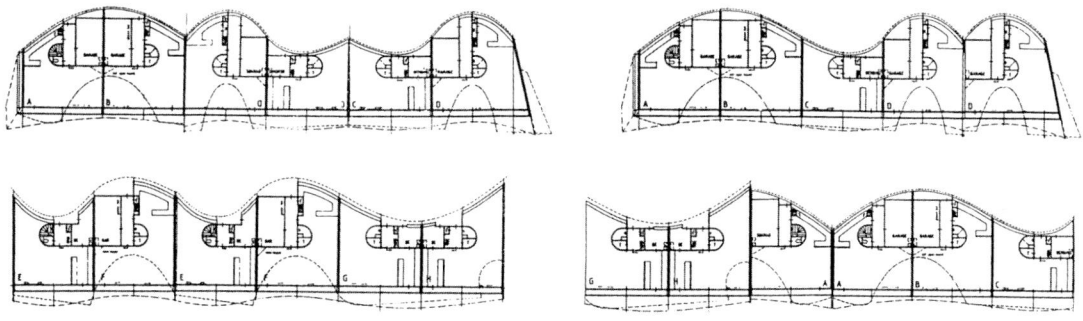

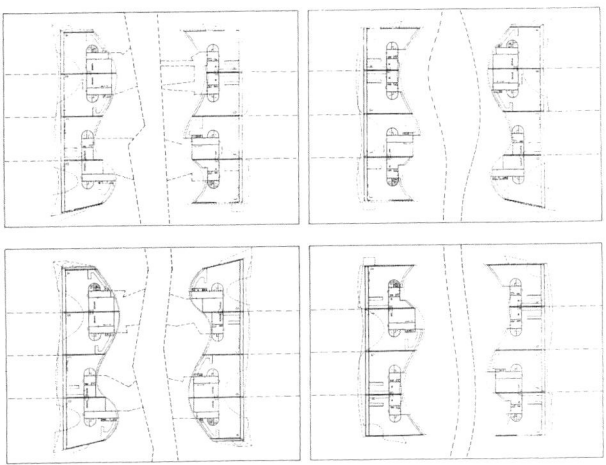

Curved building

elements are cheaper to produce in large quantities. To increase the number of applied variations, at building block level, combinations can be made with mirrored and complementary units.

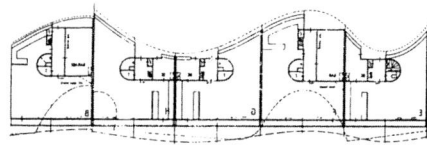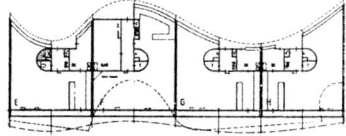

Mirroring, repetition and complementarity is also possible at the level of houses. Above, matching is achieved by equal dimensions of some side walls. Thus, various types can be combined into series that differ from the original building block.

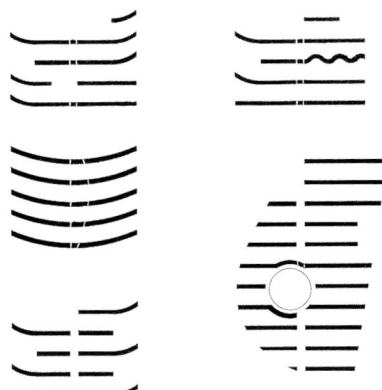

Because of the linear layout with the central path, the neighbourhood maintains its unity, even when the contours follow a free shape, e.g. along a curved road, or when large open spaces are created for playgrounds and parking lots.

ANTENNAE SHAPED TOWN PLANS

All houses have their living rooms and gardens facing south and entrances facing north. To compensate for the absence of a traditional housing orientation (face to face), a connecting path was made across the rows of houses, to act as a 'spinal column' in the urban plan. There is a great variety of houses, and the gable ends of the rows are all different.

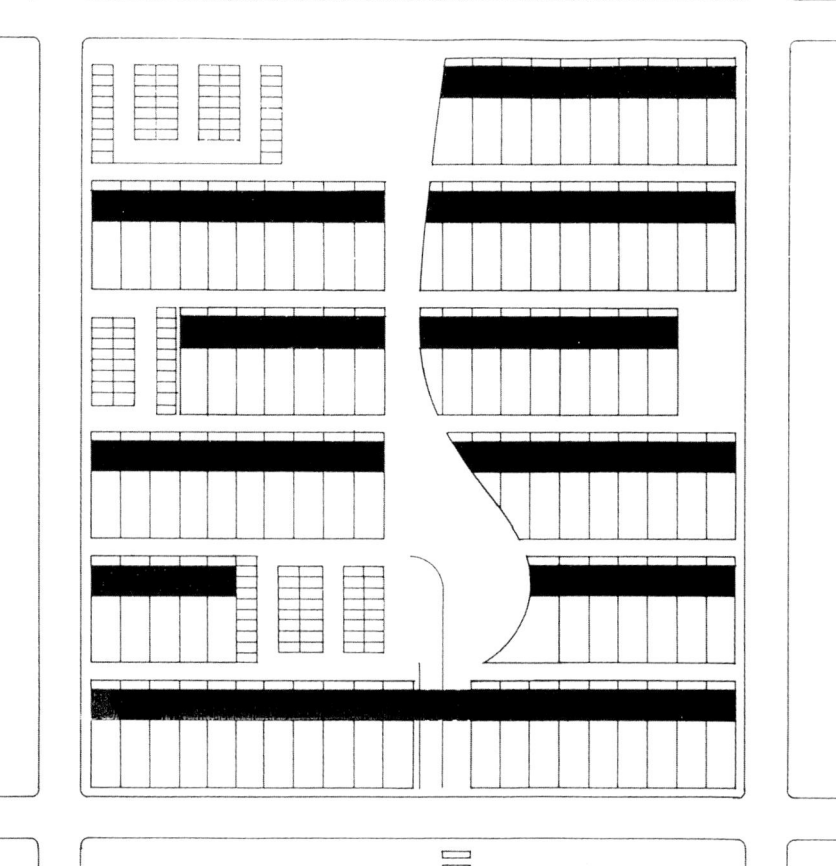

TWISTED SURFACES AND VOLUMES

POSITIONING TWISTERS IN URBAN CONTEXT

During the elaboration of the earlier described model, the VNC (the Association of Dutch Concrete Industries who sponsored that project), proposed designing an adjustable mold and making the parapets in concrete. This seemed so simple to the author that he decided to introduce a rotation of the vertical straight lines in the surface, in order to increase the image's expressive qualities. The result was an adjustable mold for twisted concrete panels.

To gain further insight, the various types of twisted surfaces were outlined. The most common torsions in the building industry to date were described separately. Then relatively simple twisted façades were studied in the models Twister A and Tordo A. As the rotation per element of one model proved to be rather strong, and too much variation in element dimensions occurred in the other model, Tordo 1 was designed. The architectural prerequisites for the elements were clearly described, with a view to finding suitable partners to develop the building and its components. Torsion per element was so small that one could apply faceting with flat or single-curved elements instead of twisted ones. 5-5

Having proved that it was feasible to produce twisted window frames as well as the matching glass panes, stronger torsions were applied to the models. Thus confusion with geometry of non-developable surfaces, as had occurred during the designing of models, was avoided. It was also less attractive for a possible principal to resort to faceting building elements for reasons of cost. The models have specific qualities:

- Twister 1 and 2 are 60 metres high and have a strong rotation (1.5° per m). Twister 1 has the same rotation as Twister 2, but a greater spatial complexity, because a cylinder intersects a twisted volume.
- Twister 3 is a 150 metre high tower with a huge recurrence of elements. The parts as such are hardly rotated (0.45° per m), but the overall effect is spectacular. By cold bending the elements, the façade is easy and cheap to produce.
- Twister 4 consisting of two contrary rotating wings, has an increased spatial complexity.
- Twister 5 is the first tower in the series without a cylindrical core.
- Several low-rise tordos show uses of the various types of twisted façades in smaller buildings, and provide insight into the different ways they reflect the surroundings.
- Angler 1 and 2 and Slider 1 and 2 are inclined tower models with cylindrical corners, that combine components developed in this research project, e.g. the window frame system and the cold bent tempered laminated glass.

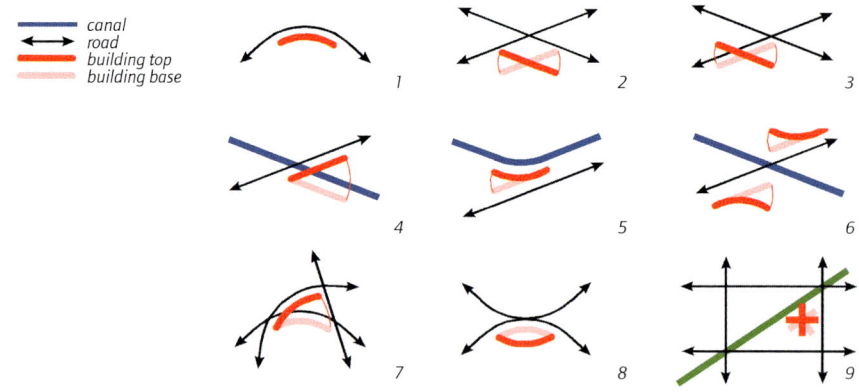

canal
road
building top
building base

1 · *2* · *3* · *4* · *5* · *6* · *7* · *8* · *9*

The positioning of twisters in
an urban context

1 A curved façade can accentu-
ate a change of direction
caused by a bend in the road
and can connect the directions of intersecting roads.

2 A twisted façade connects at
the upper and lower side to
different directions.

3 The building can sway at
great height over the road.

4 Or over a waterway.

5 Also a straight and a curved
line can flow into each other
(be 'morphed').

6 Twisted façades offer possibilities for complex interactions.

7 The slanting sides may connect to extra directions.

8 Within one façade centering
and radiating effects may
combine.

9 By adding volumes to the
design, more directions can be
incorporated.

ARCHITECTURAL ASPECTS OF THE MODELS

Geometry and industrial production, which are of major importance in this project, are expressed through strong images that combine an easy to understand, 'crystalline', geometrical composition with a large range of applications. The global geometry of twisted volumes was examined using the models Twister A and Tordo A. Subsequent models were more complex in geometry, as thickness and variation in finish were added to the outer surface of volumes. Most models feature a façade finish that accentuates the visual characteristics of horizontal and vertical screens. By only changing the lines of the predominant directions, and not the image contours (e.g. by bevelling the sides or by mixing various kinds of twisted surfaces), the geometry remains clear for all participants. This is important, because the building methods and logistics are very new and there is a danger of scaring them off if the image is too complex. This design approach is continued in the later designs: there geometry is just varied by adding shapes that are already well-known, such as a cylinder, or a mirrored twisted volume. If right angles are avoided, a shape will seem more organic and less of an independent self-sustained entity.

For the final building shapes, the programme of requirements and the urban setting are of major importance. The design of the lower levels of a model is independent of its overall shape, and can be left until later. Adding an entrance or a connection to its setting, would distract the attention from the main theme at this stage (the development of a twisted façade). As a consequence, the designs often seem to be models rather than buildings.

Twisted buildings offer a variety of images. While driving around Tordo 1, the front will first appear to taper upwards, then to be rectangular (with an unusual light reflection), and then to fan out upwards. In turn the contours look like those of a pyramid, and an inverted pyramid. An attempt was made to produce rich, playful images, in which light and dark surfaces rapidly alter in brightness. Due to the fan-like pattern of the lines and the free curvature of the contours, the perspective views show rotation rather than stacking of building layers.

The appearance of a twisted tower does not coincide with its use and function. There is no obvious link to a specific type of user. Numerous rectangular buildings show how, after meticulously studying the programme of requirements and passing through an intense design process, diverse purposes – churches, homes, offices, schools – were all optimally accommodated. Similarly, there are examples in which the design process resulted in a triangular of cylindrical tower, or in a low-rise building. The shape for a major part results from the preference of the architect, town-planner, principal or user and has no direct connection with the programme of requirements. With office buildings the ample budget often is the reason why a particular shape was feasible. It may serve a commercial interest to apply twisted glass as an aesthetic refinement: it relates the image of advanced technology to the client. With residential buildings the tight budget may be the reason for giving the shape additional value by a simple and inexpensive transformation. To save expenses only the concrete, brick or steel parapets could follow the twisted façade surface on the outer side of a gallery. The inside façade could be kept flat and relatively cheap. It is even possible to facet the façade, because the overall shape will still be quite prominent.

CONNECTION OF INNER WALLS TO FAÇADES

In a twister, the inclination of an outer wall increases according to the distance from the rotational axis and the degree of rotation. The helical connection between the inner wall and the façade is inclined in two directions. Its form is repeated on every floor and may often be identical to one of the other façades. So prefabricated parts can be used for connecting them. An example of this was drawn for 'Twister 3'. As its walls are thin, the meeting plane of an inner wall and a twisted outer façade is usually twisted just a few millimetres. It therefore hardly differs from the meeting plane between a flat inner wall and an inclined flat façade. Instead of flat inner walls, tangentially placed cylindrical walls can be used, that in their intersection with the outer façade, follow the shape of the helical mullions. An example for such a connection is drawn in 'Twister 4'.

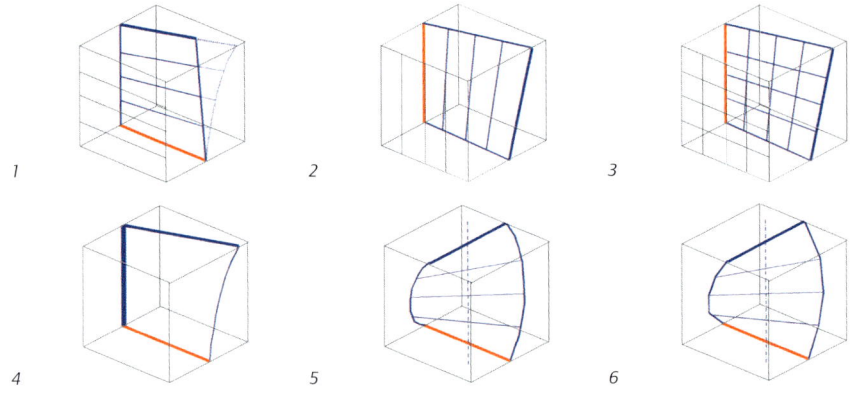

1

2

3

4

5

6

Most common twisting types

1 All rules horizontal

2 all rules in parallel vertical surfaces

3 Combination of 1 and 2

4 One vertical side line

5 Constant rotation of horizontal rules, with helical side line

6 Faceted side lines, with recurrence of surfaces

If the wall between two apartments has to be structural, it seems obvious to do this cylindrically or by twisting, because this provides the best connections to walls and the forces will flow directly downwards. It would be consistent with twisting the walls between apartments, to construct the other inner walls in the same manner, thus carrying the layout of the ground plan through to the ceiling rotatingly. But it is already unusual to twist some walls, let alone all of them. Close to the rotational axis transformations are small, so that faceting will hardly be noticed. As the distance to the axis grows, the transformations increase as well and they will become visible. One can avoid arguments by making the walls inside the building flat and vertical, to connect up with normal building methods. In that case standard cupboards and kitchen units can be used, without having to fill the gap between flat backs and the twisted wall. Particularly in a first project, all attention must be focussed on the parts that are most important, e.g. the façades.

By applying vertical inner walls, the ceiling's orthogonal structure will deviate from that of the floor. If the floor is finished with a seamless ceiling construction underneath, these deviations will hardly be visible, but with a clear grid in a suspended ceiling system, they will.

A twisted façade will usually have a far smaller inclination than a common gabled roof. Hanging the curtains will hardly be affected. The distance to the window frame has to be increased slightly and the distance from curtain to window frame will vary. Also a cord system can be selected, for instance Venetian blinds.

STRUCTURAL ASPECTS OF TWISTED BUILDING ELEMENTS

This project has left aside structural aspects of twisted elements, such as the extra rigidity that may be brought about by twisting an element. Nor was the change of material characteristics studied, or the optimization of the direction of reinforcement of concrete prefabricated elements. These aspects are secondary to demonstrating that transformation manipulations as such are possible. They may be elaborated upon in subsequent research.

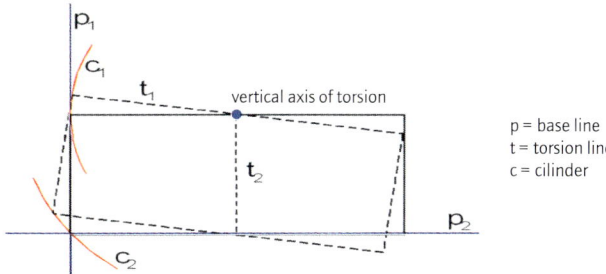

vertical axis of torsion

p = base line
t = torsion line
c = cilinder

STRUCTURAL ASPECTS: STABILITY OF TWISTED BUILDINGS

For the superstructure it is important whether the building shape introduces a twisting force, e.g. in connection with gravity or wind load. Here only the laws of gravity examined. If they cannot be compensated for, other forces need not be considered.

With regard to strength and rigidity, two building types with twisted façades can be distinguished:

1   Buildings with an orthogonal structure. Examples are the tower models Tordo A and Tordo 1 in chapters 4.2.1 and 4.2.2. The load of the projecting façades and floors will be absorbed by the structure in the usual manner. An inclined position of the columns along the twisted façades may bring about torsion load on the structure.

2   Buildings in which the ground plans, and the structure, rotate per floor.

Twisted forces may be absorbed or prevented:

- by using rigid connections between the floors and the walls or columns.
- by adding rigid cores, guys or prop up structures.
- by compensating torsion forces from the eccentric load of the building's own weight, with an opposed force in the supporting structure. This can, for instance, be achieved by positioning the columns opposite to the torsion (example: the 200 m high twister in chapter 2.1).
- by preventing an addition of twisting forces per floor by leading the vertical forces per layer to the core of the building (see Twister 3 in chapter 4.2.5).
- by compensating the torsion forces with adjacent building parts, e.g. mirrored shapes (see Twister 4 in chapter 4.2.6).

MANIPULATIONS OF FLOOR PLANS THAT RESULT IN TWISTED FAÇADES

When a ground plan is rotated around a vertical axis and simultaneously shifted upwards, the corners of the ground plan move along a helix. The sidelines of the ground plan form the basic lines that describe the twisted façades. With a twisted surface it is not called a rotational axis, but a torsion axis to indicate that, next to a rotation, also a shift in the length of the axis takes place. The torsion axis may lie in, but also adjacent to the façade. The line between base line and torsion axis is called the 'torsion arm t'. Usually the torsion axis will be straight and vertical and the shifting and rotation will be constant. It is possible to make variations, for instance by:

- applying a curved torsion axis
- varying the length of the torsion arm
- varying the rotational angle and/or the shift along the axis
- placing the torsion axis under a non-perpendicular angle with the ground plan

A complicating factor with varying parameters is that the dimensions of elements will vary as well, thus increasing the building costs.

TYPOLOGY OF FLOOR PLAN MANIPULATIONS WITH VERTICAL TORSION AXES

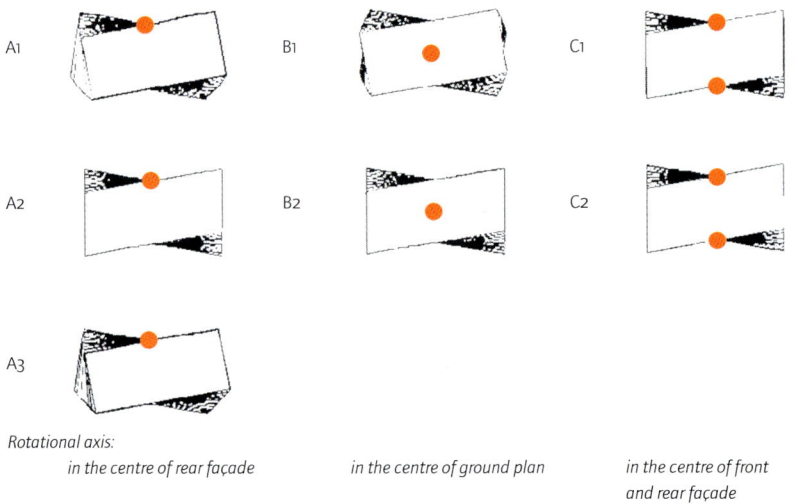

Rotational axis:
in the centre of rear façade   *in the centre of ground plan*   *in the centre of front and rear façade*

Basic types:
A   Rotational axis in the centre of one of the façades. The building's front and rear
    façade are different: one façade can be divided into two mirrored parts on each
    side of the axis; the other turns around the rotational axis at a distance.
B   Rotational axis in the centre of the plan. With an equal distance to the rotational
    axis, the front and rear façades are equal. With a square ground plan all façades
    are equal.
C   One rotational axis in the front façade and one in the rear façade. As the rotation-
    al angle increases, the front and rear façade move closer together: the ground
    plans vary in width per floor.

The diagram is based on vertical rotational axes with a horizontal rotation of the
ground plan. A possible version, with the axis in a corner, corresponds largely to half
of variant A and is therefore not drawn separately. In the same manner, a ground plan
with the axis in the centre of the side façade, is comparable to B.

Comments:
•   In office buildings, there is a preference for an open floor plan with structural
    outer walls, whereas the allocation of inner walls is free. In residential buildings
    the walls between apartments are often also structural.
•   If in normal building practice the vertical side façades are parallel, the in-between
    walls will be parallel too. In the drawn orthogonal examples, the forces that result
    from the ends of the buildingcantilevering, are relatively small. The in-between
    walls hardly project and will easily absorb the torsion forces caused by the
    extremities of the building.
•   The hypar shaped façades with straight ends of partitioning walls and straight
    sidelines imply a variation in the rotational angle as well as the lengths of the
    mullions and transoms.

Because the differences between the models in a similar group are hardly visible, only
the characteristic types A1, B1 and C1 are shown on the following pages.

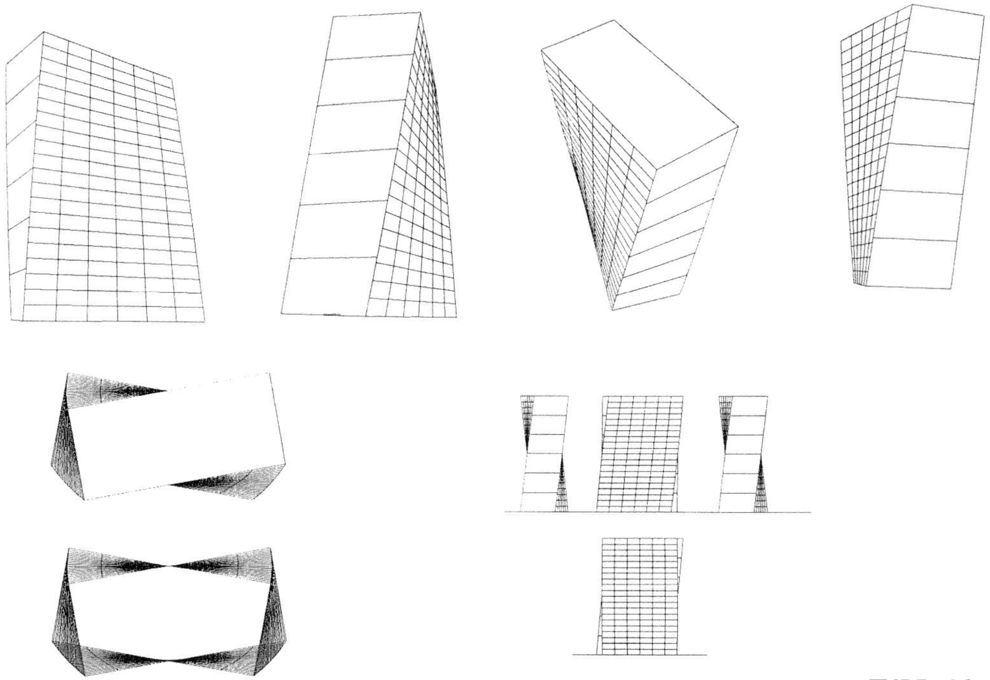

TYPE A1

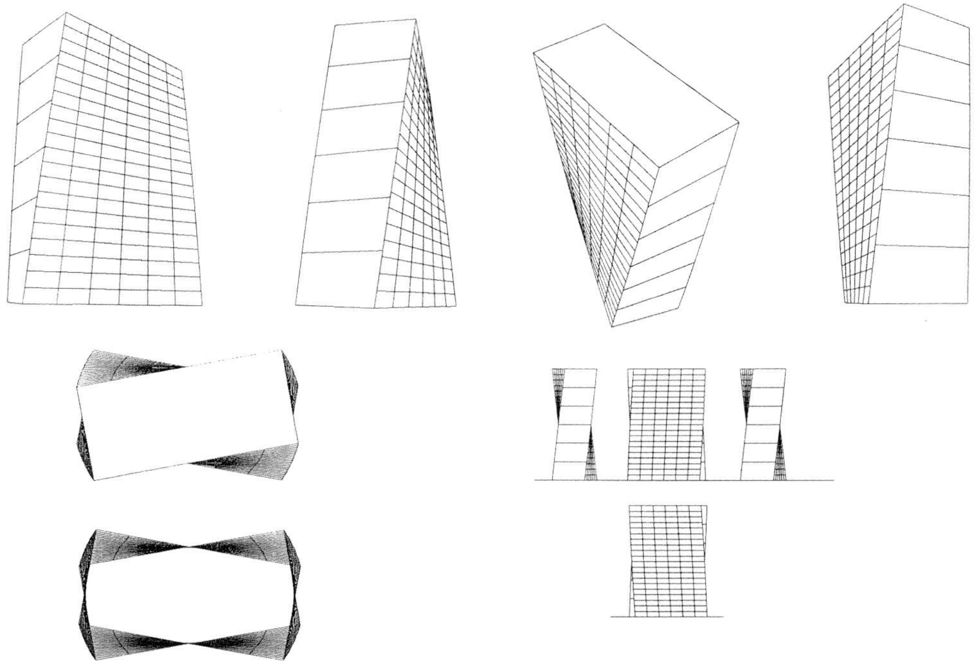

TYPE B1

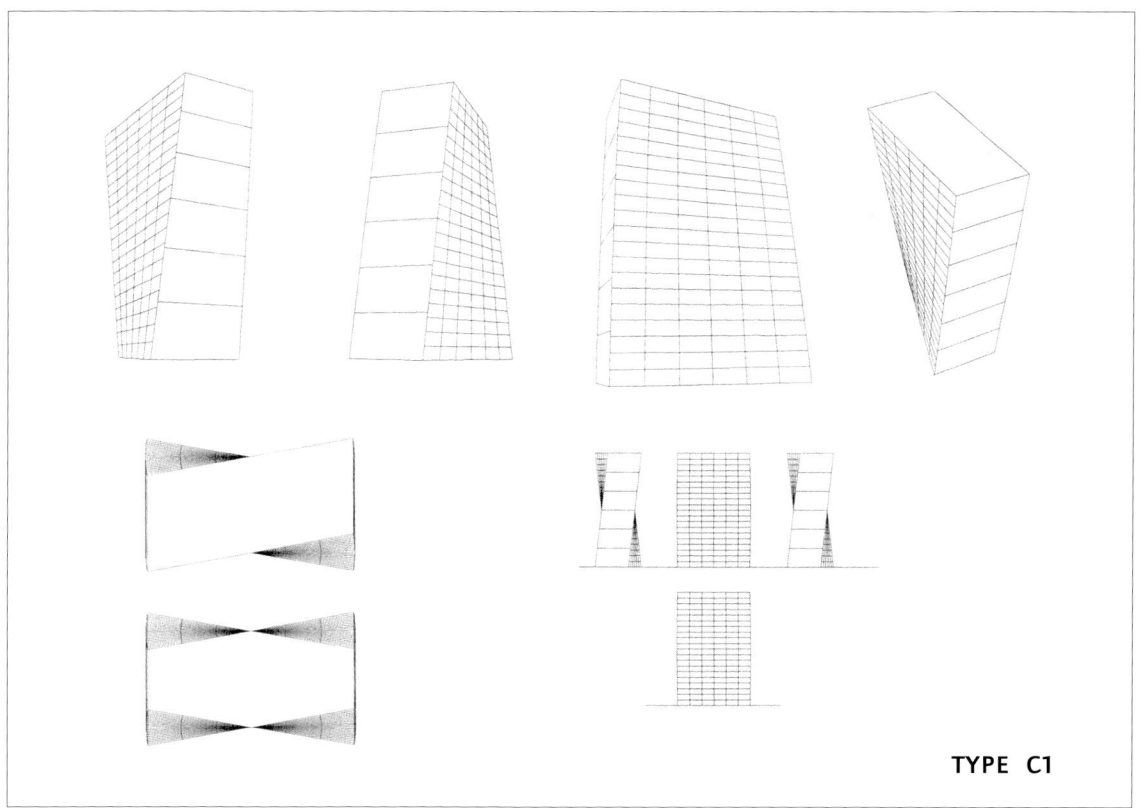

TYPE C1

CASE-STUDY: TWISTER A AND TORDO A

The small geometrical differences between the preceding models, have considerable technical implications. Their characteristics were studied in two models:

- Twister A, with a vertical rotational axis in the centre of the rear façade. All façades are twisted.
- Tordo A, with two separate vertical torsion axes. The front façade has curved transoms and the ones in the rear are straight. The side façades are flat and parallel to the inner walls.

Twister A was elaborated at a later stage, when our computer skills had improved. Tordo A had the following advantages:

- A simple structure: the shape does not cause torsion stresses. Twisting of the façades is so small that the centre of gravity of the sidewalls is always above the base.
- A conventional use of the interior since only the façade was inclined slightly.

One side of Tordo A has curved lines. All its front transoms have the same curvature; the ones in the rear are straight. As each element in the front façade is different, building costs are high. This cannot be justified by a visible additional value.

To simplify the geometry, all sidelines of the subsequent version Tordo 1 are straight. In addition the transom curvature is simplified to that of circle segments.

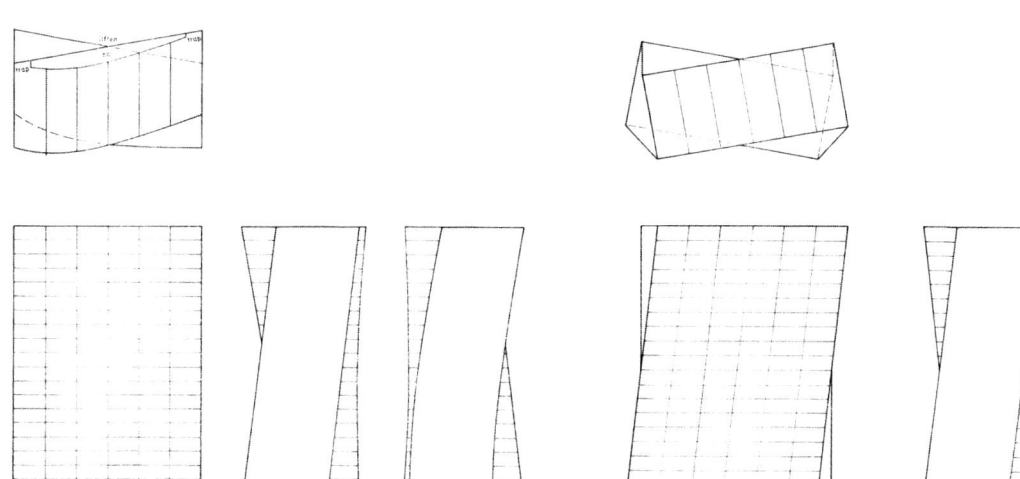

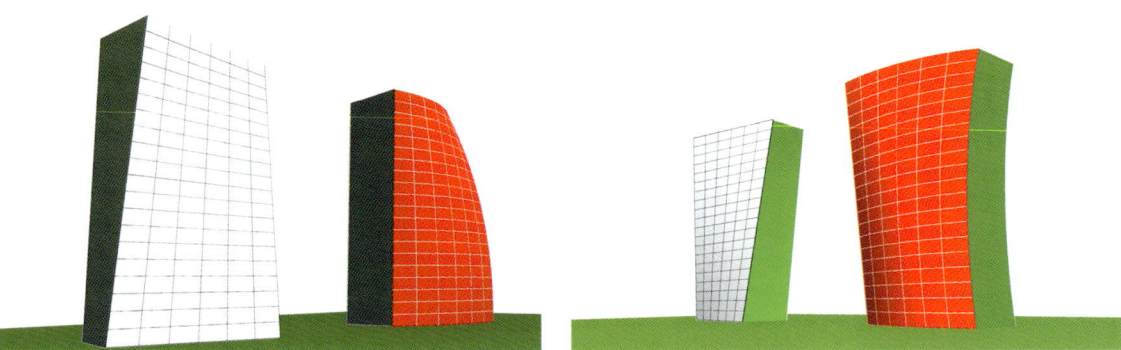

All façades of Twister A (white) are twisted. Tordo A (red) only has a twisted front and rear.
The borderlines of one side façade are straight and of the other curved.

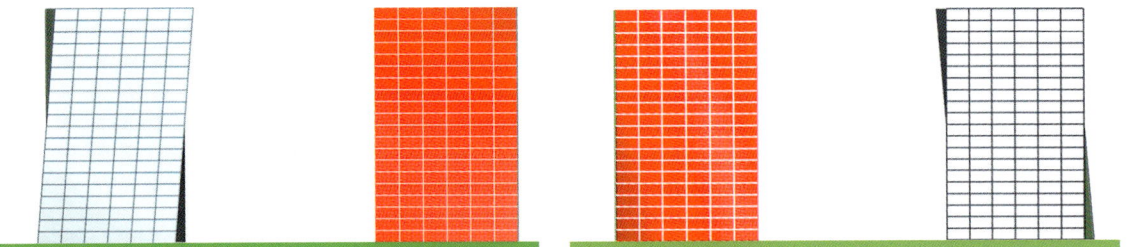

Front and rear façade of Tordo A

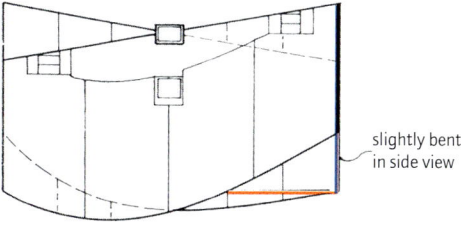

slightly bent
in side view

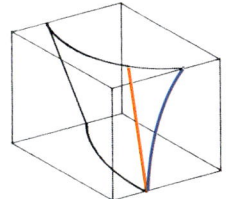

PRELIMINARY RESEARCH: CORRECTION OF THE CURVED SIDELINE

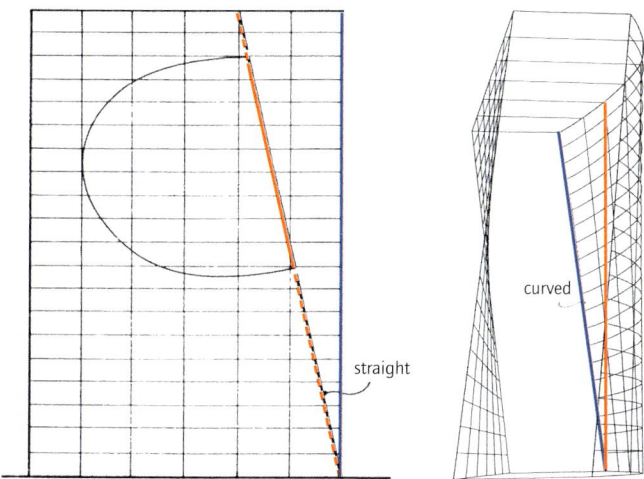

straight

curved

Tordo A initially had a twisted front with a perforation in the upper half of the surface and a curved borderline on the right. The increasing sideways inclination of the rules that describe the surface should have become visible through the perforation. And the extension of the inclined straight edge of the perforation should run through the façade's lower right corner. Unfortunately the shape of the perforation could not be constructed in this way. The façade's side contour cannot be as markedly curved as in the drawing. The computer revealed that the curvature of the sideline on the right had been overestimated in the manual sketch. In fact it only deviates by a maximum of 200 mm from a straight line through its ends. This is hardly perceivable on a line exceeding 60 metres. The next model used a simpler geometry with straight borderlines on both side façades.

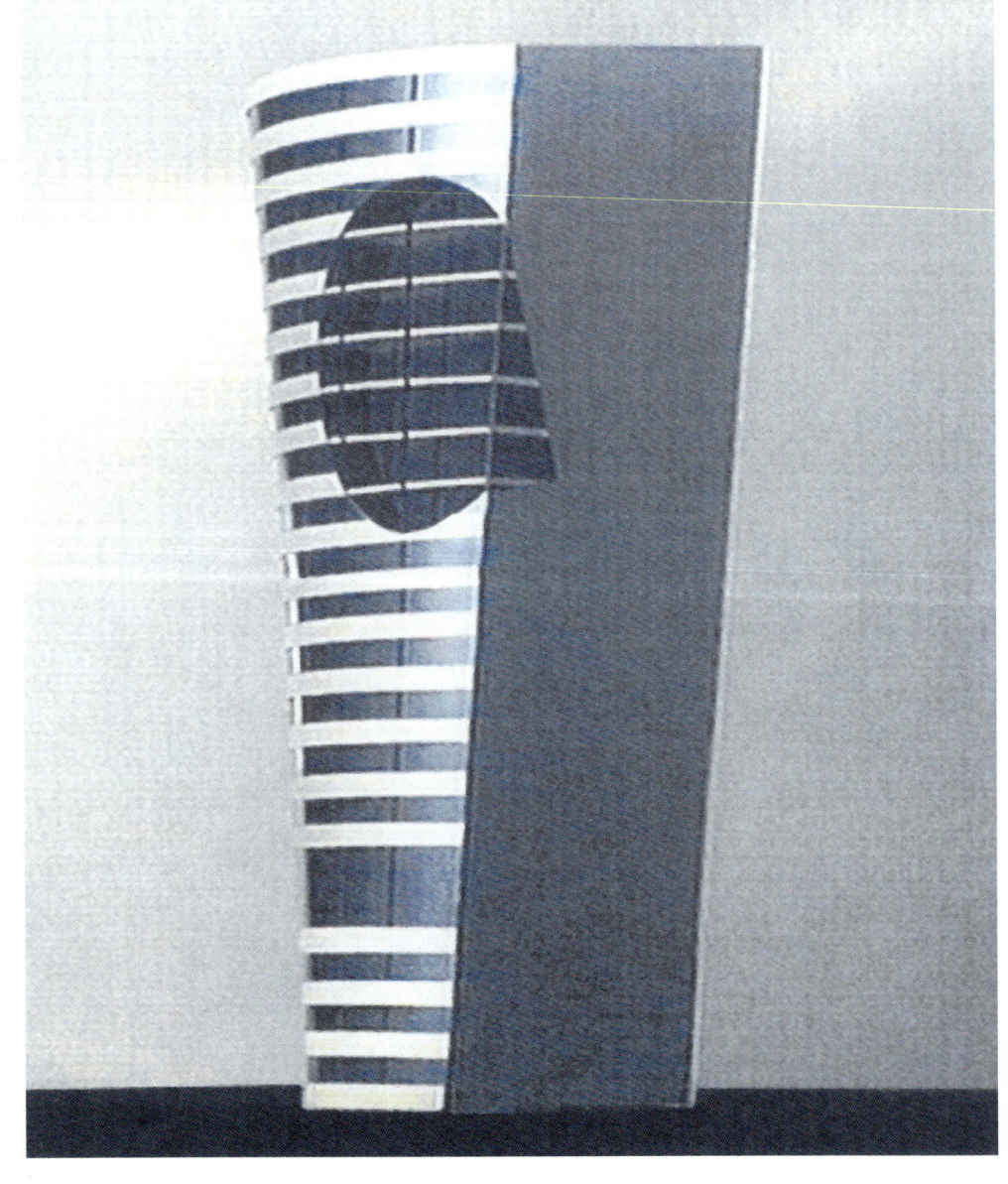

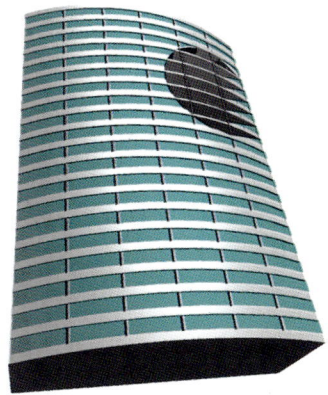

CASE-STUDY: TORDO 1

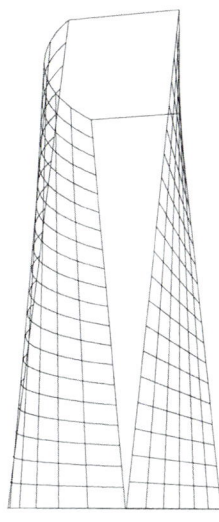

rear

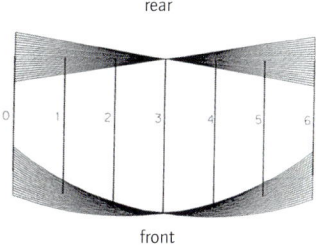

front

In the preceding models the overall geometry of twisted buildings was examined. The purpose was to design an attractive and strong image that clearly emphasizes geometrical characteristics. The model was to accommodate the twisted components of some building parts: (concrete) façade elements, glass, window frames, balustrades and hoisting system for the cleaning installation. To achieve this, a link was sought with current production techniques and the existing market.

The façade with curved mullions is, of course, the most complex. It was produced as a strip façade with concrete parapets and glass strips in window frames alternating. The façade with straight mullions (a hypar) is, in contrast, built as a curtain wall. In order to make the image more recognizable and as a technical challenge, the front façade was intersected with a cylinder to define a perforation through seven floors. If this can be produced, then almost all other types of intersection can be realized in twisted surfaces as well.

The aim was to remain realistic. For this purpose investors were contacted at an early stage to define, among other things, optimum floor plans. This resulted in the model of a 20-storey building with 500 m² gross area per floor, to be used as a hotel, office or

residential accommodation. The torsion per building element is very small (an average rotation of 1°) because, if twisting proved not to be feasible, we had to be able to resort to a facetted solution. Later this proved to be a weak point, since with facetting almost the same result could be achieved, but far cheaper. Therefore the torsion was increased in the later building designs, Twister 1 and 2.

The rotation varies from -10° at the base, via 0° halfway up, to +10° at the top of the building. In the curved façade the upright rules are visible in the joints of the concrete panels and in the mullions of the window frames. The curving of the surface reminds one of ships: flowing lines of hulls, or bulging sails.

Twisted façades usually reflect the sun as an ellipse-shape. As it moves, it creates great contrasts in light between the twisted façade and the flat surface at the rear of the perforation.
The examples in this study were drawn with Microstation. This programme enables one to position the model on a virtual globe, by entering co-ordinates. Subsequently, it is easy to study the reflections and shadows at any time of the year, with varying of of material transparency, and even with regard to atmospheric circumstances.

The round section can refer to a hawsehole for stowing the anchor, a sun (or a moon in the lateral view), a monocle or a medal pinned-on a coat.

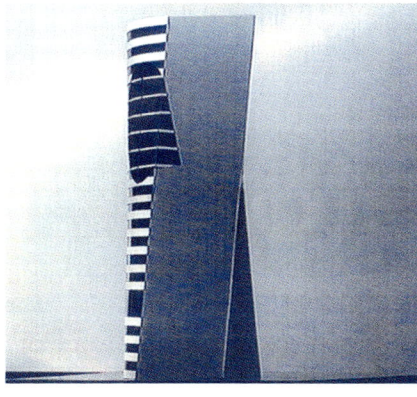

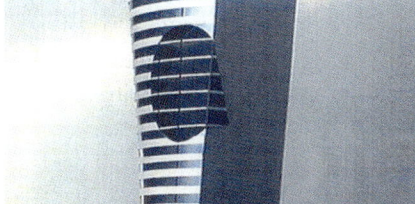

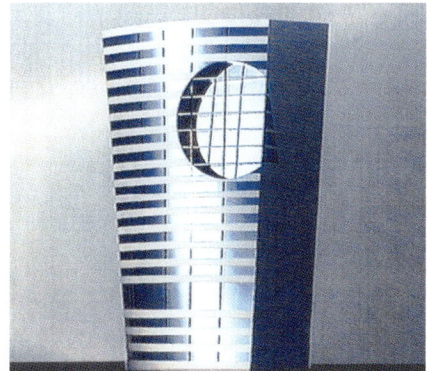

PRELIMINARY DESIGN

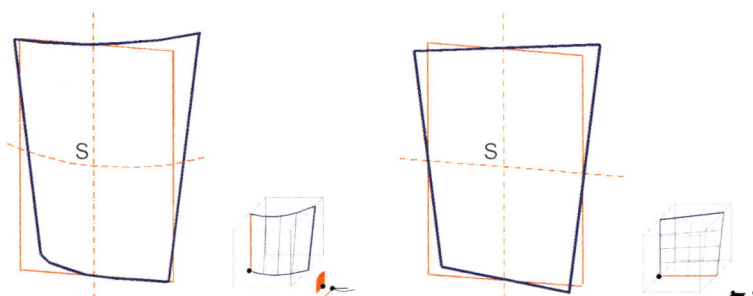

The northern façade has straight floor edges; the edges of the southern one are curved. The sides incline approximately 15°, forward at the one side of the building, backward at the other. The façades appear equal in size, but due to the curved lines the southern façade is in fact larger. Viewed from straight ahead, the superstructure forms a regular rectangular grid of columns, floors and façade elements. The upright rules of the façade connect to the superstructure.

The position of the 'symmetry point S' in the façade is the intersection of the upright symmetry axis with the upper side of the finished floor of the tenth storey. The use of symmetrical mirror images, inversed and complementary surfaces, has advantages because of the repetition of transformed façade elements. Therefore, in this model:

- The northern façade is symmetrical in two directions. Straight symmetry axes divide it into equal quadrants.
- The southern façade is inversely symmetrical: the diagonally opposite quadrants are equal.

Geometry of the southern façade

The southern façade is more complicated than the northern one, due to the curvature of the transoms. Therefore, creating concrete panels with an adjustable mold was only necessary for the south side. Various geometrical aspects of this model have been elaborated:

- The dimensions of the elements. They were derived from the twisted reference plane that runs through the middle of the elements.
- The transformations necessary to twist a flat surface.

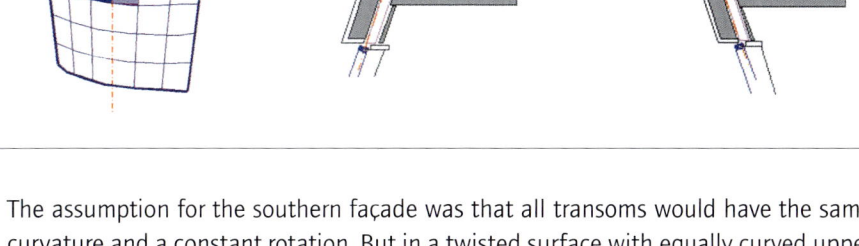

The assumption for the southern façade was that all transoms would have the same curvature and a constant rotation. But in a twisted surface with equally curved upper and lower borders, the curvature of the intermediate lines varied. These aspects are described in this chapter. In the final design the curved horizontal transoms were divided into segments with a standardized curvature.

The geometrical analysis was restricted to four segments around symmetry point S in which all dimensional aspects come together. All elements in the façade's upper half differ in size and torsion. Per quadrant the elements are inversely repeated in the diagonally opposite quadrant. Horizontal strips of concrete parapets alternate with strips of glass. Intelligent detailing allows parapet elements to be placed upside down. Thus the façade contains two of each element type.

Four segments around symmetry point

Inversion changes the position of the floor relative to the parapet

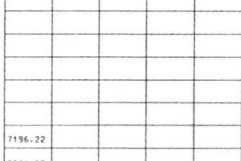

Planar grid segments and grid segments   Mullion lengths Transom lengths

The planar grid projects the façade grid on the reference plane; this holds true for each segment.

Viewed straight from the front, all panels appear equal, but per quadrant the grid segments differ. All upright sides of the stacked glass sheets are equal. But in a quadrant all transom lengths differ. The transom lengths per bay (between the mullions) vary between 6,021 and 7,262 mm. The stacked mullion segments all have the same incli-

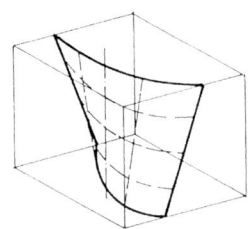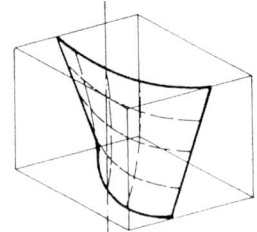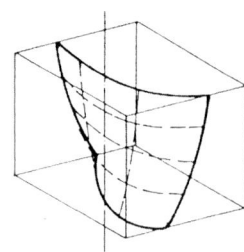

There is hardly a variation among the lengths of the mullion segments.

The size difference per segment between the models 1 and 2 is negligible.

The segments can be stacked into a straight, or slightly curved line. Therefore the model can be made in various ways, with a great degree of standardization.

In the end model 1 was opted for because it is correctly twisted.

nation but meet the transoms under a different angle. The torsion varies per grid segment: the rotation per metre along the transoms becomes smaller when the transoms get longer. The greatest torsion in the surface occurs with the shortest transoms.

Three models were studied of which only model 1 is a twisted surface. The different versions serve to acquire insight into surfaces that approximate a correct torsion. The models have:

- slightly varying curvature and rotation of the transoms, but straight mullions and sides.
- constant curvature and, per floor, a slightly varying rotation of the transoms, with straight sides. As the intermediate mullions are slightly curved, this is not a twisted surface.
- constant curvature with a constant rotation of the transoms. This results in slightly curved sidelines and mullions.

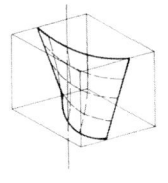

6250.31				6166.71	6534.99	7261.67
6276.94				6147.14	6494.02	7181.30
6567.94	6182.68	6021.41	6036.16	6230.99	6665.70	
6615.41	6206.02	6028.13	6028.13	6205.99	6615.42	
6665.70	6230.99	6036.16	6021.41	6182.68	6567.94	
7181.30					6276.94	
7261.67					6250.31	

3014.96	3007.08	3002.47	3000.25	3000.42	3004.04	3014.96
	3006.93					
3014.96	3006.47				3004.72	3014.96
3014.96	3005.7	3001.34	3000	3001.23	3005.54	3014.96
3014.96	3005.54	3001.23	3000	3001.34	3005.7	3014.96
3014.96	3005.38	3001.13	3000.01	3001.45	3005.86	
	3005.22	3001.02	3000.02	3001.57	3006.01	
	3005.05	3000.93	3000.03	3001.69	3006.17	
	3004.89	3000.83	3000.06	3001.81	3006.32	
	3004.72	3000.74	3000.08	3001.94	3006.47	3014.96
	3004.56	3000.65	3000.12	3002.07	3006.63	
	3004.39	3000.57	3000.16	3002.2	3006.78	
	3004.21	3000.49	3000.2	3002.33	3006.93	
3014.96	3004.04	3000.42	3000.25	3002.47	3007.08	3014.96

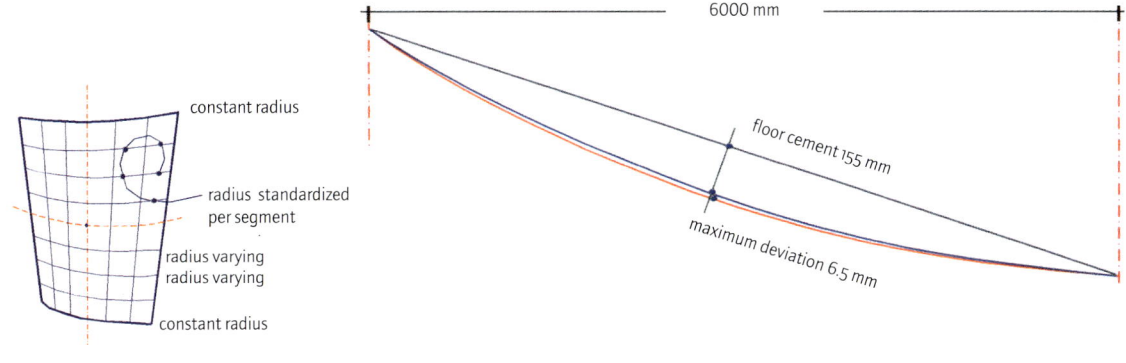

constant radius

radius standardized
per segment

radius varying
radius varying

constant radius

6000 mm

floor cement 155 mm

maximum deviation 6.5 mm

Model 1: standardization of transom curvatures

10th floor between axis 0 and 1

Within model 1, the curvature of the upper and lower edge of the façade is constant, but varies slightly in the intermediate transoms. All façade elements have straight upright edges, but differently curved horizontal ones.

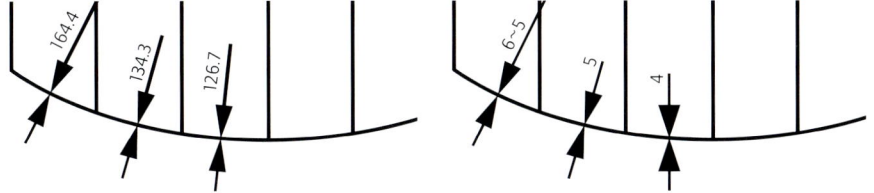

164.4 134.3 126.7

6-5 5 4

Figure A: Deviation between straight line and arc-segment with 36 m radius

Figure B: Additional deviation between b-spline and arc-segment with radius of 36 m

To standardize the curvatures, first the façade was divided into grid segments. Subsequently, the horizontal lines of each segment were curved with a standardized radius of 36 metres. The segments only blend together at the façade's lower and upper edge. Between the remaining segments an invisible buckle will occur. With the horizontal lines, the parapet and window strips will have an unnoticeable buckle. The stacked elements, however, will show no mutual deviation because they all have the same curvature.

To gain insight into the deviations by standardizing the curvatures, twisted façade elements were intersected in the middle with a horizontal plane. The drawings show the curvatures in the centre plane of the façade elements on the tenth floor. This is where the biggest distance between the standardized curvatures and the reference plane occurs.
Figure A shows the maximum deviations between the curves of 36 m radius and straight lines through their ends.
Figure B indicates how much the façade elements deviate from the reference plane (which is drawn here with B-splines through the points of the upright rules). All other elements deviate less, a maximum of 6.5 mm horizontally. This distance to the reference plane (as in all other bays) decreases to 0 mm at the baseline and at the roof edge. As size variations are small, a casing with horizontal lines of a constant curvature applies for the façade segments and the floor edges. The straight mullions simplify measurement and assembly. Their inter-element difference is less than 1 mm.

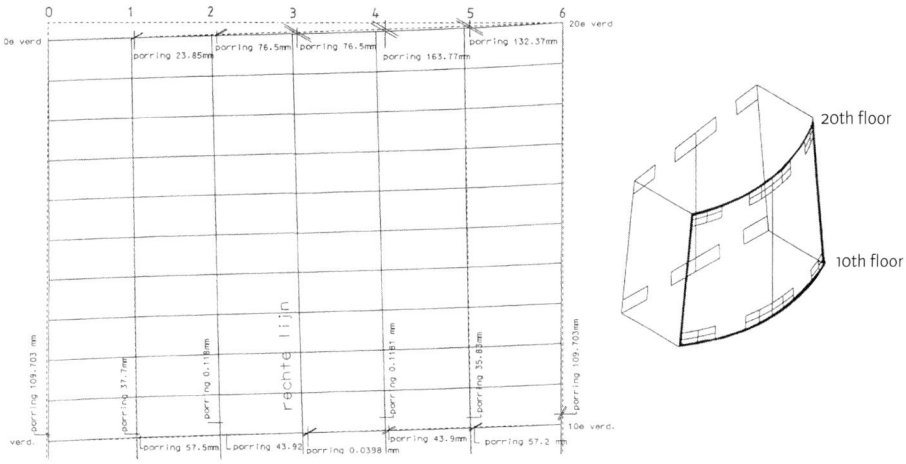

GEOMETRY OF THE NORTHERN FAÇADE

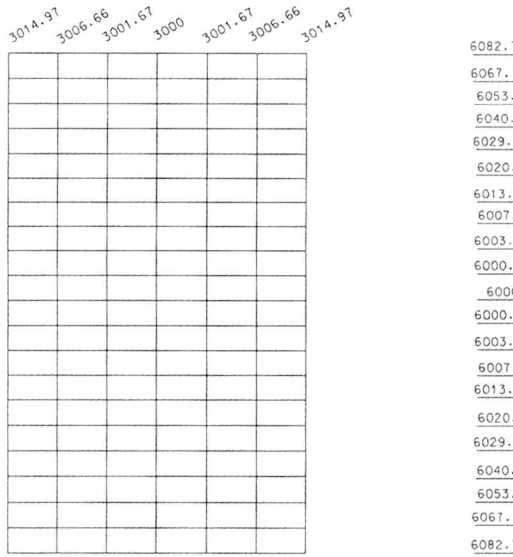

Lengths of mullions

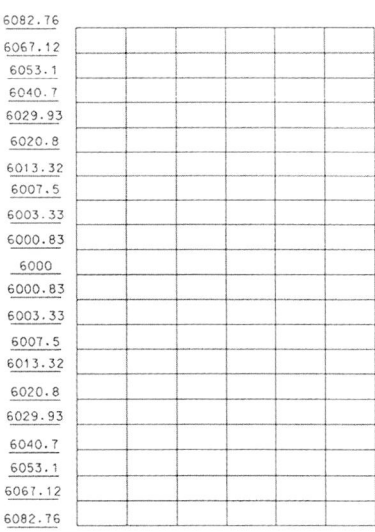

Lengths of transoms

The stacked mullion segments of a hypar-shaped façade all have the same length, as will the transom segments of window frames that line up with each other. All stacked mullion segments have the same inclination, but the rotation of the transoms per floor is different. Per quadrant all segments are different.

This hypar curtain wall's glass panels are identical and inversed in the diagonally opposite quadrant. Elements in the adjacent quadrant are mirrored: concave becomes convex, inside becomes outside and vice versa. Although the panels in adjacent quadrants are equal in size, the positioning of coated glass sheets must be reversed.

Developed planes of the southern façade and upper half

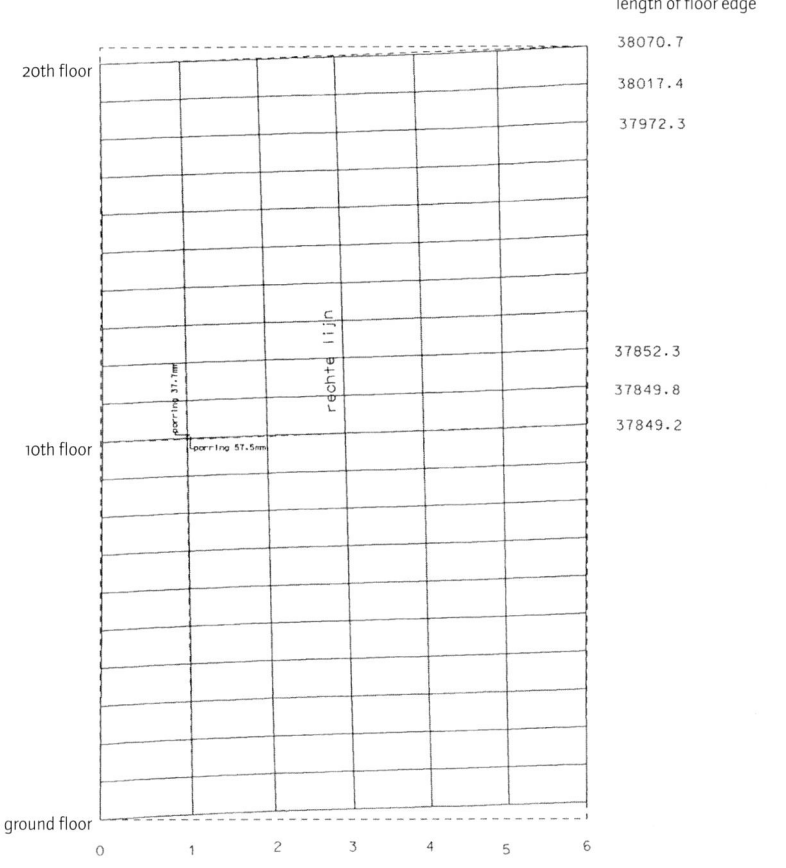

length of floor edge

38070.7

38017.4

37972.3

37852.3

37849.8

37849.2

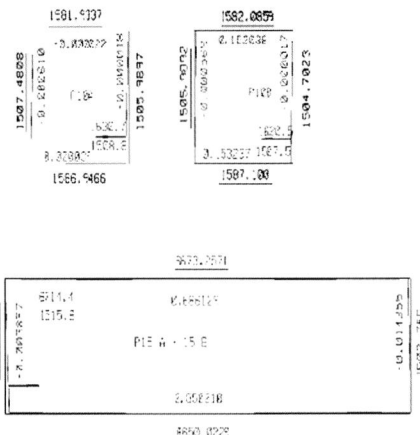

Element 10 split in two

Elements 15 and 16 as a whole

Developed planes of elements p 10 – 16

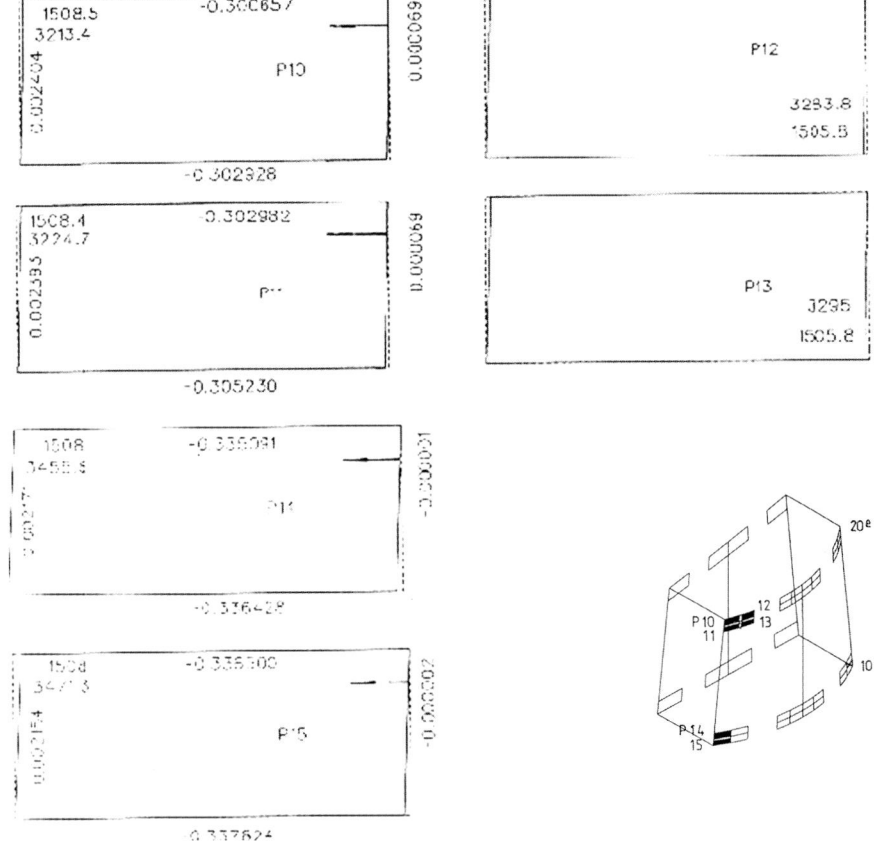

Perspective upper half of façade

The developed planes indicate the transformation along the edges of the flat surface. Torsion is minimal. The borders are slightly curved and all the corner angles are different. The dotted master plate in the drawing indicates the smallest flat rectangular plate out of which the segment can be made.

Developed planes of elements p 10 - 13

When twisted, the upright edges of this element are straight and the horizontal edges are curved; developed, all sides are curved.

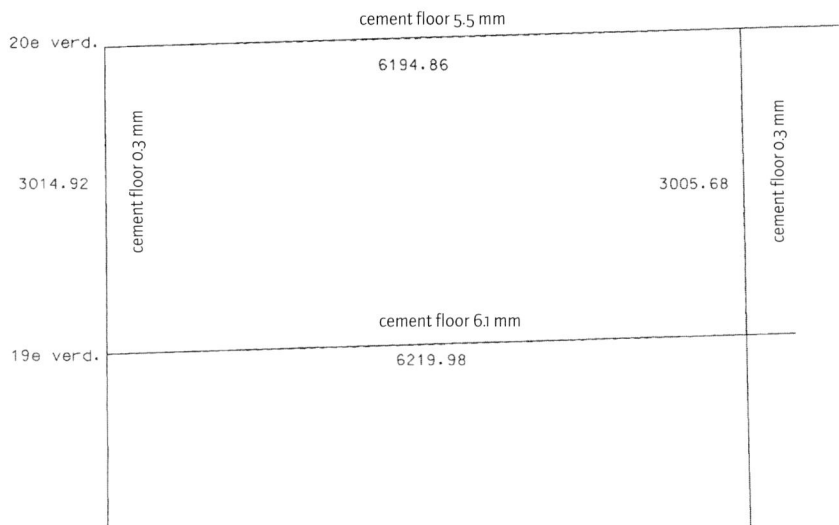

The 'pitch' indicates the degree of curvature: it is the greatest distance between the curve and the straight line through its ends. The upright edges of this element have a maximum pitch of 0.5 mm; the horizontal pitch is 6.1 mm maximum. By dividing the element into smaller parts, the edges become shorter and every pitch decreases. The parapet elements, as applied in the southern wall, are half the height of the above element. The pitch of their vertical sides is less than 0.2 mm and can be disregarded. Also strain and crimp strongly decline when the dimensions are reduced. Strain and crimp within one large element are bigger than the sum of part transformations when it is divided up.

The minimum curvatures in a surface

The colour diagrams show the minimal curving radii per façade zone of the northern and southern façade, surface types R1a and R3a, respectively. The maximum radius in a twisted surface is infinitely large, because a straight line runs through each point. The curvature of the diagonals is represented separately. These drawings are simple to provide an indication that it might be possible to use one mold for various panels - with restricted tolerances.

The hypar surface is the easiest to analyse. Both the horizontal and vertical lines are straight and it can be divided into four equal quadrants. The surface transformation is a result of mere torsion. The transformation of the southern façade is more complex, because there the horizontal lines are curved, not straight.

The rotation of the transoms varies slightly. The transom halfway up the façade is the shortest one. Similarly, the centre mullion is the shortest. The rotation of approximately 1° per 3 metres height is divided in the corners over a greater length than in the centre of the façade, therefore the rotation in a segment decreases towards the corners, whereas the minimum curvature radius increases.

The inclined figures of the minimal curvature radiuses indicate that neither the adjacent, nor the lower or upper façade parts (molds, glass) have an equal rotation. The differences, however, are very small. The minimum radius varies in the northern façade between 180 and 184.97 metres and in the southern one between 34.52 and 35.74 metres. The parabolic diagonals have a larger curvature, with radius between 204 and 213.5 metres in the northern façade.

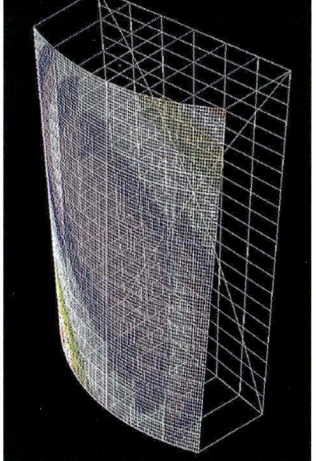

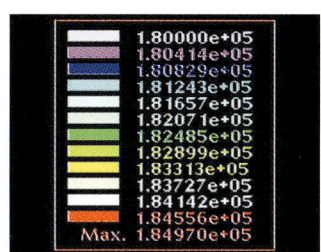

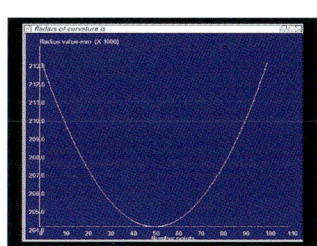

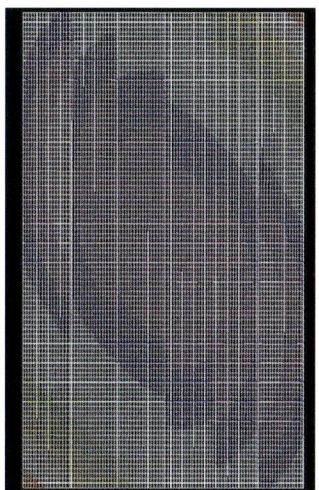

Maximum curving radii of the hypar-shaped northern façade

Ditto southern façade

CASE-STUDY: TWISTERS 1 AND 2

Both Twisters 1 and 2 were rotated 90° over twenty floors. The ground plans were repeated upwards and so window frames and glass sheets are equal to those above and below at every point. Because of the repetition of components, this type of façade is considerably cheaper than the previously designed Tordo 1. Outstanding building models and a prototype of the window frame were drawn to stimulate the building industry to develop twisted window frames and glass sheets. Simultaneously, the feasibility of the building shape, the application possibilities and the façade finishing were examined.

Due to their greater rotation, Twisters 1 and 2 proved to be more suitable for research into the shape characteristics of twisted surfaces and volumes than Tordo 1. Because of the constant 2.25° rotation per floor, flowing through the compass points, there is no front or back, nor a univocal favourable side as far as sunlight is concerned.

TWISTER 1

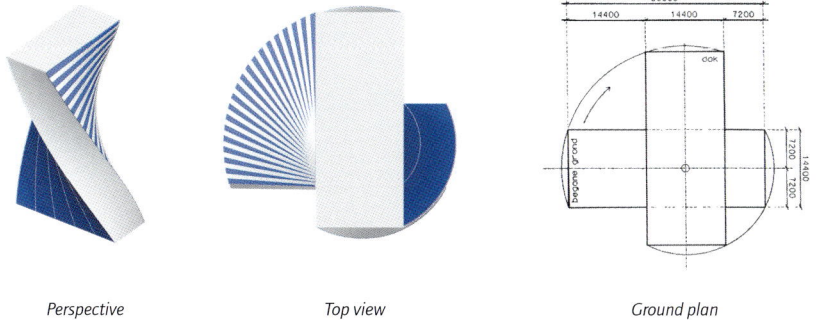

| Perspective | Top view | Ground plan |

The two longitudinal façades are equal in size, but have different finishes. With the horizontal and vertical lining, they show the characteristic effects of the model's geometry. When walking around the building every view is unique, because the building contours are curved differently and the images of the buildings are asymmetrical (due to the eccentric rotational axis). The contours evoke various associations and they interact.

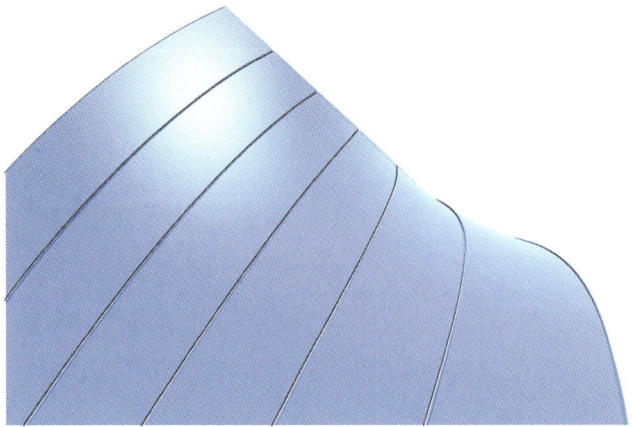

Views when rounding twister 1

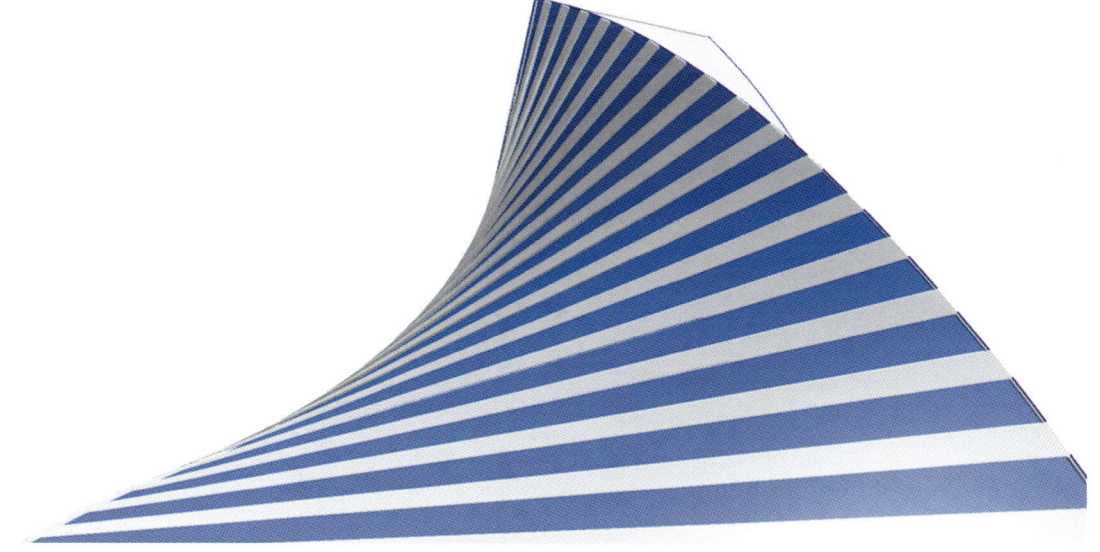

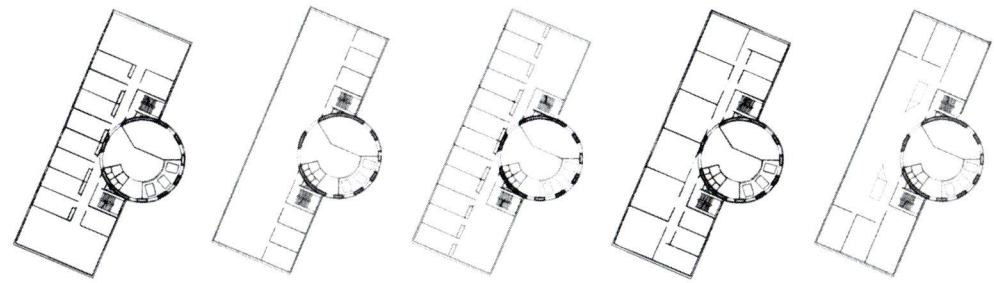

TWISTER 2

Lay-out variants for office use

This tower, an assembly of a twisted volume and a cylinder, has two different longitudinal façades. The one with vertical lines makes a theatrical 'great swing', having a hidden rotational axis, far outside the surface. Due to the difference in the façades, it features less repetition in components than Twister 1.

The addition of the cylinder provides extra space for a central hall with elevators. The wings always connect to the elevator hall at a different angle. The rigid cylindrical core is cheap to build, and plays an important role in the structure.

Side view

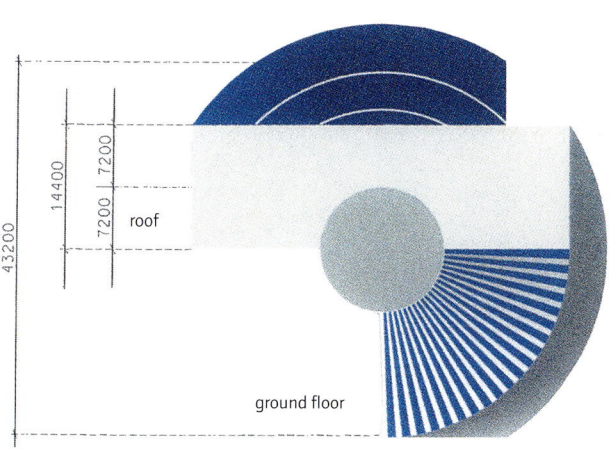

Top view

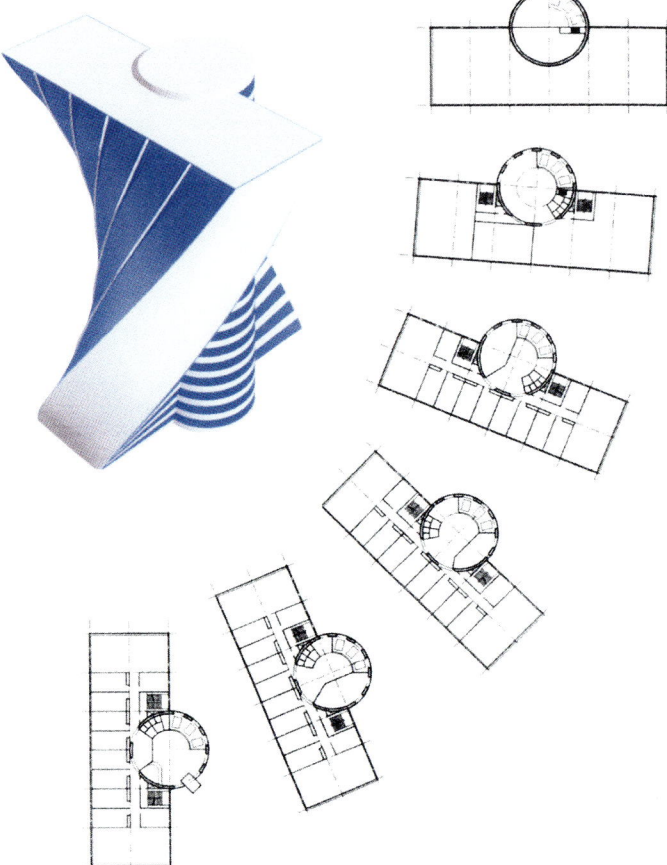

Rotation wings with relative to core

The core goes straight upwards. The sanitary core with pantry and toilets turns with the wings. Consequently the remaining spaces (conference room and sitting area) in the core are different on each floor. When ascending or descending by elevator, one can see how the building makes a large sway. The surface of approximately 500 m² is very suitable for apartments, offices and hotels.

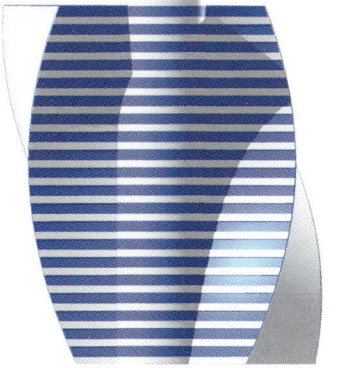
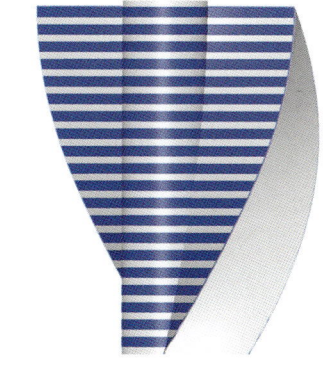

Appearances when rounding twister 2

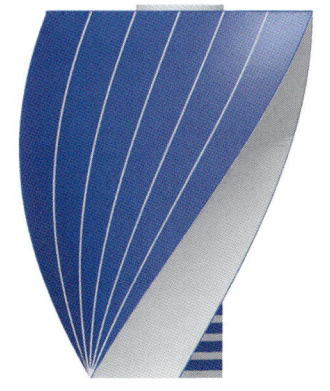

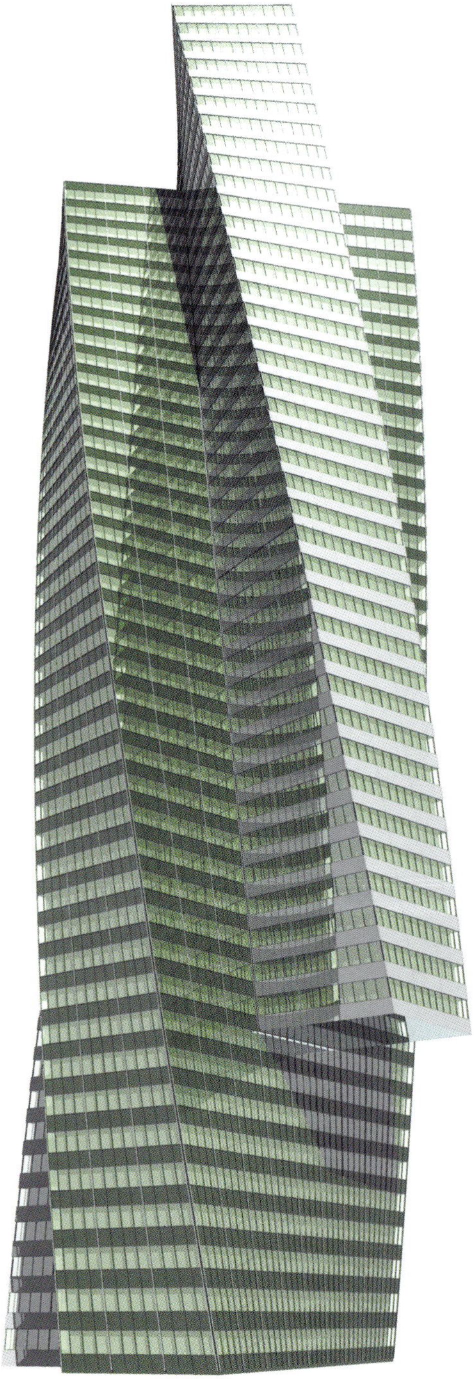

CASE-STUDY: TWISTER 3

The concept of twisted buildings was tried out at a possible location in Amsterdam. This took place in co-operation with the Dutch architect Pi de Bruijn. First the required cross-shaped building was examined with various façade finishes and degrees of rotation. When the building volume appeared to fit the location, the ground plans were drawn. ABT made a structural plan. A central concrete cylinder carries the wings. Each floor is hung individually. Since the torsion was small, a relatively cheap cold-bent aluminium curtain wall was developed. A prototype of part of the façade was designed and subsequently realized by Van Dool Geveltechniek, The Netherlands (see Chapter 6). The building developer Wessels Zeist, the Netherlands, then approached Grondzaken, the governmental office in charge with exploiting of the Municipality's building sites with a request to allow the tower to be built at the stipulated location. However, another developer, who was first in line, was invited to plan another tower at that site.

Upward view, next to the core.

By omitting the lower nine floors of one wing and putting a mirror finish on the lower side, a spectacular focus point was created. As one looks up, one sees reflections of the twisted façade and the activities on the boulevard.

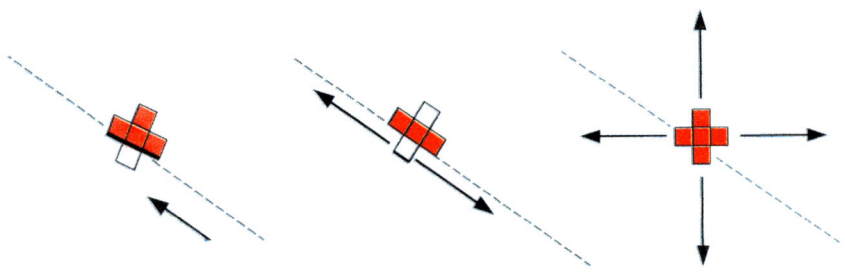

URBAN SETTING AND ARCHITECTURAL DESCRIPTION

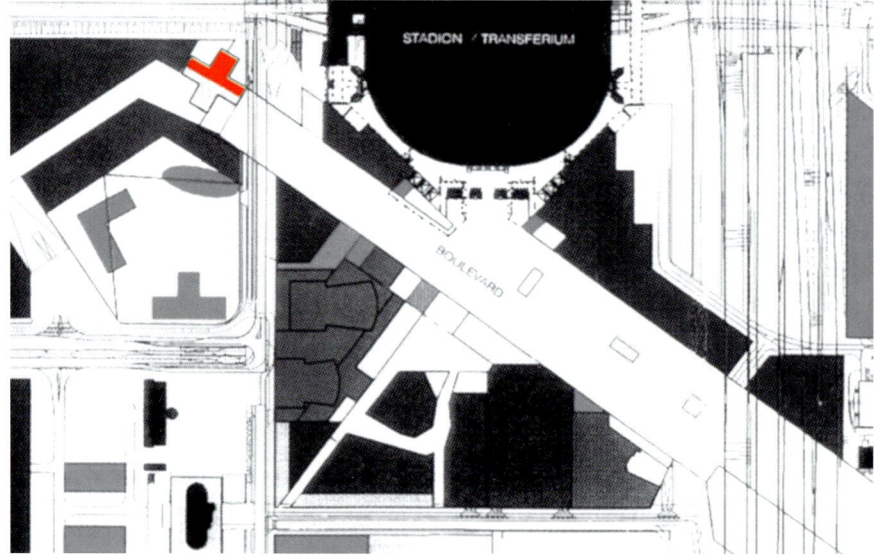

Connection to the directions of surrounding elements: the façade's base with the entrance is visible from the far end of the boulevard. The far end of the protruding wing points is parallel to the boulevard. The tops of the wings adopt the directions of the orthogonal urban structure. The urban plan for South-East Amsterdam provides the district with a lively centre. Characteristic is a wide boulevard through the middle, lined by many public facilities. Its position is diagonal, at an angle of 34° to the orthogonal road structure. At one end, next to the football stadium 'ArenA', one turns a slight corner and the boulevard changes into a pedestrian shopping street. The 150 metre high tower pegs down the entertainment area in the landscape. It rotates through 66°. From a distance the shape of the twisted building emphasizes the characteristic position of the boulevard within the district.

By omitting the nine floors, every view around the building is different. The images will change unexpectedly, as it constricts in the centre and at the ends. Taking a closer look, the mirror under the wing that protrudes over the boulevard will offer a spectac-

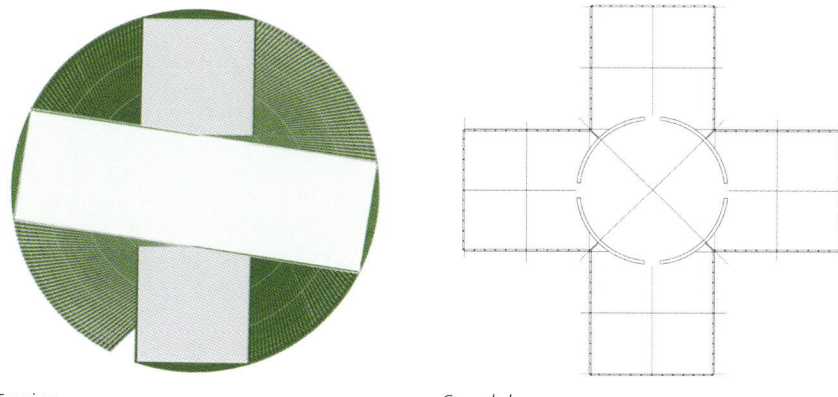

Top view   *Ground plan*

ular focal point, with unexpected prismatic effects of the adjoining façade together with reflections of life in the street. The shelter of the overhanging wing, with the entrance to the building, will become an intensely visited location, because this is also where the escalators for the garage emerge.

By completing the façade with two types of parapet, the building looks like a composition of two slender, intertwining volumes. One is composed of alternating white and dark-green horizontal strips; the other is smoothly crystalline, entirely covered with green reflecting glass. The dark-green grids of mullions and transoms acquire a vertical lining, by making the ones for the façade cleaning installation white, and somewhat thicker. Thus an architectural game evolves of heavy and light, transparent and massive, supporting and being supported.

The cross-shaped ground plan, composed of five 14.40 x 14.40 metre squares, is suitable for offices as well as apartments. All rooms can be positioned on the outside.

At the top of the two green glass wings large open spaces can be created to house functions like a health club with an elegant swimming pool, restaurants or communal facilities for residents or visitors. The wings with horizontal white strips rise a further six floors. They offer space for quality conference rooms, dining rooms or stylish penthouses. Additional areas at the lower levels to be designed at a later date should reinforce the urban structure. Public utilities, e.g. shops, restaurants and service industries, will intensify the life in the streets. There are spacious parking facilities underneath the boulevard and the ArenA.

The torsion of the building as a whole is impressive but per building element it is moderate, approximately 1.4° per 3 metres floor height. The twisting of the outer façade can be sensed in the interior, particularly at the extreme corners of the building. The rotation is clearly visible there, due to the slope of approximately 490 mm over 3 metres height. In use the rooms hardly differ from the ones in traditional towers.

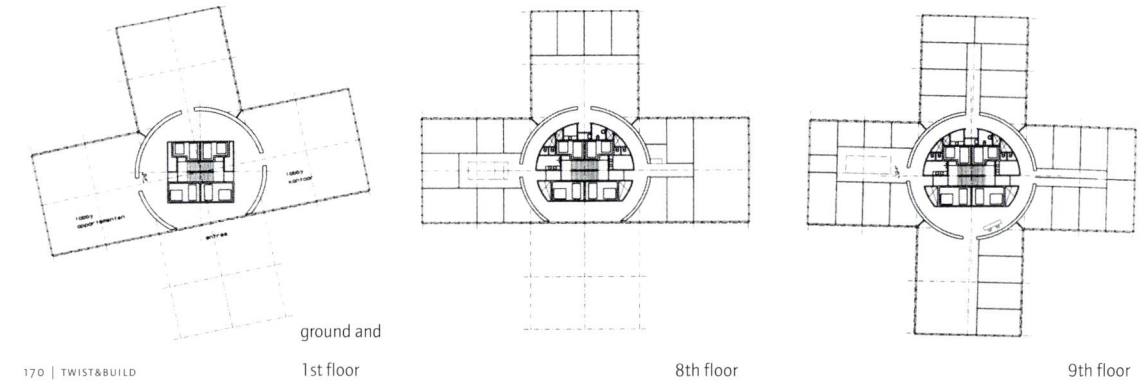

ground and
1st floor

8th floor

9th floor

View of the building, at right
angles with the boulevard

There is a clear view over the
boulevard because the lower
nine floors of the wings have
been omitted

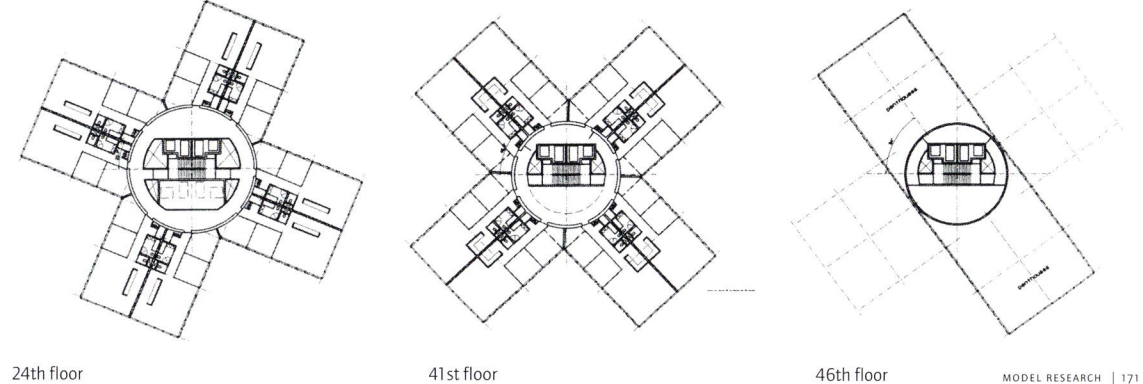

| 24th floor | 41st floor | 46th floor | MODEL RESEARCH | 171 |

SUPERSTRUCTURE

Relative to the core with the central hall, the wings turn an additional 1.4° per floor

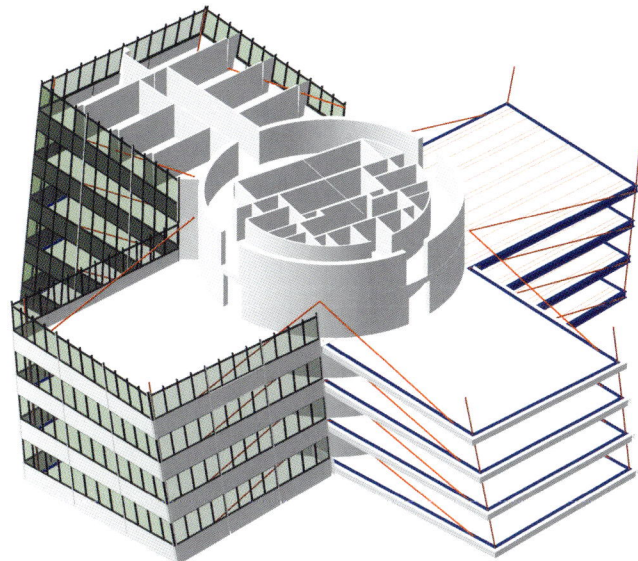

The structural design was made by ABT engineers, The Netherlands [5-6] The total height of a storey (3,200 mm. for the offices and 3,000 mm. for the apartments) is kept to a minimum, in order to maximise the number of floors within the permitted height of 150 metres. In both cases, the clear height is 2,700 mm, leaving a construction height of 500 mm for the office floors and 300 mm for the apartment floors.

A cheap solution for the protruding wing is to hang its steel floor constructions from a rigid core. This principle was subsequently carried through everywhere. The core is a concrete cylinder whose wall thickness decreases as one travels upwards. As the outer diameter becomes smaller, the space in the adjacent wings increases. Since the wings are suspended, torsion forces on the core are avoided and no columns are needed along the façade. Due to the hanging principle, the vertical thrust on the concrete ring is so strong that tensile forces by wind load are almost completely compensated for. Therefore, the reinforcement in the concrete can be kept light.

Because of the chosen structural principle the degree of rotation is of little relevance. The 1.4° rotation per floor arises from the required connection to the urban setting and the desired architectural impact. The envisioned system allows the height per floor to vary, which is interesting when, for example, high conference rooms are programmed. It also allows independent structures at the lower levels, to connect up with the surroundings. Their foundations may extend from the cross shape. Because only the cylinder-shaped core of the building runs down to the basement, and not a forest of supporting elements, the disturbance of the parking grid in the garage is kept to a minimum.

INSTALLATIONS: DUCTS AND WIRING, FAÇADE CLEANING

The helix-shaped upright ducts may be realized in various ways: doubly-curved, facetted with straight sections or staged with a small sideways replacement at each floor. In theory, the path it follows twists, but this only influences an angular duct. A round channel does not twist along its longitudinal axis. Here faceted canals, composed of straight pieces, were chosen. The connection angle between the segments is almost 180°, even when ducts are two storeys high. When the distance between the duct and the tower axis increases, its inclination will also increase. Most of the ducts and wires for the air conditioning system are close to the core. The rotation and slope angles are so small there, that the connection tolerances between right-angled standard fittings will suffice to absorb the twist. The horizontal branches can be either rectangular or round. Rotation plays no part here. The ventilation ducts lie in a zone along the façade, within the height of the construction. The ducts remain short because the wings are shallow. By applying fan-coil units, the air-duct along the façade only needs to feed fresh air. The used air is discharged via a central duct above the corridor.
Torsion has no implications for electricity/gas/water/sewage/data-cables because they are round. Vertical rectangular cable ducts can easily absorb the small amount of torsion; the horizontal ducts are identical to those of a standard office building.

The cradle for the cleaning installation has to be fastened to the façade, otherwise it would hang too far away from a forward sloping façade, or could swing sideways of a backward sloping façade.

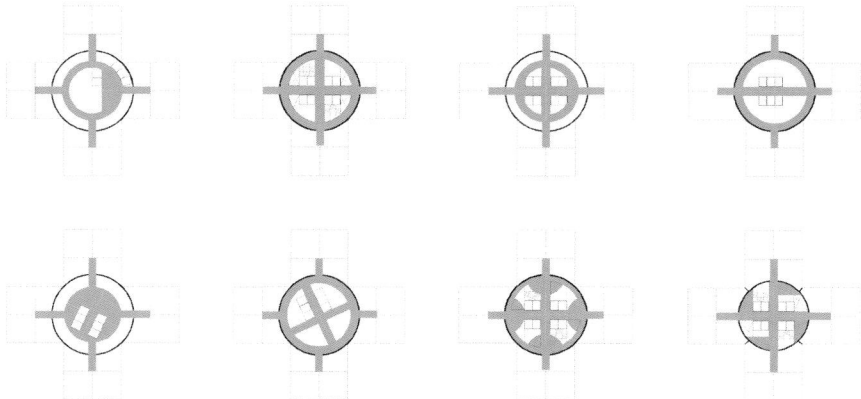

In a twister the width between the guiding transoms is constant per bay over the entire height of the building. The helical transformation of the transom is so small that it can be considered identical to the straight one of a conventional façade. The sloping angle is constant within an upright bay, but differs from the adjacent ones.

Core lay-out versions

PRELIMINARY DESIGN: CORE LAY-OUT VERSIONS
Twisting a building offers new possibilities. With identical building components, a spatial and functional combination can be designed that is different on every floor. Within the core the lifts can be positioned centrally, tangentially or radially. An important consideration for a circular corridor: the larger its radius, the more floor area it will occupy.

PRELIMINARY DESIGN: GEOMETRICAL DATA
Within the height of one storey a sloping twisted panel has longer sides, than a vertical panel would have. The torsion of a sloping façade panel is, therefore, divided over a greater length. The façade lies adjacent to the building axis. As the lengths of the mullions hardly differ, the rotation of the horizontal lines within the elements is roughly identical at all points.
If the tower twisted 1° per 3 m height, the twisting difference of one corner of the panels is, for the façade panels with the greatest difference, less than 1 mm per panel (1,500 x 1,500 mm). For each façade panel we measured, that the outward twist can be rounded off to 13 mm. The twisting of a panel this size is equal to that of a panel of 1,000 x 2,250 mm or 500 x 4,500 mm. In other words, a glass sheet of 1,500 x 3,000 mm in this case twists 2 x 13 = 26 mm.
Depending on the wing side, the façade leans either inward or outward. The further away the outer walls are from the core, the more their slope increases: with the clear floor height of 2,700 mm. this increase is 20 mm. per metre; it increases from 160 mm at the enclosed corner of the façades, up to a maximum of 460 mm at the outer corner. The maximum deviation between a helix and a straight line between the ends of a 3,200 mm high mullion is less than 1 mm. Therefore, the mullions may as well be straight.

45° to the left

In the wings and the core, following building customs, vertical walls were positioned in a rectangular grid. Only the connection of the inner and outer walls demands a specific solution. It is comparable to that of a flat vertical inner wall to a flat inclined outer wall. The meeting plane is in fact twisted, but this transformation can be ignored: the difference in horizontal rotation between the lower and upper edge of an inner wall is less than 1 mm. An attachment had to be added though, as an intermediate between vertical inner wall and sideways sloping façade mullion. It is repeated on each floor and is equal to that of the other (identical) wings at that position. So, if prefabricated, it will not be costly.

The interior walls were aligned to the rectangular grid at floor level. As the walls rise vertically, they meet the 1.4° rotated ceiling at an angle with its grid. If the ceiling has a smooth finish, as is normal in apartments, the rotation will scarcely be noticeable. But with a suspended ceiling system, as is often applied in offices, it will result in tapering border panels. In this case, a choice must be made between allining the walls with either the floor grid or that of the ceiling.

PRELIMINARY STUDY: DEGREE OF TORSION, FAÇADE FINISHING

Before the directions at the top and bottom of the building were tuned to the directions of the adjacent and surrounding streets (which in hindsight is obvious), the visual qualities of various degrees of twisting were examined, as well as the interplay of lines with the various façade finishing.

The image on the left is reserved and dignified, stubborn even. From the basic connotation of a positive line, the accent here was diagonally downwards. This pegs down the building to the surrounding area. The mirror image, to the right, places the accent upwards. The attention is drawn up and disappears into the air. It expresses more of a longing than the rotation to the left. It is flamboyant and dance-like.

With a strong twist, the image becomes spectacular and less stately. The torsion is rather extreme, from surprising to grotesque. It is interesting to see the varying contour lines of the wings in the upward view.

Only after deciding to have the building in line with the surrounding roads, the volume was visually divided into two slabs differing in façade finish and height. The blue colour of the glass was later changed to green, because of the more neutral shading when looking out, and because of the more favourable cold bending properties.

90° to the right

180° twisted, to the right

50° to the left

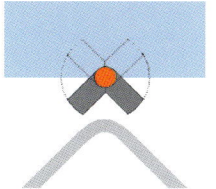   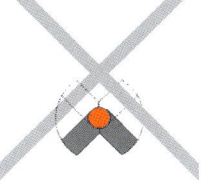 

CASE-STUDY: TWISTER 4

View from above

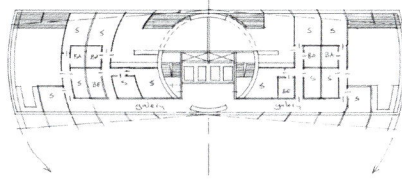

ground plan of the tenth floor

setting in a landscape

At the waterside

Accentuation of a corner

Along a quay

At the crossing of (water) ways

At a bend in the road

In Twister 4 the wings connect to a cylinder, the angle differing per floor. This model features a varying structural principle: the symmetrical twisted wings exert compensating torsion forces on the cylinder. The façades could only be executed more cheaply if the parapets (in concrete, brick or steel) were twisted, and the closing windows were placed as flat surfaces along the inner side of the galleries and balconies. A floor plan was designed for apartments with such openings in the façade. This model has tangential cylindrical walls, in order to connect along helical intersections to the mullions in the façades. Unlike the earlier models with flat inner walls, no intermediate elements are needed to connect to the helical mullions.

The cylindrical and twisted façades blend. The view from inside is unusual and impressive: at one side of the building, one looks down upon the slanting facade. At the other side the room from which one looks outside appears to 'hang in the air'.
Because of the way the wings turn in opposite directions, the ground floor and the top floor share intimacy on one façade, and a view on the other. This phenomenon is also apparent in a cylindrical building block with a central open core, but in this case the gradual rotation per floor is added. Between the wings a theatrical transfer takes place: from looking out into the distance to overlooking a semi-secluded area, from isolation to cherishing. Approach and estrangement are fundamental feelings associated with twisted surfaces.

Views when rounding twister 4

The unexpected transformation of the reflection of the opposite twisted building wing is striking, as is the double reflection of sunlight.

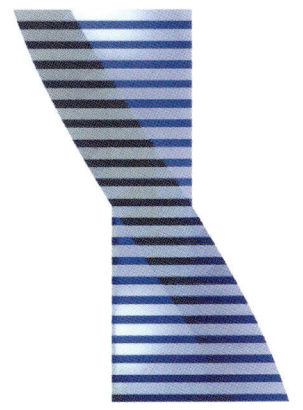

View upwards, from the floor, next to the core

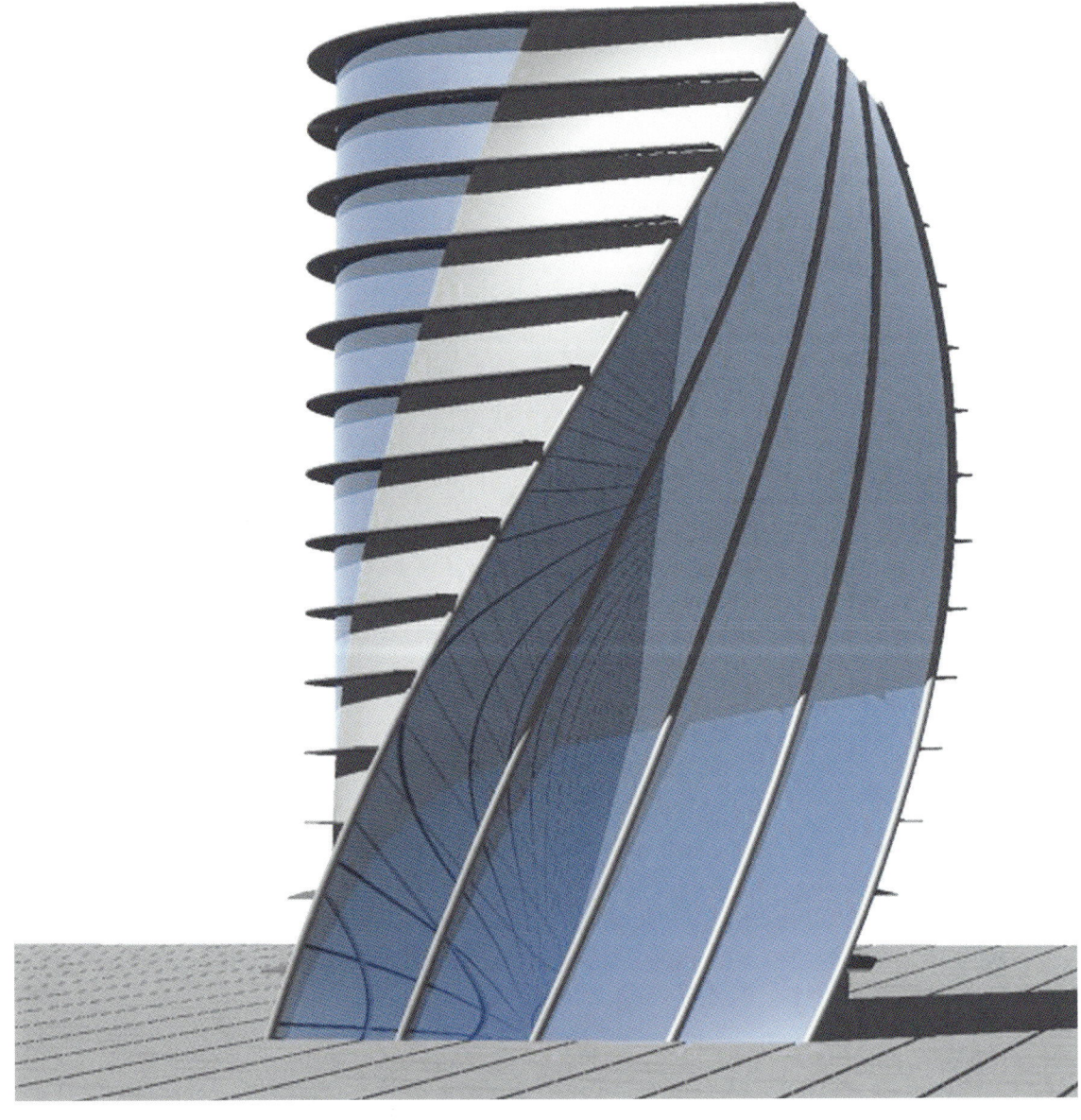

CASE-STUDY: TWISTER 5

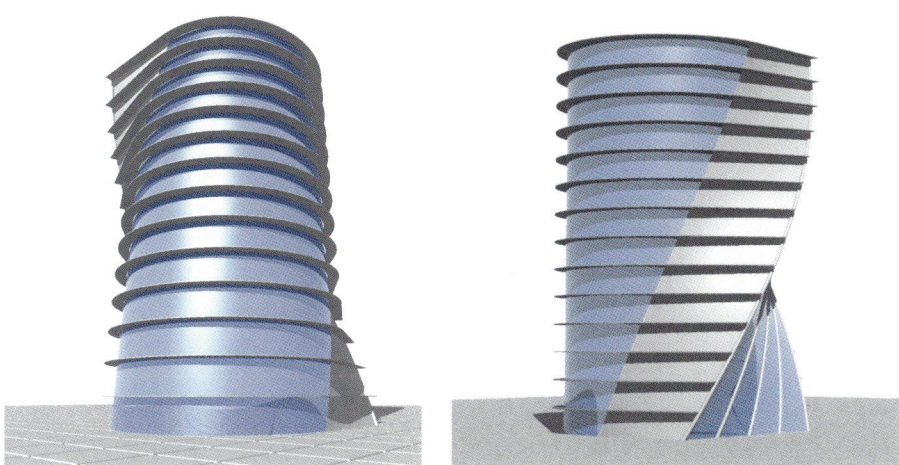

The corners of these buildings are cylindrical.

In this tower – 14 storeys high – the façades provide the structural stability. By rotating the floors around a square, variations in floorplans are studied.
The façade provides a – distorted – view over the surrounding. During the night the traffic will produce continuously changing images.

Preliminary studies

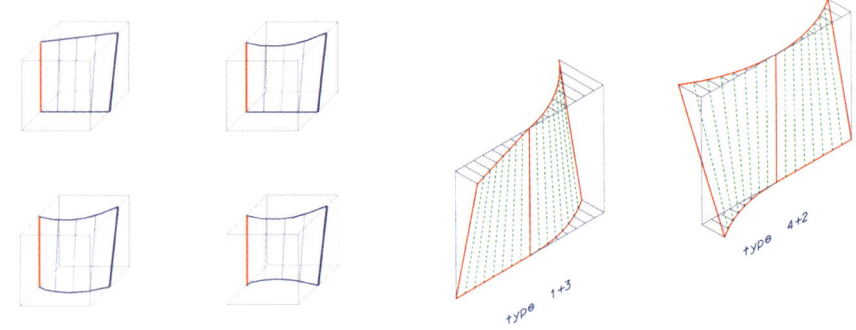

CASE-STUDY: LOW-RISE TORDOS

Torsion types

Study models of window frames

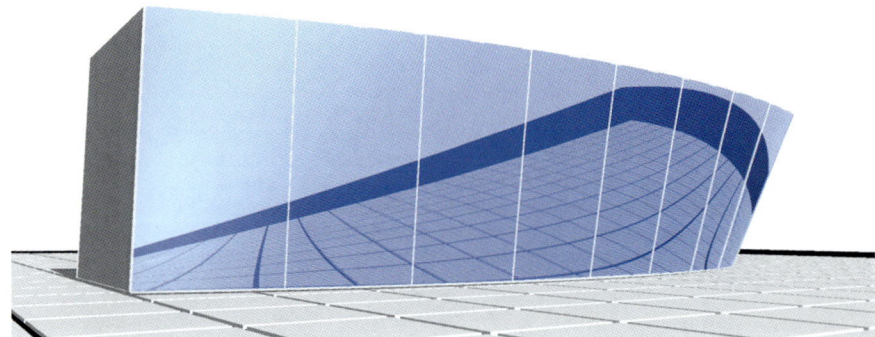

With 'orthogonal' torsion the rules lie in horizontal or parallel vertical surfaces. They mostly coincide with the floors, columns, or partitioning walls of the super-structure. Starting from the four versions of orthogonal torsion, examples were drawn of window frames and low-rise buildings. All floor level areas in the low-rise are approximately the same, so when divided into equal units, e.g. for houses, each dwelling will acquire more or less similar floor areas.

Perspective of low-rise type 2

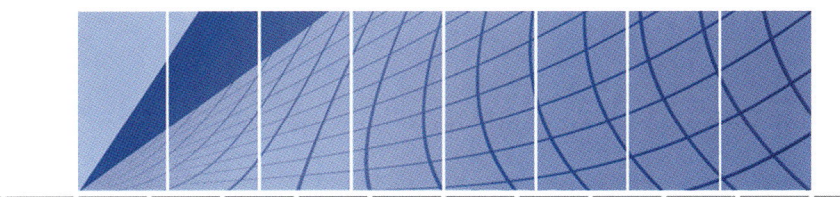

Straight front view of low-rise type 3

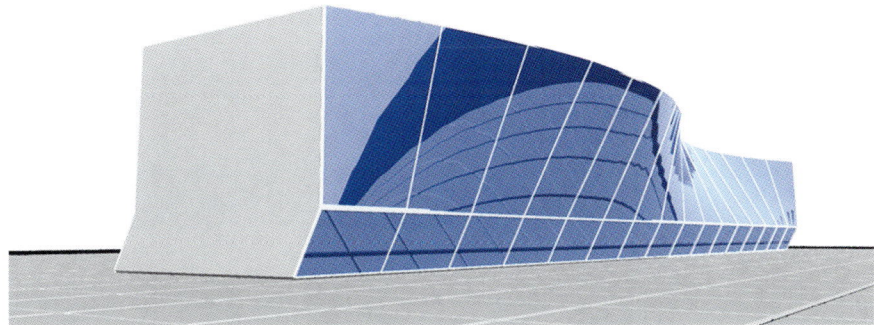

Perspective of a combination of low-rise types 2a and 2b

With strong transformations, the subconsciously experienced relation between the reflection and the real surroundings is lost, and fictional surroundings, in which volumes suddenly turn up or disappear, are suggested. They appear to change in shape and position when one moves.

EXAMPLES OF APPLICATION

By placing the low-rise buildings on a 4,800 x 4,800 m grid, one can gain insight into the reflections. The models are four storeys high and consist of eight modules, each 6 metres in width. These buildings have conventional superstructures. As opposed to twisters, they feature little repetition of elements.

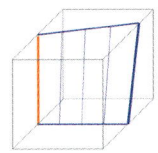

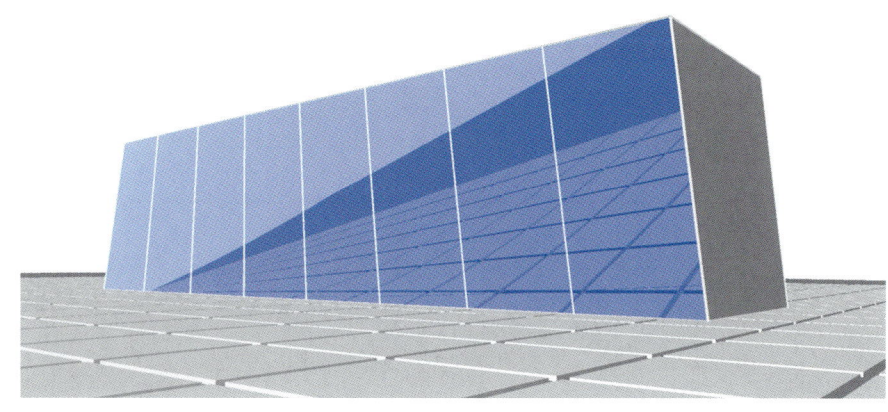

Low- rise tordo 1

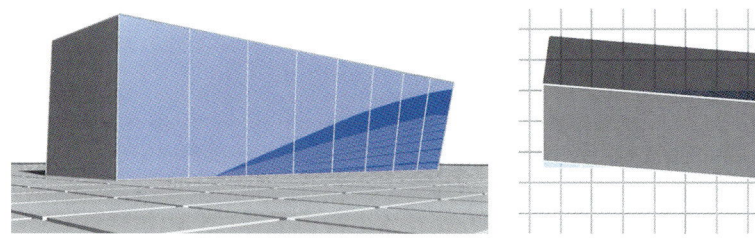

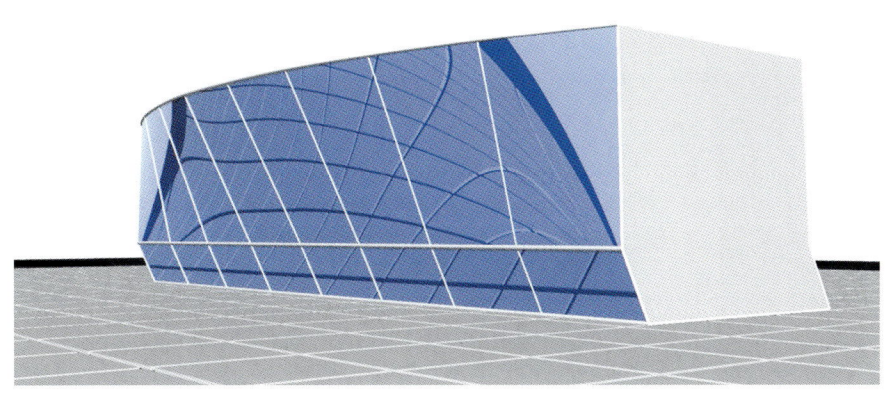

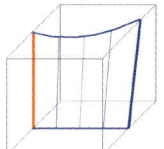

Low- rise tordo 2a

The shape contrast between flat lower and twisted upper façade, enlarges the spectacle

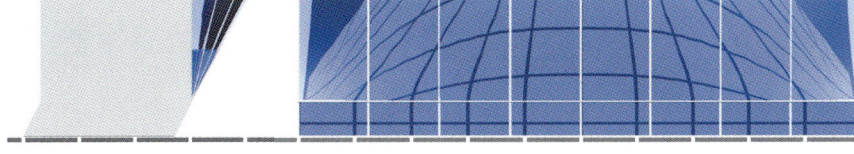

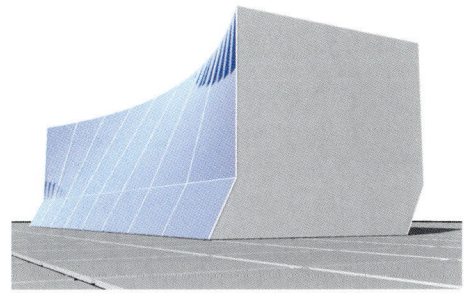

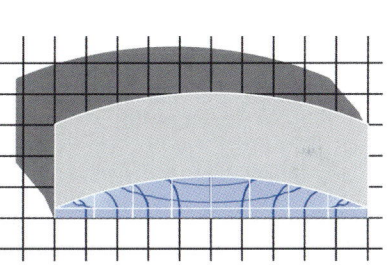

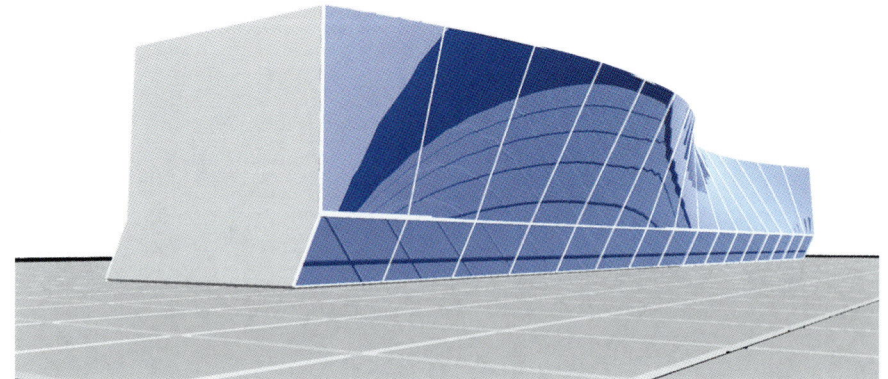

Combination of low-rise tordos 2a and 2b

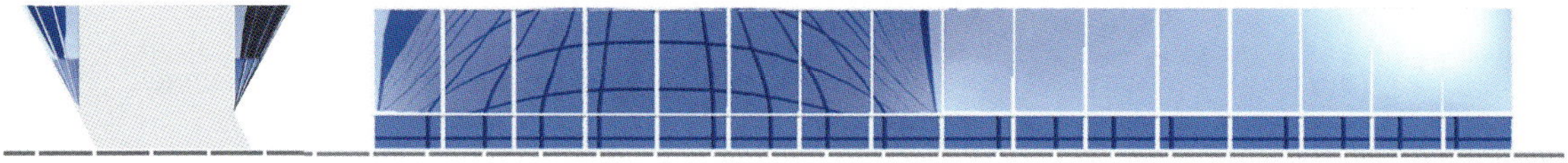

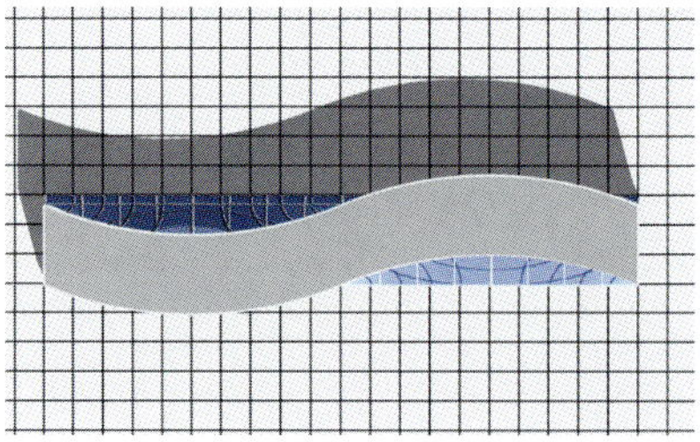

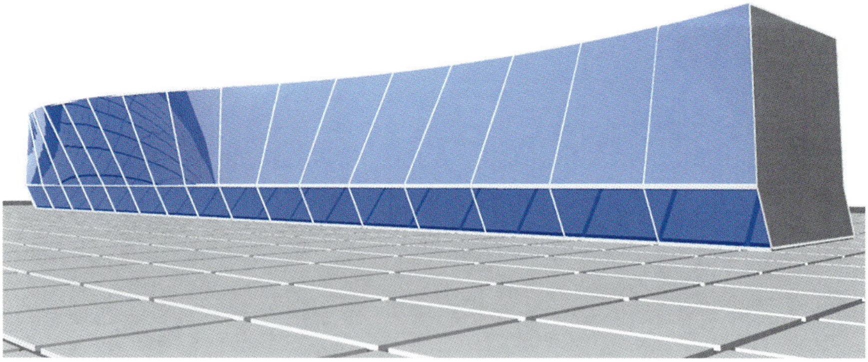

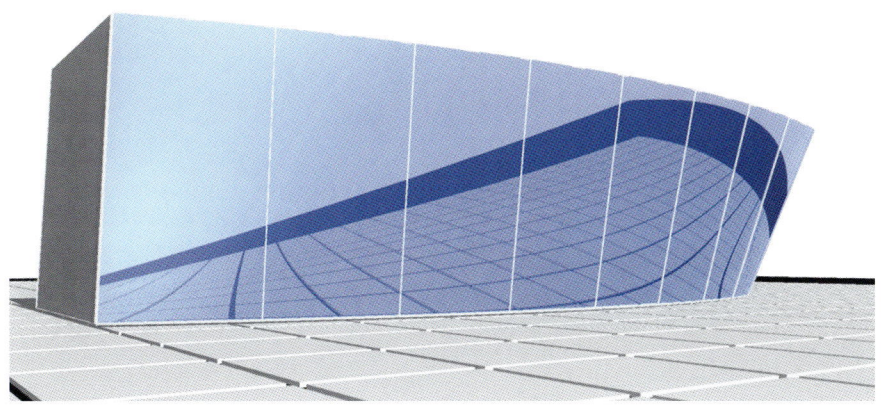

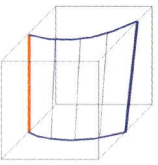

Low- rise tordo 3

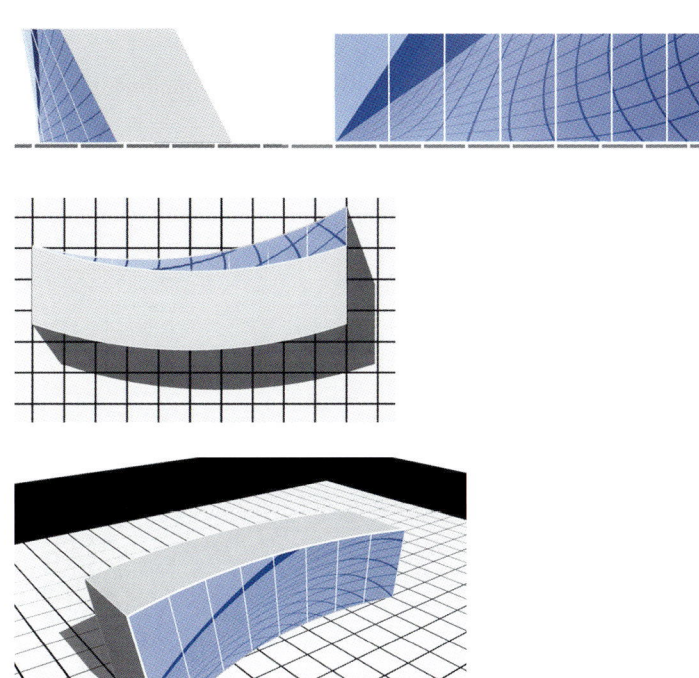

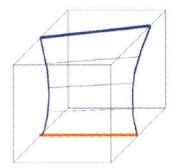

Low- rise tordo 4

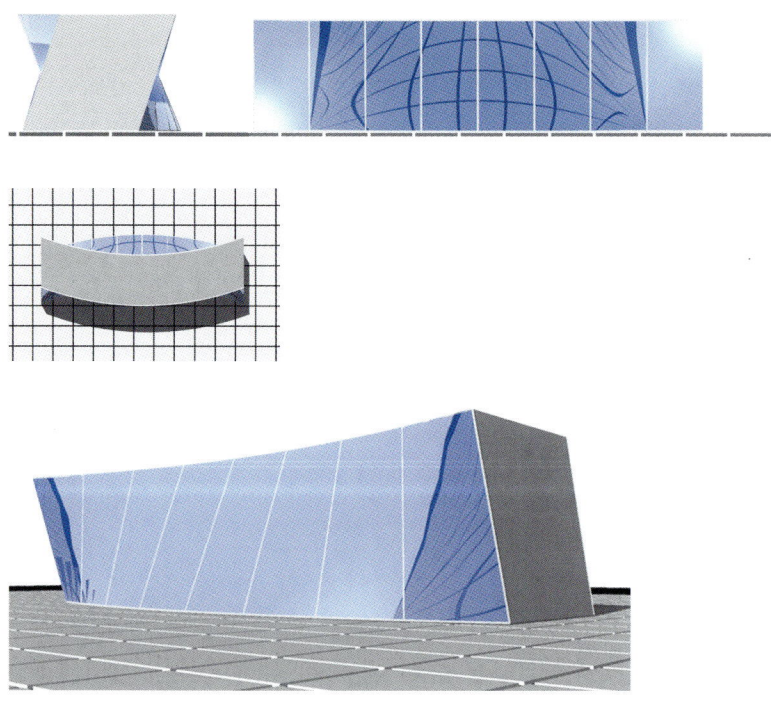

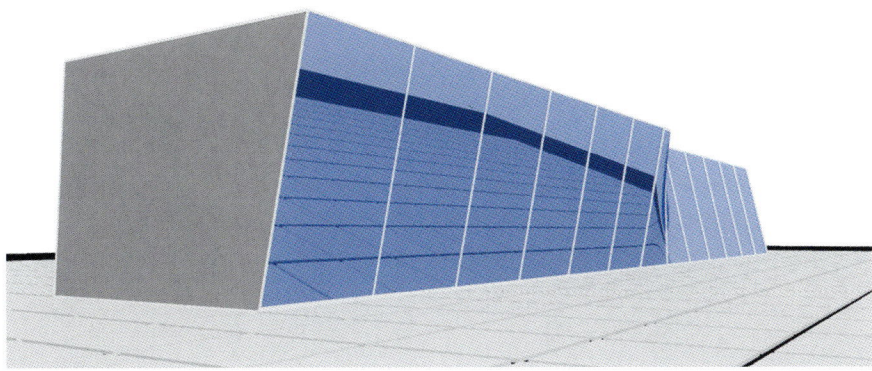

Exchange part

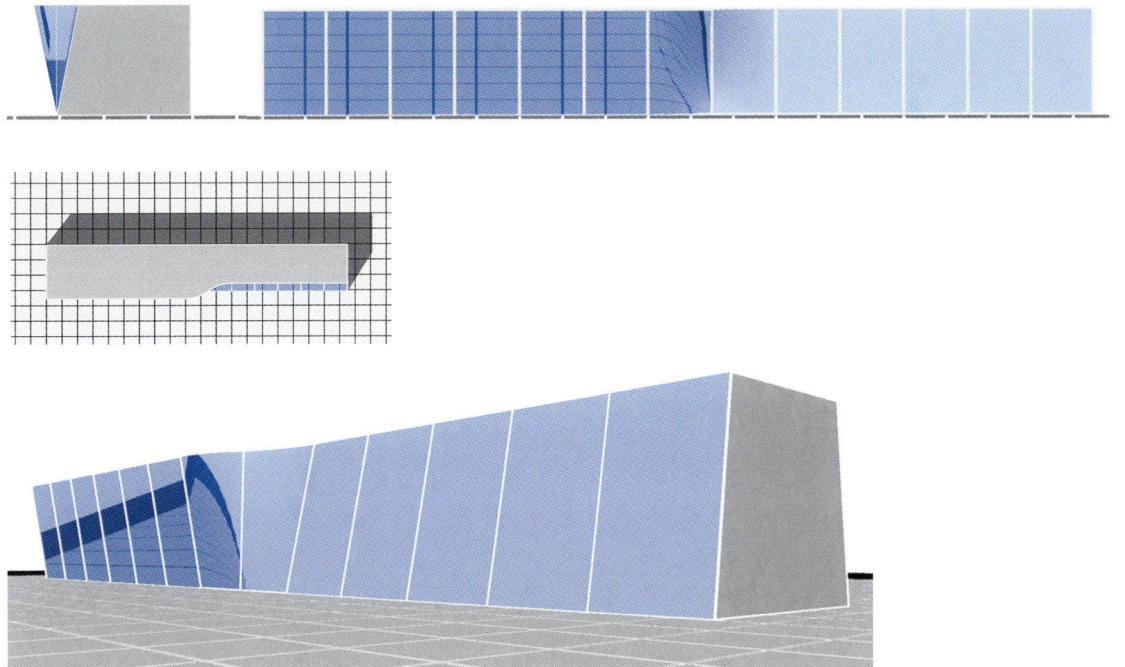

To save expenses, one can opt for the façades to be mainly flat with a few twisted elements. The transformed parts are called 'corner pieces' and 'exchange parts'.

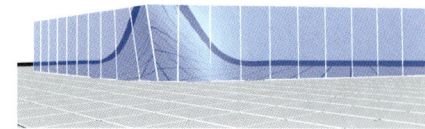

Corner-piece 1

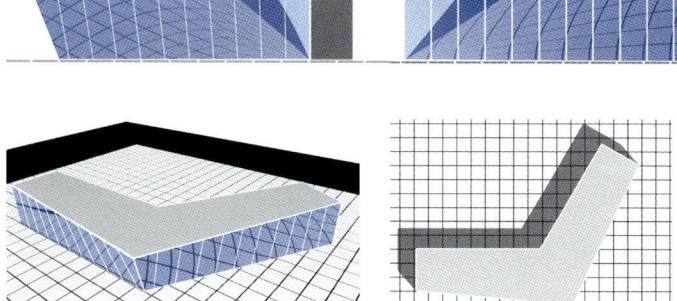

Corner-piece 2

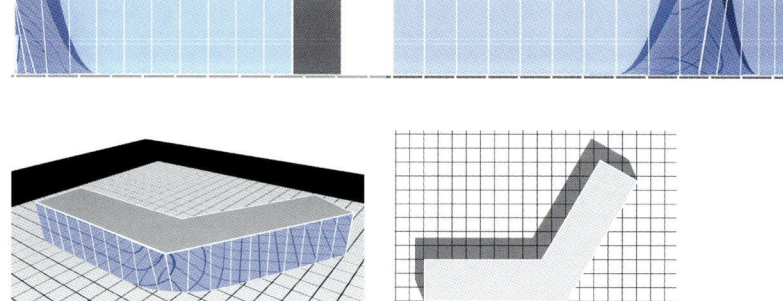

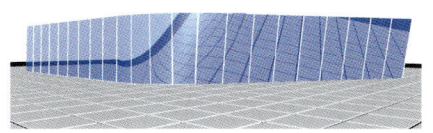

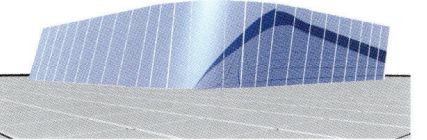

Corner-piece 3

Corner-piece 3

Corner-piece 4

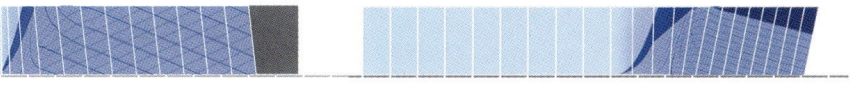

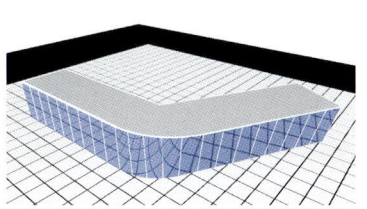

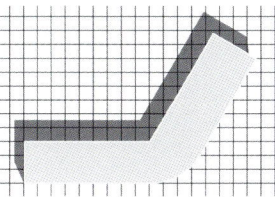

Corner-piece 4

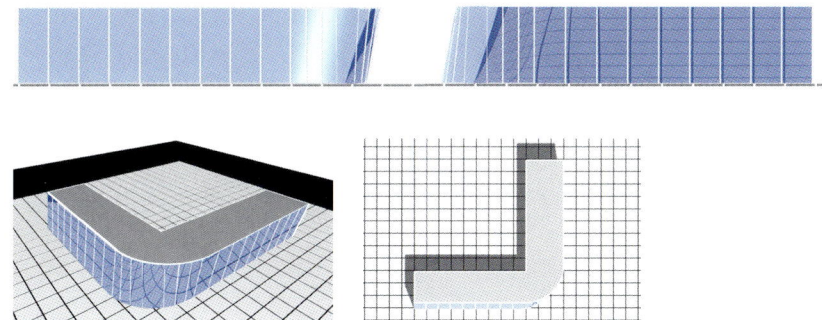

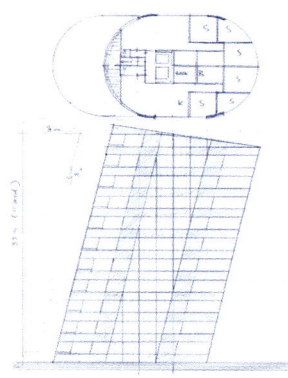
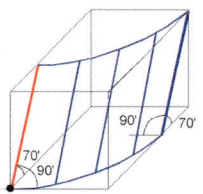

CASE-STUDY: SLIDERS AND ANGLERS

SINGLY CURVED SURFACES AND TWISTED PROFILES

With the window framing system designed for twisted façades, glass sheets can be connected at varying angles to floors or walls. Such details do not only occur in twisted and double-curved façades, but also in sloping cylindrical façades and singly curved façades with a varying curvature. This chapter presents pilot projects of the 'Twist (window frame) system' applied in non-twisted façades.

An 'angler' is a building of which the ground plans are shifted along an inclined straight line. 'Sliders' are buildings whose floor plans are shifted along a curve. The drawn examples are shifted along an elliptical curve, which results in cylindrical façades.

The anglers shown here have cylindrical corners. When an inclined cylinder is connected to a horizontal surface, e.g. a floor construction or a parapet, the angle at which the glass meets the transom varies. To make the connection possible, the profile must be assembled with torsion. In this study the 'Twist' system was developed. No such window frame system was available beforehand.

A curved, slanting façade can also be manufactured with heat-strengthened glass without window frames. The material that would be needed for this, is expensive, due to the non-rectangular shape of the panel. The laminated cold bent heat-strengthened glass developed in this project, however, allows such façades to be produced relatively cheaply and easily.

With regard to the façade, the core of this building has a different position on each floor; therefore, each floor has a different lay-out.

Angle of incidence upon the horizontal surface varies

ANGLERS

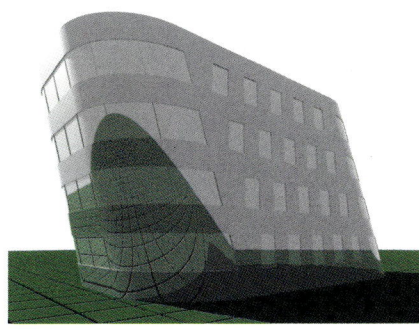
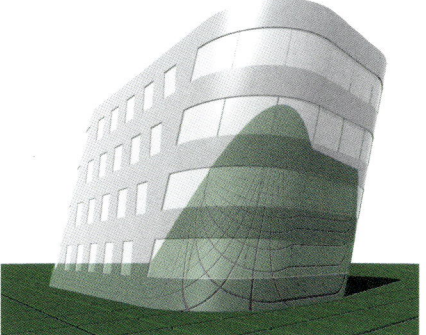

SLIDERS

The façades are cylindrical, with horizontal axes. Therefore the glass sheets always connect to floors and parapets with straight lines. The angles of incidence, of which the glass sheets enter transoms, differ per floor but are constant within each transom. For the window frame, the Twist system (see Chapter 6) can be applied by mounting the standardised glazing profiles without a twist per floor, under a different but constant angle to the rear profile.

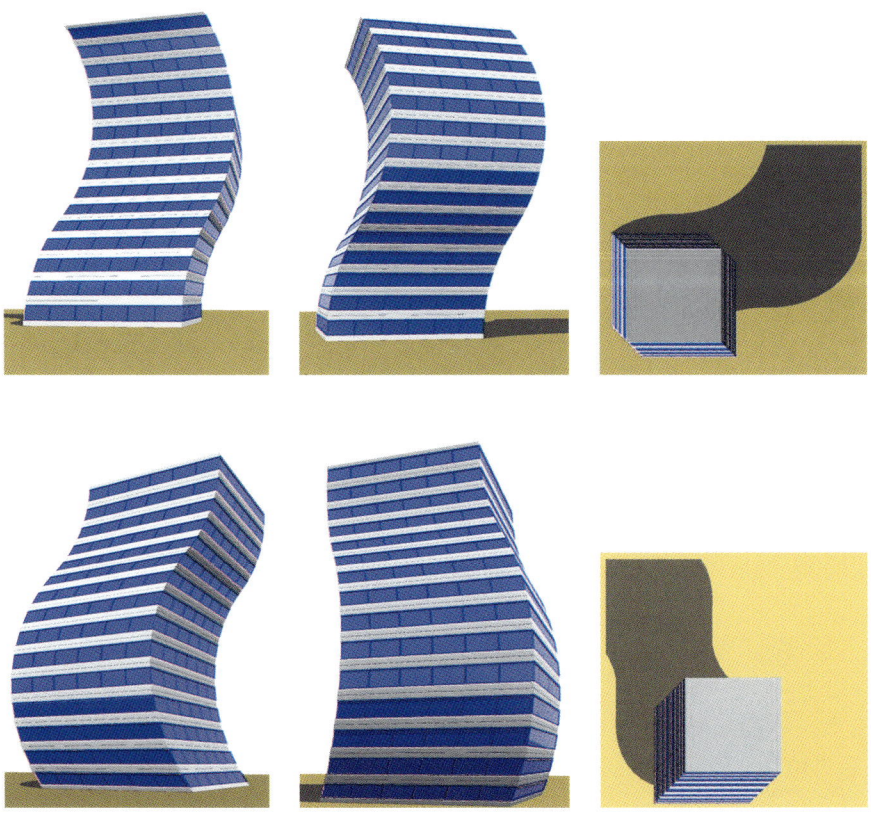

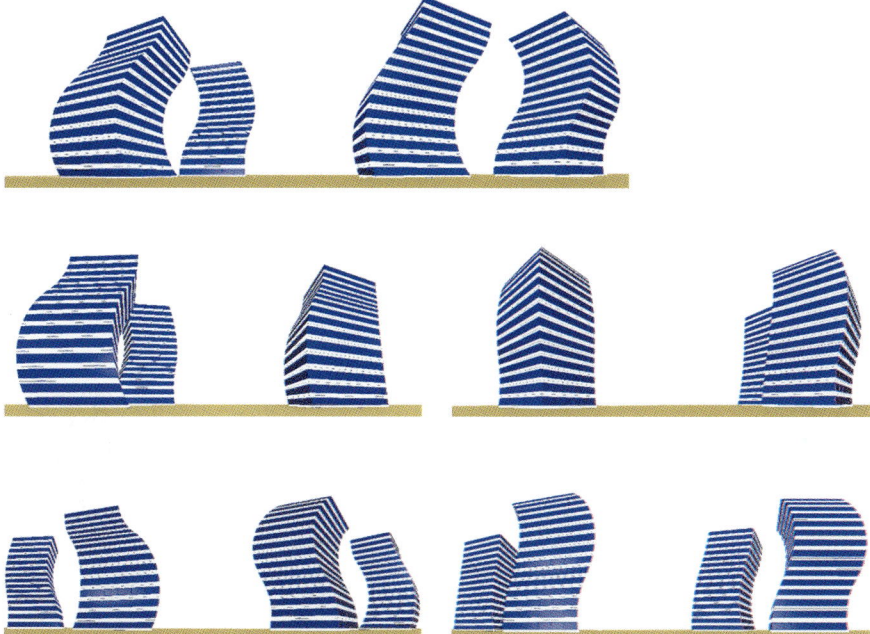

The interaction between the curved contours of adjacent buildings will be a striking phenomenon in the landscape. The application of twisted façades will allow more complex interactions. Both buildings are composed of three-quarters of a complete undulation, the difference being that one starts at maximum amplitude and the other in its centre.

06

MATERIALIZATION

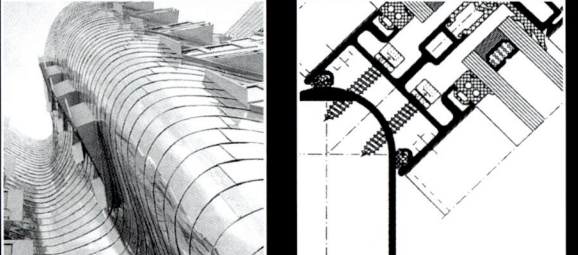
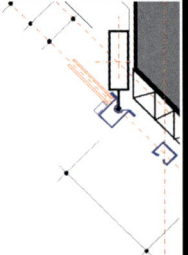

This chapter presents geometric and production aspects of twisted façades. Initially, no specific materials were selected, thus avoiding prior exclusion of options. Given the large investments involved in developing completely new materials, it was later decided to start from existing materials. To obtain a broad range of twisted elements, a façade composition of parapets, window frames and window panes was developed. The three components are described separately, with their characteristic sizes, material properties and production methods. The geometry of the overall shape of twisted towers was examined with Twister A and Tordo A. The geometry of building parts and their production were elaborated in a series of models, starting with Tordo 1. After listing the drawing and dimensioning problems and analyzing the distortions found in models, adjustable molds were designed for concrete and glass parts, and an appropriate window frame system. The development of a mold for the concrete elements proved to be relatively simple once the geometrical preconditions had been established. This point of view was supported by various manufacturers, who stated that they saw the project fit for realization and would gladly co-operate. Therefore, having prepared a preliminary design, creating the prototype of the mold and testing it with a cast was abandoned. Research then concentrated on the twisted window frame and glass. The resulting prototypes are described in Chapter 7.

DIMENSIONS

COMPUTER DRAWINGS OF RULED SURFACES

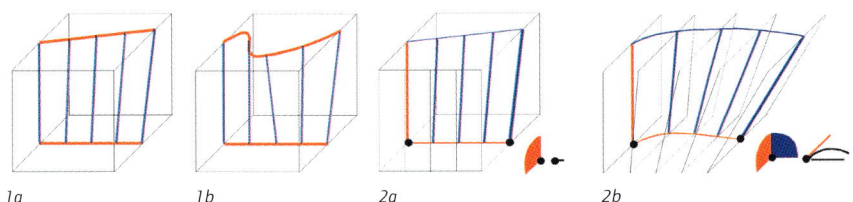

1a   *1b*   *2a*   *2b*

A twisted surface can be drawn on the computer in various ways:

1   By determining a number of equally interspaced points on an upper and lower line. Subsequently a surface is drawn through straight lines that connect these points. (1a).

If they are spread equally over curved upper and/or lower lines, the connecting straight lines will not lie in parallel surfaces. Control over positioning of the rules, for example to be sure that they connect to an orthogonal building grid, is often required(1b).

2   By shifting and rotating rules, with at least one shift component perpendicular to the direction of rotation. (2a)

By rotating the rule in various directions. The shift line can either be curved or straight. Currently only a few programmes are able to rotate a line in two or more directions. Appropriate software commands have to be written for this purpose. (2b)

THE UNIVERSAL DETAIL

The conventional way of drawing is inadequate for representing a node in 3D curved components. A cross-section can be produced relatively easily with the computer, but the image is too complicated, because the cross-sections are supplemented with contour lines of the curved or twisted components that are behind the cross-section. Drawing a non-right-angled intersection through a curved profile by hand, is time-consuming. Even if drawn correctly, the result will often be difficult to understand, since the intersection is larger than the smallest one possible, which traditionally is the standard representation.

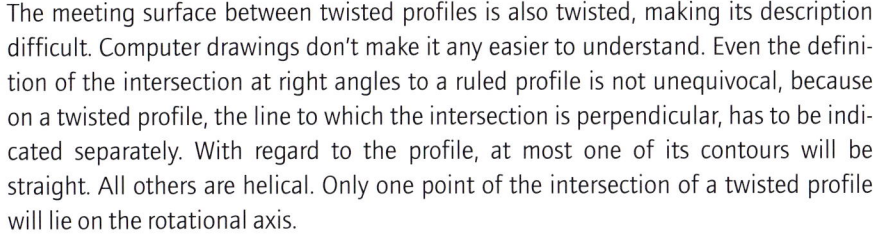

The meeting surface between twisted profiles is also twisted, making its description difficult. Computer drawings don't make it any easier to understand. Even the definition of the intersection at right angles to a ruled profile is not unequivocal, because on a twisted profile, the line to which the intersection is perpendicular, has to be indicated separately. With regard to the profile, at most one of its contours will be straight. All others are helical. Only one point of the intersection of a twisted profile will lie on the rotational axis.

With 3D designs, the mutual positions and connections of inclined and possibly curved profiles can better be represented by **universal details**, than **basic details**.

The basic detail is the geometrically correct representation of the meeting between objects. When one profile connects to another, that lies at an angle to the former or that is curved, each profile is entirely shown behind the intersection. The cross-sections deviate from the standard. Intersections with twisted profiles are even more complex. Correct though it may be, such a representation is laborious to produce and hard to understand.

The universal detail is a simplified reproduction of a group of profiles, possibly curved or twisted, that meet at an angle. It shows a unique position of the parts: the exceptional situation in which the profiles are straight and perpendicular or parallel to each other. Thus, the non-orthogonal meeting may be reproduced in one drawing, where each component has the size of the right-angled intersection or the front view. Consequently, the connection often looks simpler than it is. This simplified reproduction of the meeting is wrong, according to established drawing agreements, because the cross-section of only one component is represented correctly, whereas the others are inappropriately illustrated as right-angled intersections. The advantage, however, is that the profiles have been reproduced in their actual mutual measurement proportions and distances in one drawing. Angles and profile curvatures can be indicated additionally, with their maximum and minimum dimensions.

Isometric view

Universal detail

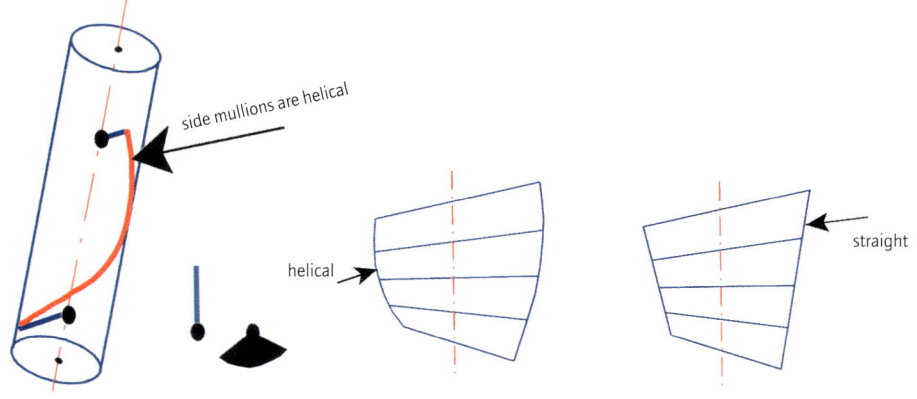

side mullions are helical

helical

straight

Torsion type R2b, with helical
sides (conoid, not a hypar)

Torsion type R1a (hypar)

THE HYPAR

A hypar has rules in both the horizontal, and the vertical direction. This has many advantages when construing a twisted shape and calculating the strains inside, for example when it is being used as a concrete shell. The sidelines of the drawn hypar are straight; the rotation angle varies and the transoms are not all equally long. In a hypar-shaped window the angle of incidence of the glass in the glazing profile varies, as well as the twisting degree per profile length.

When a straight rotational axis in the centre of the glass sheet has a constant rotational angle, and all horizontal rules are of equal length, the side mullions are helical.

THE 'ARCHITECTURAL' HYPAR

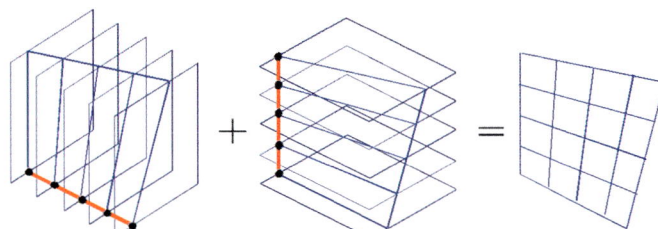

All rules connect to an orthogonal grid

In the architectural hypar, rotation of the rules takes place within parallel surfaces. The transoms and mullions coincide with the rules in the surface and connect to straight floor edges, walls and columns.

The stacked mullion segments in the drawn hypar are of equal length, as are the adjacent transom segments. In a mullion, all segments have the same inclination, but the transoms turn away at a different angle per layer. The sheet sizes differ within each bay, unless a mirroring of parts occurs, due to symmetry.

THE REFERENCE SURFACE

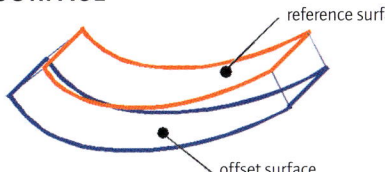

All measures are derived from the reference surface. This of any geometrical shape one desires; in this case it is twisted. It has no thickness and it contains the base lines. The geometry and dimensioning always relate to the reference surface, unless otherwise stated.

Offset lines and surfaces

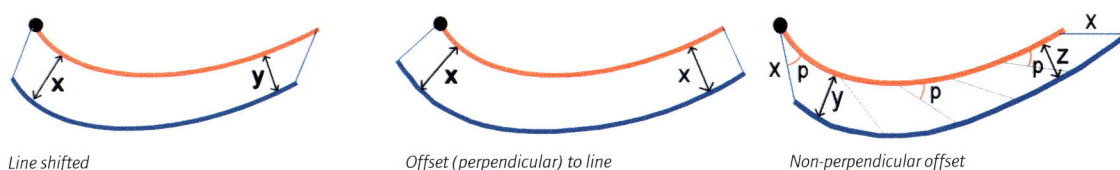

Line shifted   *Offset (perpendicular) to line*   *Non-perpendicular offset*

When the outer surface of a twisted panel is drawn by shifting the inner surface to the outside, they will have the same shape. The thickness of an element, however, will vary. Since a constant thickness of elements such as double glazing and window frames is usually preferred, their inner and outer sides are drawn by making offsets. These are derived from the reference surface. This may lie within or adjacent to the elements. The offset is at all points made perpendicular to the reference surface. Therefore the rims of elements are also perpendicular to their reference surface. With a non-perpendicular offset the thickness will vary.

Just as the length of a 2D curve differs from its offset, the sizes of curved surfaces are different from their offset. Differences between the inner and outer surface of a thin curved window pane can be ignored with regard to the tolerances that occur in production and assembly. With thick building parts (window frames or concrete façade elements), deviations must be taken into account. The offset distance is important. For example, trusses will have different curvatures than the glass sheets they support.

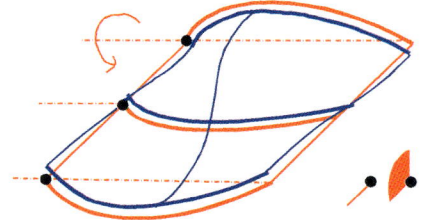

1 Right-angled offset of surface   *2 Surface through offsets of curve lines*

1   When a surface is composed of 'curve lines' (identically curved base lines), all their offsets are equal.

2   Through curve lines, that are rotated around a horizontal axis, a surface can be drawn, as well as through the offsets of curve lines. Both surfaces will intersect, as can be seen in the drawing. Similarly, when identical roof girders with glazing profiles are rotated, the angle of incidence of the glass varies with regard to the profiles on the trusses. With a large rotation, such a glass surface is not feasible because it would pierce the trusses.

Offset of a hypar

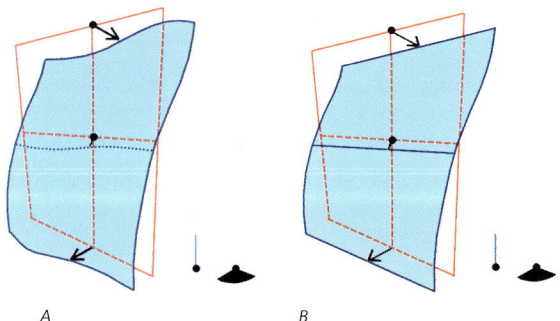

A   B

A   The offset of a hypar is not a ruled surface. The offsets of a hypar's rules are helical, because all points of each line are offset perpendicular to the twisted surface and, therefore, have moved in a different direction. In case of a small torsion, the offset only slightly deviates from a twisted surface, because the helical lines hardly deviate from straight lines. When dimensioning the window elements, offsets of ruled surfaces can be regarded as straight. But size deviations often result in drawing problems, due to the high accuracy of computers.

B   A twisted surface can be made by drawing straight lines in one of the directions of the hypar, and using them as rules. The distance between this twisted surface and the reference surface varies.

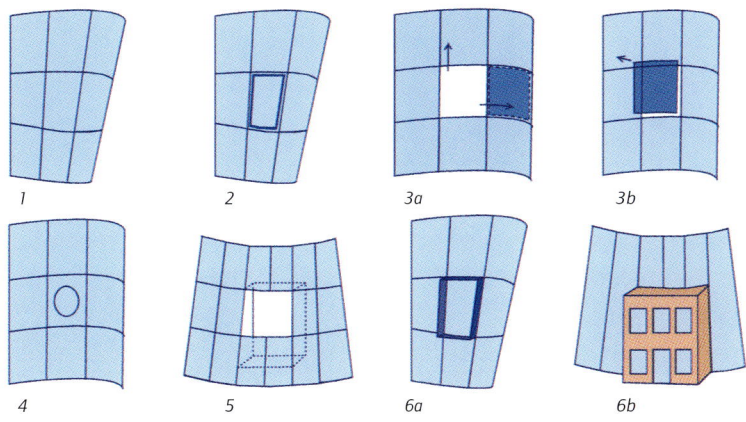

OPENINGS IN CURVED FAÇADES

Openings in curved façades

Openings in curtain walls:

1 Ventilation through openings in the window profiles or between doubled profiles.
2 Side hung, pivoted or cantilever window against the window frame profile.
3a Parallel moving sliding or sash window, with a constant curvature and/or rotation in the sliding direction.
3b Non-parallel sliding window, e.g. moving along straight slide ways.
4 Flat frontal face with windows that can be opened; the sides vary in size.
5 Opening in glass, free of window frame.
6a Opening with walled-in balcony with flat doors/windows.
6b Conventional building element with flat elements that can be opened, sticking out of the curved wall.

The connection details of hinged windows in twisted surfaces are, in case of modest rotation, comparable to those of common windows. A sliding window with its guide way and complicated wind and water tightening, is more difficult to design than one with hinges. In addition, heavy windows need a compensating force (counterweight or balance spring) when displacing the centre of gravity in a vertical direction. The window does not have to be displaced parallel to the façade surface. It is also possible to fasten it to a straight guide.

The problems of moving parts can be avoided by flattening them in a surface which is in the front or the rear of the façade, e.g. with a walled-in balcony or a protruding orthogonal volume.

Windows made of flexible materials are left aside in this diagram.

Option 5: all windows in this complex are flat and identical. Only the framing varies in size. The window may be either in front of, or behind the façade, or intersect it.

Sliding windows in singly curved surfaces

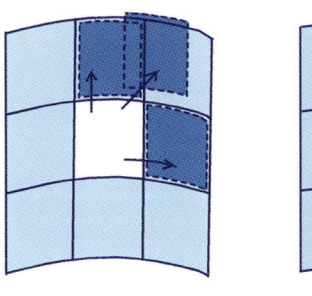 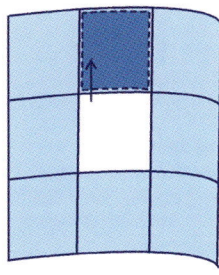

Fixed radius   *Freely curved*

Sliding windows can move in any direction in flat and cylindrically curved surfaces. In a freely singly curved surface, they can only be made to slide in the direction of the straight lines. Usually, they are vertical with horizontal guides.

Sliding windows in surfaces of revolution

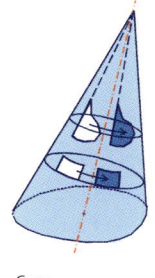 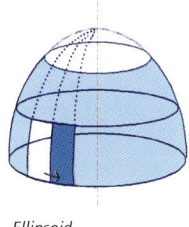 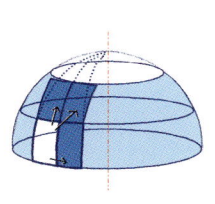 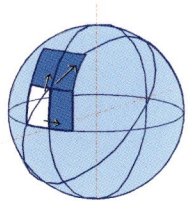

Cone   *Ellipsoid*   *Sphere*

In a surface of revolution a part (e.g. a glass sheet) can be shifted as well. This is only possible when the adjacent surface part has an equal curvature and the displacement line is circular, within a surface at right angles with the rotational axis. Each point in the surface must undergo a constant bending and rotation in the sliding direction.

With a cone, it is obvious to create sliding surfaces with straight sidelines and circular lower and upper lines, but different contours are possible. With a sphere, a surface part can be slid in all surface directions.

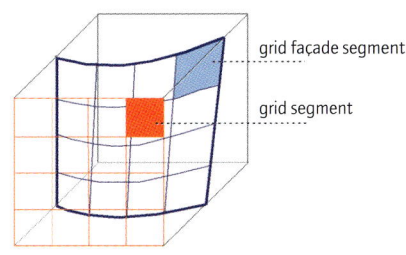

grid façade segment

grid segment

The screen projects the grid segments upon the façade.

Rotating and roller windows in a sphere

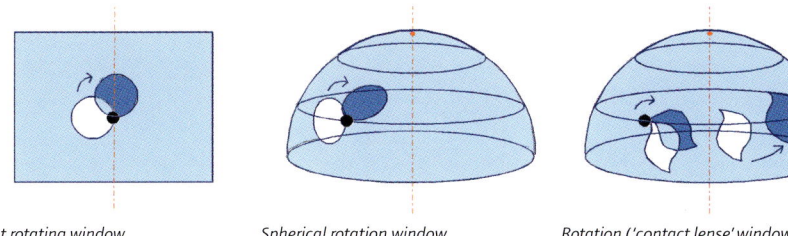

Flat rotating window   *Spherical rotation window*   *Rotation ('contact lense' window)
and sliding windows with free contours*

A flat surface is a sphere with an infinite radius. A figure within a flat surface can be shifted in all directions. The window shape can be chosen at will. The window, whether flat or spherical, does not have to slide along a line, but can also rotate around a point: a one-point rotating window with a axis at right angles with the rotation surface. In a sphere, it is obvious to use the meridians for vertical sidelines for rotating windows, and circle segments at right angles with the rotational axis for horizontal sidelines.

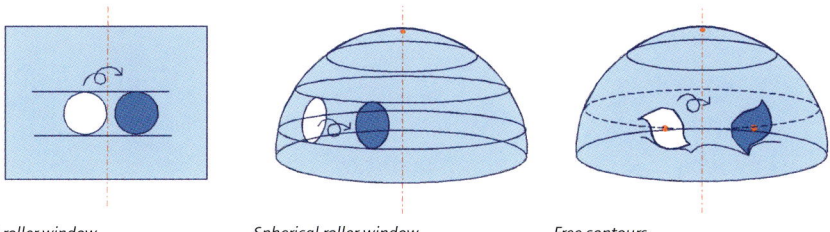

Flat roller window   *Spherical roller window*   *Free contours*

With the window rolling over a slide profile, a second profile was drawn to prevent it falling out. On a sphere, the window can be rolled in any direction because the surface curvature is equal in every direction. By tuning the guide way to the contours, the point of gravity can remain at a constant height, so that the window does not become heavier or lighter to displace. A rough profiling of the guide must prevent the window from gliding sideways.

Sliding windows in ruled and curve surfaces

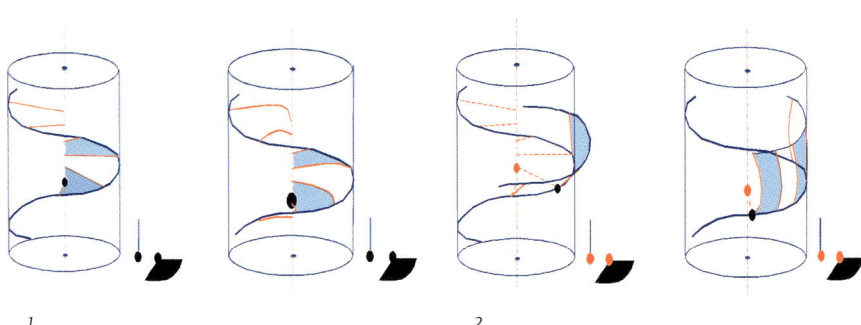

1

2

1   Right-angled ruled surface, respectively curve surface
2   Non right-angled ruled surface, respectively curve surface (here, with adjacent centres of rotation)

In most twisted surfaces, like in freely doubly curved surfaces, sliding windows are no option, due to the panels varying in size and distortion. Only in at right angles rotating surfaces, as illustrated in chapter 4, can sliding windows be made.

For twisters, a distinction can be made between the twisted surface types:

- **right-angled ruled, and curve surfaces.** They have a straight rotational axis; the base line and the direction in which the rotation takes place, are in a surface that is at right angles with the rotational axis. If the base line does not intersect with the rotational axis, it is a right-angled ruled or curve surface with an adjacent centre of rotation.

- **non right-angled ruled, and curve surfaces.** These also have a straight rotational axis and a constant rotation in a surface that is at right angles to the rotational axis, but the base line of these surfaces is not in a surface that is at right angles to the rotational axis. In both right-angled and non right-angled twisted surfaces, the parts are repeated (and sliding windows are possible) if rotation and displacement are constant.

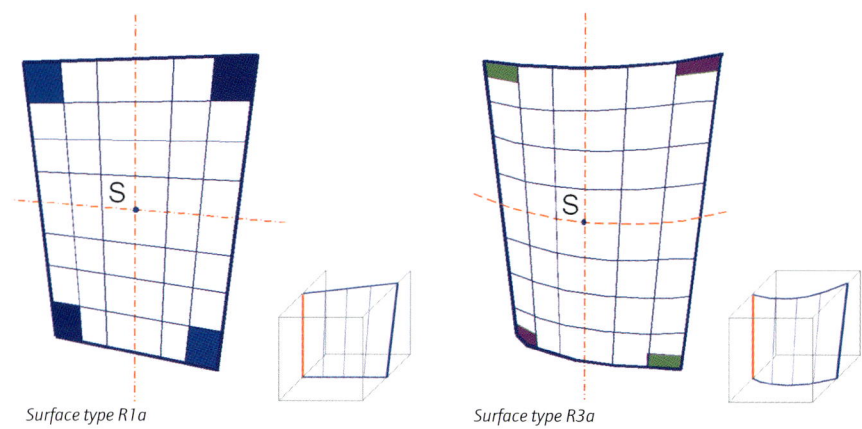

Surface type R1a   Surface type R3a

LARGEST TYPE, STACKED AND ADJACENT ELEMENT

In the above façade, the largest elements are in the corners. The hypar type R1a with two symmetry axes has four elements that qualify as **largest type**, whereas torsion surface type R3a has two: at the top right and the bottom left. The size of the corner elements determines the dimensions of the adjustable glass mold and the concrete shuttering. All elements that connect to a vertical axis, have an equal sideline length.

Façade parts situated on top or below each other, are called **stacked elements**. The parts in the same horizontal strip are the **adjacent elements**.

SYMMETRY IN A FAÇADE

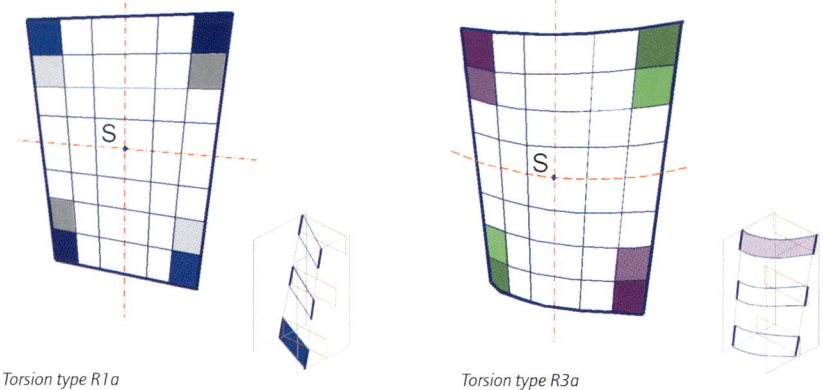

Torsion type R1a   Torsion type R3a

Hypar type R1a is divided into four equal quadrants by straight vertical and horizontal symmetry axes. The adjacent quadrants are mirrored as well as placed back to front. Diagonally opposite quadrants are identical, and inverted.
Façade type R3a has symmetry axes in the centres, but the horizontal one is curved. This façade, only has equal diagonally opposite quadrants. The intersection point of the symmetry axes is called **symmetry point S.** The symmetry axes of torsion type R1a are also the **shortest connecting lines**.

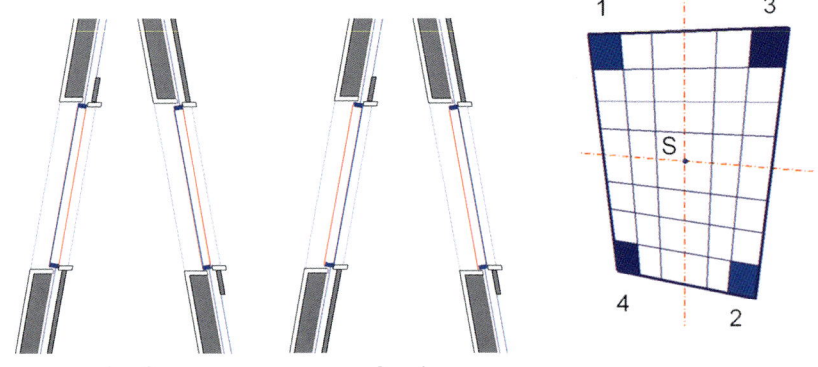

1   Common position

2   Identical and upside down

3   Identical and mirrored

4   Identical, mirrored and

*   upside down*

Inversion and mirroring of window frames and panels

When the hypar-shaped reference surface lies in the centre of the element, the panels can also be repeated inside out and upside down. This is not possible with torsion type 3, because the shape will then bulge in the wrong direction. Details of the window frame must be tuned to the position inside out and/or upside down, because in that case windows can, for instance, turn inwards instead of outwards.

Mirrored positioning of window frame and panels

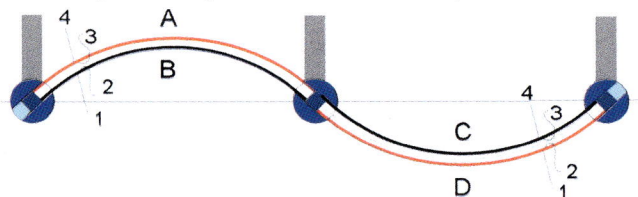

With this sinus-shaped window frame, the rotational axis of the frame profile lies on the intersection of reference surface and structural surface. The panels are centred on the reference surface. The size of inner panel A is equal to that of outer panel D, but layer 3 changes with window D to layer 2. In other words: in a mirrored position, the coating of double-glazing is no longer on the same surface. Reflection coatings are usually designed for a specific layer and not effective otherwise.

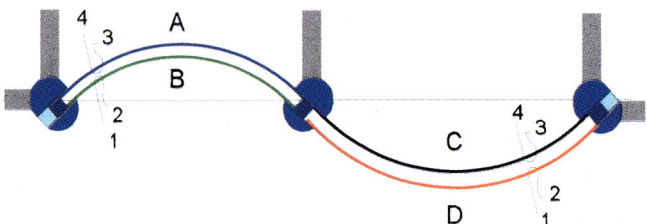

If the reference surface does not lie in the centre of the double glazing but in the centre of inner panels A and C, all sheets will be of a different size, due to the curvature of the glazing profile in the drawn window frame system.

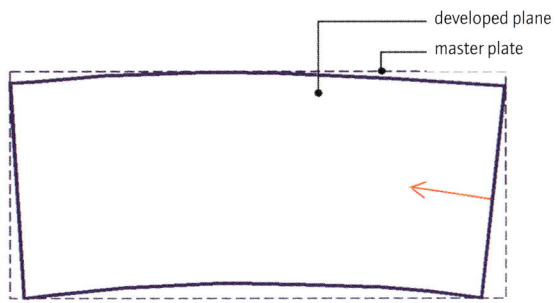

GEOMETRICAL SIMILARITIES TO SHIP-BUILDING

DEVELOPED PLANE AND MASTER PLATE, SHRINKAGE AND STRAIN

Developed plane upon master plate, with edge strain

Most computer programmes that support developed planes of (double-)curved surfaces, can also draw (as a matter of course) the smallest rectangular flat plate out of which the planes can be cut: the **master plate**. The lower contour of the developed plate 'rests' on the lower edge of the master plate. Due to the fact that the opposite contours of the developed plane are not parallel, and its corners are not right-angled, the size of the master plate is used to define its measurements. An arrow indicates from what point and in which direction the distortions were calculated. This is important for the transforming process. The pitch is the greatest distance between a curve and a straight line through its extremities. For a hypar window pane, the pitch of the edge of a developed plane can usually be neglected. Then, the sides can be assumed to be straight.

To twist a plate, it has to be stretched or butted within its surface. The choice between butting and stretching depends on the material and the transforming process. The software, because of its application in the shipbuilding industry, is often geared to processing steel plates by rolling. The distortion can be indicated in the developed plane as a lengthening or a shortening (stretch or butt, strain or shrinkage). In the above developed plane, only the side stretch has been indicated. The stretch or butt within each part of a surface grid is shown in the next paragraph. The shipbuilding industry does not mention the x, y and z-axes in drawings, but the f, p and d axes (forward, port and down). In the developed planes, the x-axis indicates the width direction, the z-axis shows height. The fpd directions were indicated in the developed plane.

DEVELOPED PLANES

A developed plane of a twisted surface with a small degree of distortion can be made by dividing it into a 'mesh' of very small triangles and subsequently putting them next to each other on a flat surface. This is time-consuming. Therefore, automating these actions by computer is advantageous.

Most of the current software is developed for the transformation of steel plates by rolling, pressing or by local electric heating. During transformation, glass behaves differently from steel. Depending on the process, it will often not transform from one side, but from the centre, or from all points at the same time. Although specific software can be designed for determining the transformation in a certain process, the cur-

0.006082	-0.024211	-0.003391	-0.015774	-0.934922	0.015007	0.026140	0.003645	0.030604
0.757766	0.722649	0.733877	0.707964	-0.126708	0.697371	0.685294	0.637920	0.638599
1.330796	1.292135	1.296122	1.26001	0.51429	1.217165	1.187107	1.121126	1.101794
1.720508	1.679604	1.678737	1.635817	0.983360	1.569996	1.528185	1.449080	1.418131
1.922678	1.880852	1.877558	1.831272	1.276656	1.751913	1.703775	1.618038	1.577981
1.933585	1.892180	1.888926	1.842774	1.390555	1.759469	1.710827	1.624738	1.584216
1.750074	1.710453	1.709749	1.667283	1.322067	1.589781	1.548554	1.468554	1.432258
1.369601	1.33151	1.337535	1.302376	1.065818	1.240582	1.208779	1.141348	1.120132
0.790281	0.758411	0.770475	0.746289	0.629095	0.710261	0.695983	0.647778	0.646508
0.010921	-0.014938	0.007434	-0.002049	0.001871	-0.002101	0.007332	-0.015085	0.010734

Developed plane of prototype glass sheet 1 Lb, with stretch per grid section

rent programmes for steel processing, provide insight into the type of transformation behaviour one might expect from a window pane. It is also sufficient for the calculation of transformation requirements for shuttering materials for concrete elements.

With many programmes for unfolding double-curved surfaces, a straight line must be indicated from which the developed plane can be built. More advanced software does this by itself.

Many kinds of data can be made visible:

- Starting line for the calculation of the developed plane, and the starting point or line, e.g. for rolling.
- The rules within the twisted surface.
- Stretching from the centre or the edge, and the stretch and butt involved.
- The dimensions of the master plate.
- The outer dimensions of the developed plane before stretching and butting.
- Data for processing the plate (e.g. pressing of steel: pressing points, pressing power and number of pressings).

It is important to establish the purpose of the developed plane: for dimensioning, processing or to acquire insight into the play of transformation stress. Each material has its own preconditions when it is processed. Depending on the material, it has to be determined what amount of transformation can be tolerated.

To make a 3D distortion within the surface, it only needs to be stretched or butted in one direction. The software cannot always be adjusted to stretch direction. Often it chooses an optimum by itself.

The developed planes made during this project show how metal sheets behave when bent in two directions. This is different from the behaviour of glass, but will suffice as an approximation. Due to the small stretch and butt that occur in the glass sheets of the tower models, the developed plane programme can be used directly to cut the sheets. The transformation in the prototypes is so small that no optical change occurs. Because the thickness of the sheet remains almost the same everywhere, structural variations can be ignored.

For concrete panels stretch and butt indicate for example the necessary forces to press shuttering material into a mold and the required elasticity of a synthetic mat inside.

DIMENSIONING AND STEEL PLATE PROCESSING IN THE
SHIP-BUILDING INDUSTRY; CENTRE STRETCH AND EDGE STRETCH

In the ship-building industry, centre and edge stretch indicate where the plates transform. Preferences for one of these depend on regional traditions. In the Netherlands, one usually works with **edge stretch**; the United States of America and Japan work with **centre stretch**. Poland applies both. The software is tuned to this. The type of stretch can be selected by the draftsman.

The distortion at various points is indicated in a grid of one's own choice. It is also possible to butt the material; in that case distortion has a negative value. Butt is usually avoided because sheet may buckle.

The choice between centre and edge stretch has consequences for plate dimensioning: if the edges are to be stretched, the element can be made from a smaller master plate. Often only one of the two stretching variants is actually possible. In the Netherlands the edges are stretched by pressing and rolling.

The material characteristics, the adjustment of the rollers and the tolerances are very important. For a large part the work is done intuitively, directed by elderly employees. To determine how the plate has to run through the roller, 'roller lines' are drawn on it. They connect points of the same direction vector. These are straight lines. If a strip of wood is placed on a plate while it is being rolled, this will generate a bulge in the sheet. After rolling, there is not much left of the wood. Determining the thickness of the strip is a matter of intuition and experience.

Another method is local pressing of the plates. The force of compression, and the number of times this is done can be indicated with dots in the drawing. The shape of the bulge can be improved by working intuitively with pressure adjustments.

By temporarily heating certain points with electrodes, the steel plate will shrink at these points after cooling. With this method the distortions are kept well under control: the duration of heating, temperature and locations can be accurately determined. Line or point heating can also be applied with welding torches.

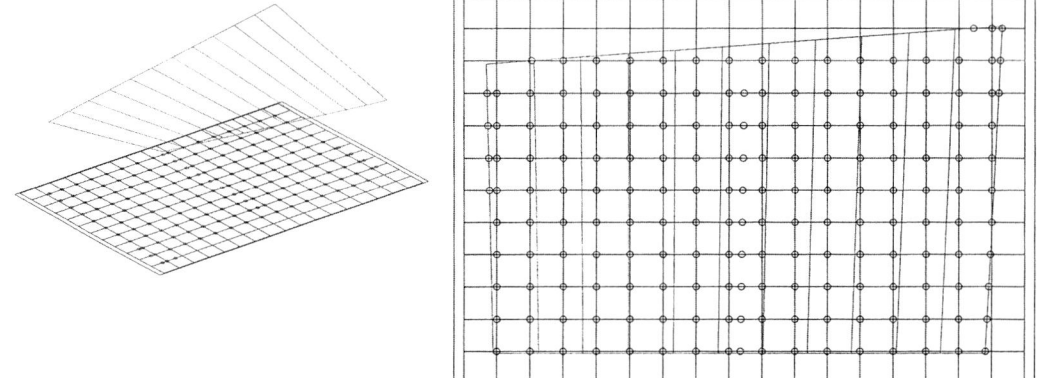

Perspective of glass sheet
above pin bed

Top view of pin bed

THE PIN-BED

A pin-bed in the ship-building industry is a collection of H-profiles that can be adjust-ed in height, and on which a hull segment can be built. It is placed on the floor in an orthogonal grid of approximately 750 x 750 mm. with a total surface of, for instance, 10 x 10 metres. The angle of the plates at the top of the H-profiles can be adjusted to provide supports parallel to the hull skin. The height adjustment of the H-profiles is derived from a 3D drawing of a hull, with the command 'pin jigs'.

APPROXIMATION OF TWISTED A SURFACE WITH A DEVELOPABLE SURFACE

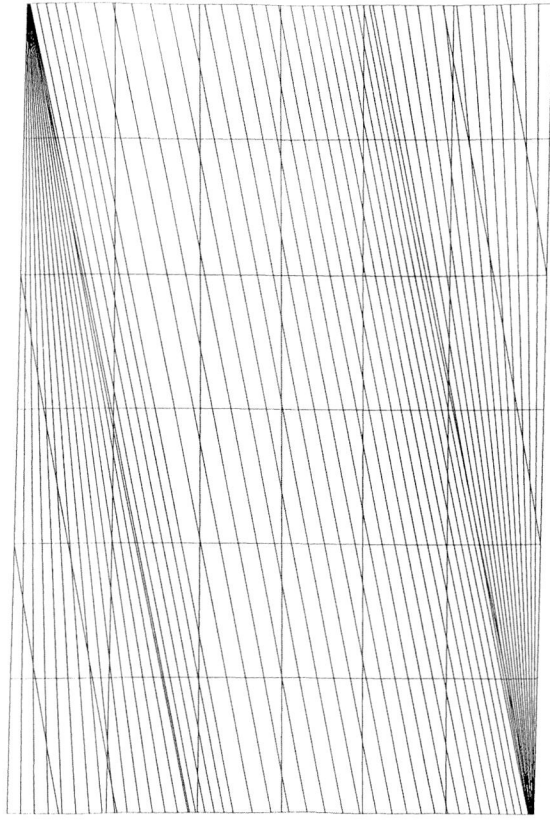

Many of the ship-building industry programmes can approximate a twisted surface with a developable plane. For this purpose the surface is divided into conical fragments and single-curved surfaces. In the drawn developed plane of façade type R3a, the main part of the surface is approximated by a singly curved surface. Adjacent to the upright sides, conical parts are drawn. The software dictates that the surfaces acquire a regular distortion. Yet, the cone fragments are visible by their increased curvature. If the surface is to be made with cold-bent glass, large bending stresses will occur in the glass sheets, at the points where the curvature is very strong, in this case at the tops of the cones.

With a strong degree of twist, the material will offer resistance and the bending stresses will try to spread. Great forces will bear down on the frame, because the material tends to flatten out at the maximum curve. The bending tension is not compensated for by, for instance, a window frame.

Due to the spread of tension within a cold-bent glass sheet, the surface will, at best, approach the desired shape. The greater the radius, the smaller both the deviation from a flat surface and bending forces in the sheet will be. Thus, the visible deviations are also smaller. With large cold-bent sheets, strong bending will probably create flat 'terraces' in the middle of the panels, particularly visible in reflecting glass. With little bending, such deviations will be negligible, compared to distortions caused by the glass tempering process.

GEOMETRICAL ASPECTS

FAÇADE GRIDS

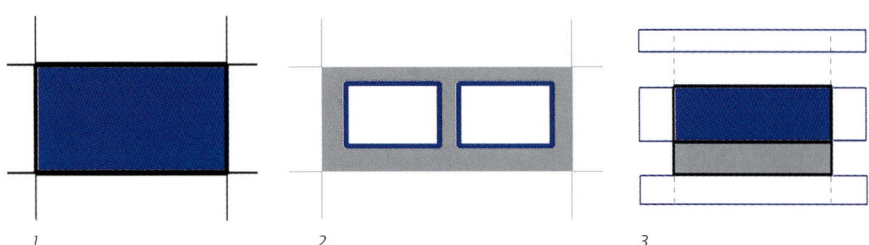

1   2   3

Façades predominantly are built of:
1   Structural glazing or curtain walls.
2   Concrete bay-filling elements, load bearing or not.
3   Alternating bands of parapets and windows.

A self-supporting material, that is not only waterproof, but also meets the demands for energy and light insulation, would be ideal. It would make the zoning of a façade in parapets and windows, as well as a layered façade build-up superfluous. The inside and outside of a building could be the same. But in practice, it does not rain from the ceiling and the sun does not shine from under a table.

This project is based on a conventional façade build-up, with specific, zone-related requirements. This keeps investments for the participants low, provides them with a longer period to become familiar with the new transformations methods and enables a gradual change-over to a new production system.

Taking the overall geometry of building models as a starting point, the zones (whether or not with a specified thickness) were elaborated. With the proposed build-up, the change of façade design, dimensions and technology, only comes down to variation on a theme. Architectural and economic optimization are only possible if the feasibility of the product is proven. By providing building element combinations that are currently common in the industry, a broad application of newly made components will be easier to swallow, than completely new products.

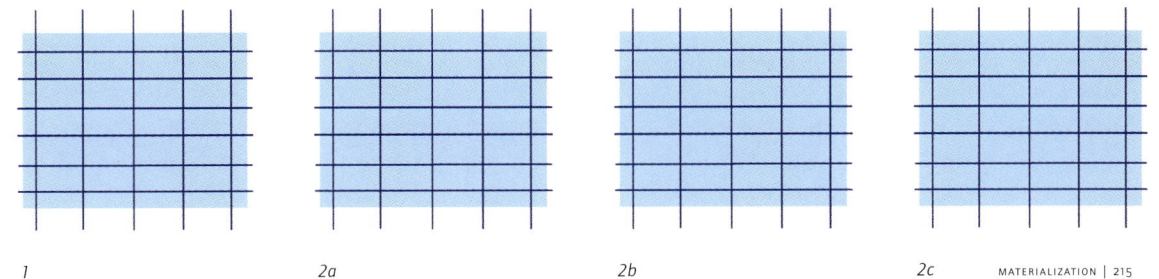

Examples of frontal orthogonal window frame structures

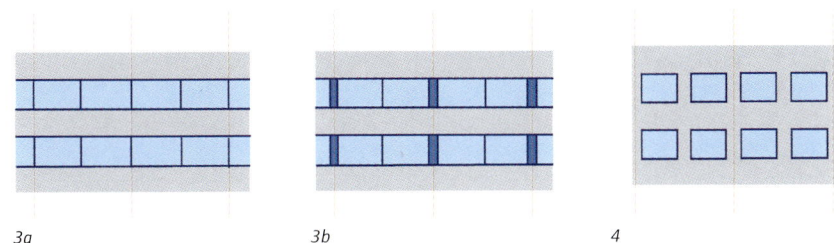

3a   3b   4

1   Screen pattern of single profiles in two directions.
2a   Double mullions in one direction.
2b   Double mullions in two directions.
2c   Double mullions with, in each case, four window panes assembled into
     prefabricated segments.
3a   Strips of windows, running through.
3b   Strips of windows, with intermediate elements.
2   Freely positioned windows.

Usually a curtain wall is built up from coupled mullions, two floors in height per profile, with assembled transoms in between. This construction system is very light (and
cheap), because the profiles do not require extra rigidity for transportation or assembly. The mullions in particular, produce rigidity. The transoms may be thinner.
They only need to bear the wind load and their own weight. Virtually all façades
(90 percent) have window pane widths of 1200 mm.
Because it may be advantageous to build the façade as a prefab system in which prefabricated frameworks are fixed, resulting in double mullions and/or transoms, such
structures are also included in this scheme. However, the assembly of glass into prefabricated window frames implies a greater weight, and therefore a larger construction strength, that increases costs.

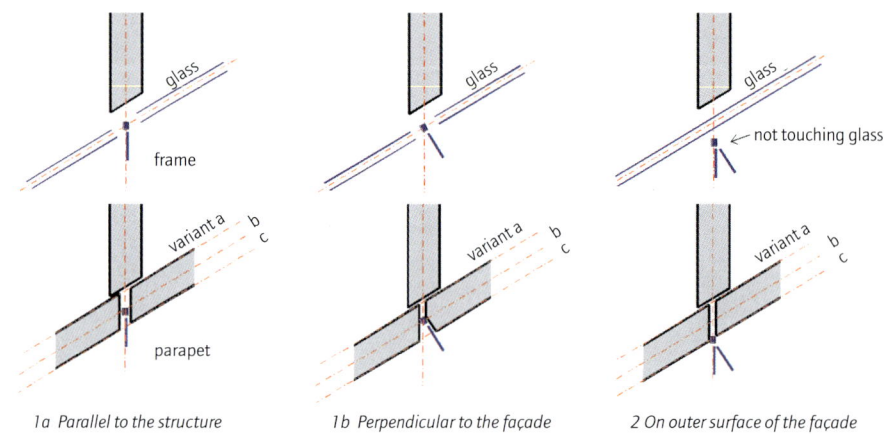

1a Parallel to the structure *1b Perpendicular to the façade* *2 On outer surface of the façade*

CLEANING GUIDE POSITION ON A FAÇADE WITH HORIZONTAL BANDS

A twisted façade's mullions are inclined; often one of the façade's sidelines curves forward and the other backward. The façade cleaning cradle produces forces perpendicular and parallel to the façade. It wants to sway sideways or hang loose from the surface. Some type of guiding rail for the installation is essential. For it to run straight, the axis of the rail must coincide with the intersection of the reference and the structure surface. The axis can be:

1a In between the window frame mullions and in the vertical joints of the concrete panels, for instance the centre between the inner and outer surfaces. In this case, the guides may all be in parallel surfaces, e.g. coinciding with that of the superstructure.

1b Same as 1a, but with the cradle connected perpendicular to the façade. The guiding rail is now twisted. If it is in the middle of the parapet, the joint has to be very wide (or V-shaped).

2 On the outside of the façade. In this case the hanging direction of the cradle can be chosen freely.

With a horizontal guide, for instance branched off from a vertical centre course, the cradle would have to be hanging from the façade, or some installation on the roof. This is more complicated and vulnerable than one that hangs only vertically.

In a 'Tordo', with an 'architecturally twisted' surface, the façade in front view is orthogonally divided. Due to the mullions leaning forward or backward to a varying degree, and the transoms having different horizontal angles, they both will vary in length per façade segment. The cradle attachments must be able to deal with these variations.

TARGET MODEL FOR THE FAÇADE

Tordo 1 was used as a test model, to ascertain the geometrical requirements that transformed building elements had to meet. Its façades are built up on an orthogonal grid, 3,000 x 6,600 millimetres, as is often used in housings and office buildings.

In the front façade the horizontal lines are curved; in the rear façade they are straight. The façade twists 1° per floor per height of 3 m.

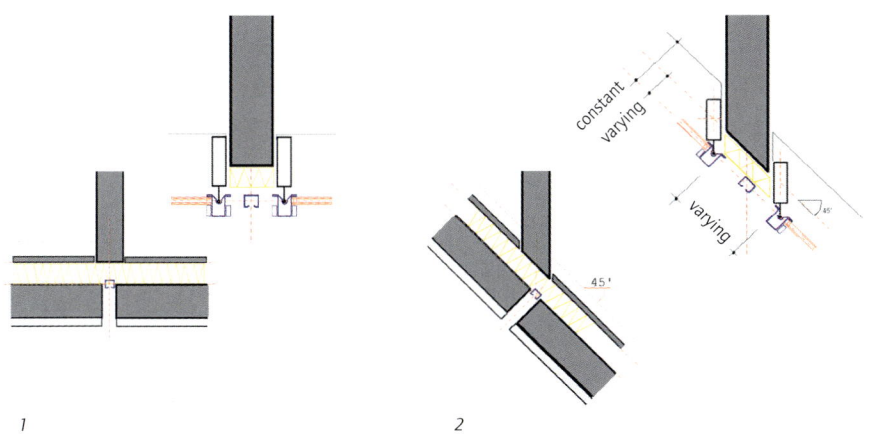

1   2

Geometrical preconditions

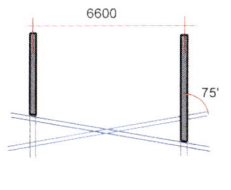

6600

75'

Hypar-shaped façade: straight transoms

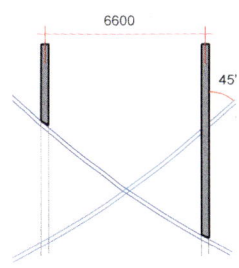

6600

45'

Conoidal façade: curved transoms

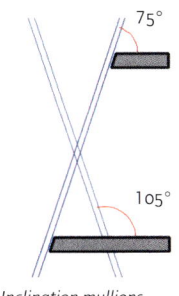

75°

105°

Inclination mullions

Horizontal cross-sections
of the connections
between elements

1 *Parapet to be elaborated:*
   rims perpendicular to façade

2 *Window frame parallel to*
   structural surface yet to be
   elaborated: the connecting
   direction to the guiding sys-
   tem of the window-cleaning
   cradle is perpendicular to the
   outer surface of the façade

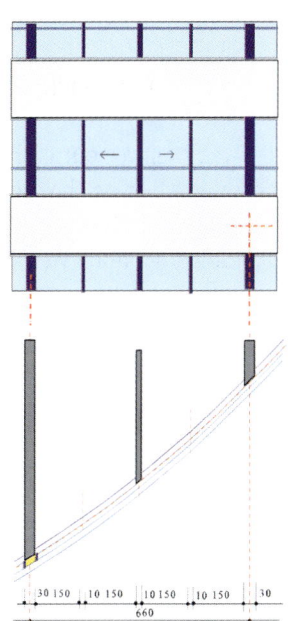

Window frame

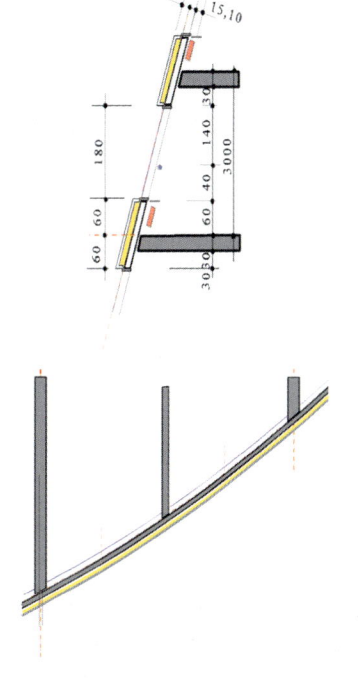

Parapet

CONCRETE

With model Tordo 1 as a reference, the geometry of a conoidal façade with parapets was examined. The façade and its main elements were measured, and developed planes were made to gain insight into the stretch and butt of the elements with the greatest mutual differences.

CASE-STUDY: THE PARAPET ELEMENTS OF TORDO 1

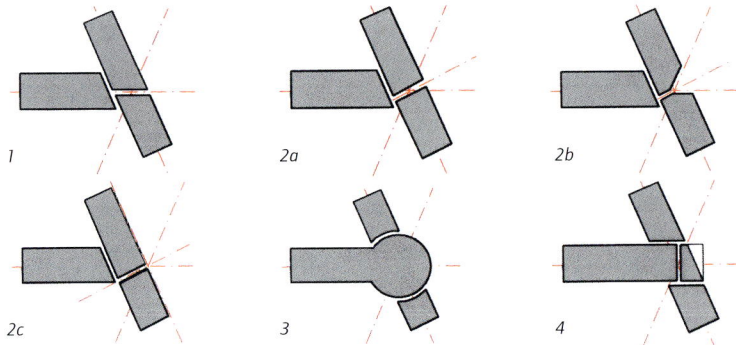

CONNECTION VARIANTS BETWEEN CONCRETE ELEMENTS

Examples of connections between concrete elements:

1 Rims between parallel elements, for instance parallel to the orthogonal grid of the superstructure: horizontal or vertical. The reference surface and structural surfaces intersect, e.g. in between the façade elements. All rims are at a constant distance from each other, and at varying angles to the façade surface.

2a Rims between elements at all points perpendicular to the reference surface in the centre of the façade.

2b Partly tapering joints that enable the cleaning installation to be connected perpendicular to the outer side of the façade. Reference surface and main axis intersect in between the façade elements. The tapering can be executed as a constant V-shape.

2c Joints perpendicular to the façade, with the intersecting line of structural surface and reference surface on the outside of the façade.

3 Cylindrical contact surfaces between façade panels and superstructure.

4 Medium between elements made in situ at all points of the façade.

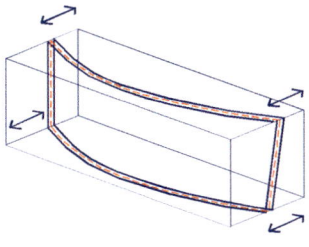
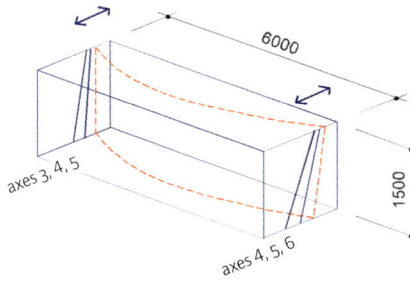

1

2

THE GEOMETRY OF THE ADJUSTABLE MOLD

- Corner positions individually adjustable; mold surfaces are offsets of the reference surface in the centre of the element.
- Inclination and length of edges are equal for the elements that connect to the same axis of the building; the sideline is adjusted separately per element.

The sidelines are shifted in parallel surfaces, within an orthogonal mold. Due to mirroring of elements, repetition occurs. The segments of the left half of the building (between axes 0 and 3) are repeated upside down in the right half (between axes 3 and 6).

Adjusting the mold to produce stacked elements

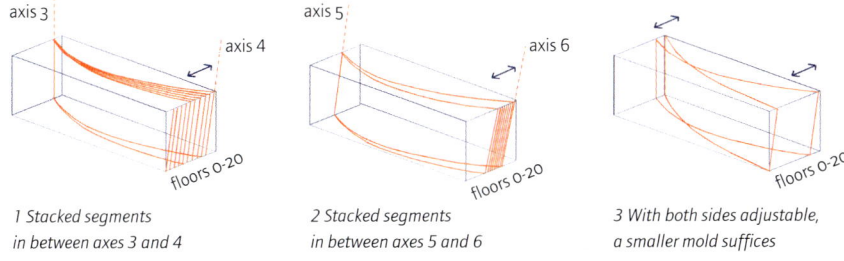

1 Stacked segments in between axes 3 and 4

2 Stacked segments in between axes 5 and 6

3 With both sides adjustable, a smaller mold suffices

1,2 Both sides of shuttering inclined, one of which is fixed. Per stacked series of façade elements (placed above and below each other), one side per element is adjusted every time.

The size of shuttering surfaces

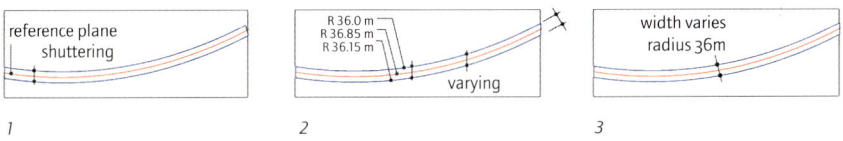

1

2

3

1 Rims perpendicular to reference surface. The panel has the same thickness everywhere, but in parallel surfaces the thickness varies.

2 The shutterings are offsets of the reference surface and have different curvatures.

3 When both shutterings have the same curvature as the reference surface, the thickness of the concrete panels will vary.

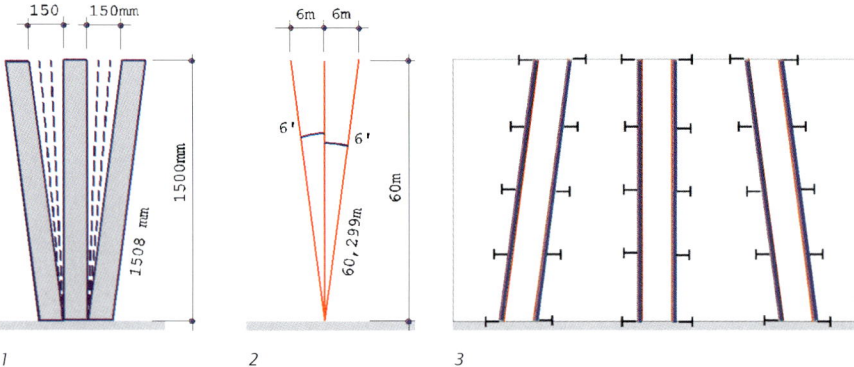

1   2   3

1 Maximum angle of building inclination

2 Maximum angle of mold inclination

3 Maximum shuttering transformations

The shutterings cannot have the same curvature if the thickness of the concrete panel must be constant. Therefore, a choice must be made between:

1   The side rims perpendicular to the façade surface, so they have the same width at all points, but are twisted.

2   A constant thickness of the panel, with parallel vertical side rims, and varying sizes of the connection in the joint. This means that head partitions between the shuttering plates will vary in size. The two plates, as offsets of the reference surface in the centre, have different curvatures. With a panel thickness of 300 millimetres, they have a radius of 35.85 and 36.15 metres, respectively.

3   Standard sizes for the head partitions at the vertical sides and shutterings, both with the same radius of 36 metres. The thickness of the panels will vary, which introduces new size variations when producing a layered build-up. These are too small to be visible.

Option 2 was chosen. First of all because it was expected that a detailing system for parallel connections of window frames and parapets to an orthogonal superstructure might offer new possibilities. The vertical rims are different for all elements, which complicates production, but a cheap solution may be found. The sidelines are straight and in parallel surfaces. The stacked sidelines all have an equal length.

Some data:

- The tower has seven upright axes; axes 0, 1 and 2 are equal to axes 6, 5 and 4, respectively.
- The four sides of each bay-wide segment all have different lengths.
- The vertical sidelines of the elements at axes 0+6, 1+5, 2+4 and 3 are 1,507.5, 1,503, 1,501 and 1,500 mm, respectively.
- The horizontal sidelines all have a radius of 36 metres in the reference surface. Their lengths differ per façade segment and vary between 6,022 and 7,262 mm.
- The elements are only repeated in the diagonally opposite quadrants of the façade.

Projection of the concrete panels on axes 0-6, is -300, -200, -100, 0, 100, 200 and 300 mm.

The curves of the horizontal lines of both the form work sides are standardized to the radii of 35.85 and 36.15 metres. All steel profiles of the construction behind the shuttering can also be made with standard curvatures. The surface must be stretched or butted to allow twisting.

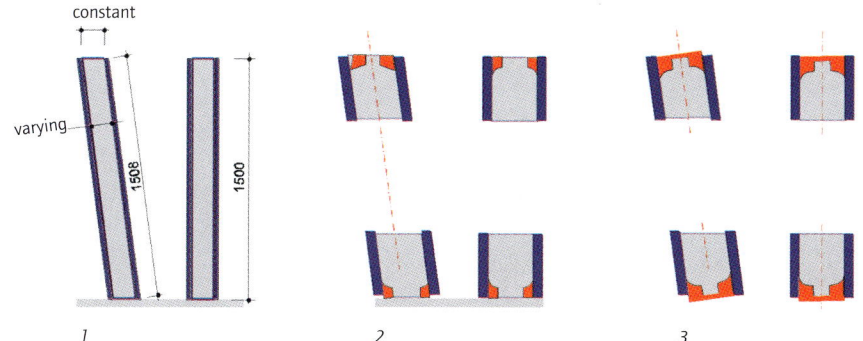

constant

varying

1508

1500

1

2

3

The extension of the plate in the reference surface is a maximum of 2.85 mm in length direction when the plate is 1,500 mm high and 6,000 mm long and when the rotation is 0.5° per panel height.

A wooden or steel form board can hardly be stretched.

With regard to the surface distortion, variants for the shuttering are:

1   Individually adjustable surfaces, in a grid of, e.g. 100 x 100 mm.
2   Strips of, for instance, 100 mm. wide.
3   Plate material that can be stretched within its surface.

Version 1 can be dropped for this building, due to the high cost of the mold and its one-off nature. If more buildings had to be produced, this variant could be considered.

Version 2 offers a fair possibility. The light facetting that occurs in the surface will not stand out with a rough outer surface. The seams can also be emphasized.

Version 3 is now preferred, with a synthetic plate for shuttering that will be kept in shape by a steel structure with curved girders.

Connection of window frame to parapet

1   The thickness of the panel will vary when a constant horizontal distance between the panels is maintained. A shuttering may be chosen that is always constructed to the required panel height of 1,500 mm. Also a board of constant size may be chosen that at its maximum inclination, will result in elements that are slightly too low (1,500 mm, instead of 1,508 mm).
2   The inserted profile can narrow the upper edge to a minimum width, in order to reduce the torsion problems of a surface strip to that of a line connection.
    By narrowing the parapet where it connects to the window frame, width variations can be absorbed in the joints. For the tower, the upright rims will connect to a panel with an equal thickness. The rims that are in sight at the upper and lower side of the panel will have a smooth finish, because of the filling. The upper side has to be inclined in order to allow the water to drain outwards, preferably as steeply as possible to prevent local pollution.
3   A rounded profile provides for drainage at the upper edge.

1   Element thickness varies between 298.5 and 300 mm

2   Varying profiles to make a raised horizontal edge in the centre

3   Profiles fitted to the shutterings to make rounded edges

WINDOW FRAME

After defining geometrical preconditions and designing feasible solutions, a window frame system was developed in cooperation with Reynolds Architectuursystemen, Harderwijk, NL: the Reyno-Twist system. It fits in well with their new system for the European market. By using existing profile components, already tested for water-proofing, assembly, etc., the development costs of this completely new system could be kept relatively low. The system's requirements were distilled from many factors. Model research played a great part in this. Twisted building applications were drawn on various scales and with various degrees of rotation. Serial sizes, expected market demand and technical aspects of production were taken into account. The connections to adjacent building elements of different materials (concrete parapets) were presented in diagrams and the geometry of possible façade openings described (see supplement 4).

Window frames with moving parts, however, still have to be designed. First, the reaction of the market to the prototype of the Twist (window frame) system will be probed. The drawings are sketchy and offer insight into the subject, without pretending to be complete. Problems and possibilities are categorized, to optimize the development trajectory of a twisted façade element. Their elaboration was not the aim of this study and therefore kept for later. The prototype serves as a basis for optimizing components. The hypothesis that the Twist system would also be applicable to types of twisted façades other than the hypar-shaped one of Tordo 1 – for which it was initially designed – proved to be true. It was even applicable for volumes with freely double-curved façades (blobs).

A strategy was established for the development of increasingly complex material distortions. This is attuned to parallel developments in the transformation of glass. Possible applications of the Twist system are connected to developments of alternative panel materials (steel, synthetics, aluminium), but the glass ones are most important. Glass, obviously, will appear in almost every double-curved building. The Twist system is more expensive than conventional window framing, because it is more labour-intensive. These surplus costs were foreseen and considered to be of secondary importance. First and foremost, it had to be demonstrated that it was, in fact, feasible for industrial manufacturing. In line with this, the refinement of material usage with regard to environmental aspects, for example energy management, are considered to be follow-up studies.

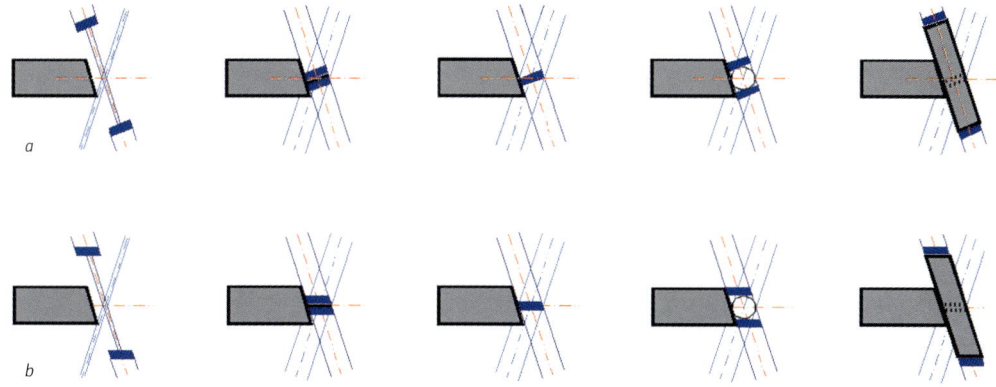

POSITIONING

Within various conventional façade compositions, window frame profiles were drawn, to gain insight into the consequences of twisting a façade. Two basic positions of the profiles were distinguished:

a   Perpendicular to the glass sheets. Here, connecting angle and distance between window frame and superstructure (walls/floor) vary. In frontal view, the profiles have different widths.

b   Parallel to the superstructure and to each other. In frontal view, the profiles are straight and have the same width.

a Profiles perpendicular to façade

b Profiles parallel to floor/wall

1a   1b   2   3   4

Profiles perpendicular to façade

Perpendicular junctions between façade and floor/wall, as drawn in the lower series, depict an intermediate stage of longitudinal twisting of a profile, when the mullion is vertical. Many connections between façade and superstructure are possible:

1   Twisting profiles. The floor/wall has been cut off under a varying angle parallel to the façade. Along the profiles, the connecting angle to the building varies. (1a)
    If the profiles were placed parallel to each other and the width of the façade were to be constant, the cross-sections of the profiles would have to vary in size transversely. This is not feasible in aluminium. (1b).

2   Equal connections at all points. The cylindrical contact surface may be part of the floor/wall, or a separate steel tube. A tube by definition does not need to be twisted.

3   A large twisted medium with a cylindrical edge that may connect to a thin structure.

4   A small twisted medium, that may connect to a thick structure. The smaller the medium, the easier it can be twisted.

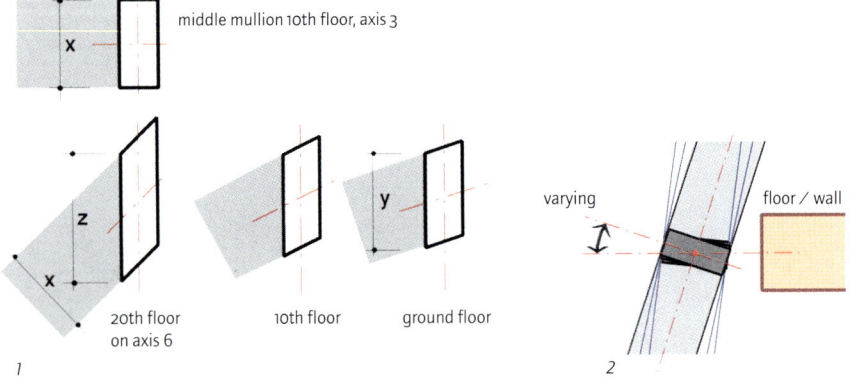

middle mullion 10th floor, axis 3

z

x

20th floor
on axis 6

10th floor

y

ground floor

varying

floor / wall

1

2

1 *Horizontal cross-sections*

PRODUCTION AND CONNECTION PROBLEMS

1 **If one side of the profiles connects to a building at a constant angle, and the other is parallel to the façade at all points, then the profiles will transversely vary in cross-section and their connection surfaces will vary in shape.**

The drawings show transoms and their connecting angles to the mullion on the extreme right of the façade of Tordo 1. The varying horizontal cross-sections of the mullion are drawn; similar transformations occur in cross-sections of transoms.

The mullion leans 15° backwards. At this point the largest connecting angle of the transoms occurs: 45°. The greater the angle between transom and mullion, the wider the mullion must be, to prevent the transom extending beyond it. (Size z is larger than the minimum size x). Along with the two twisted outer surfaces, rebates and other profiling will have to transform. This severely complicates dimensioning and production.

2 **When a profile is twisted, the connecting angle and the position of profile edges vary with regard to wall and/or floor edges.**

Here the reference and structural surfaces were in the centre of the façade and the construction, respectively, but the problem with different positions is identical. The variations imply an excessive amount of drawing work and a great number of different components.

3 **Drawing, dimensioning and producing a twisted profile with a complex cross-section is labour-intensive**

In a conventional façade, a glass sheet connects to the profiles at a constant angle. Its connection surface is parallel to the panel, to allow optimal fixing and waterproofing. For a twisted façade, mullions and transoms must be twisted. This is difficult if profiles are rigid, e.g. to absorb wind load, and particularly problematic if profile cross-sections are complex, e.g. with internal insulating fixtures.

In conoid surfaces transoms and mullions must be twisted as well as curved, to connect to curved floor edges, parapets, or walls. This is difficult and labour-intensive.

Here the inside and outside surfaces of the window frame are drawn as offsets of the twisted reference surface in the centre of the façade. These are approximations of twisted surfaces, and not composed of straight lines (see Chapter 4). This implies that

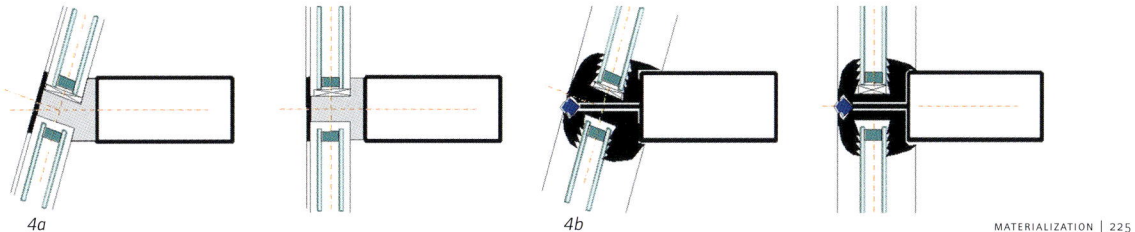

straight lines can be used for dimensioning the building construction, but that they will acquire small deviations everywhere. The same is true for the sizes of glass panels. If the centre of the window does not coincide with the reference surface, the window pane is not a twisted surface, but an approximation. This too implies complexity.

4a *Aluminium fillers*
    with standardized angles

4b *Synthetic profiles*
    with standardized angles

4 Approximation of a twisting connection to glass by facetting, leads to poor sealing.

A twisted glazing profile can be approximated by facetting with non-twisted segments, that are connected to a stiff profile for support and anchoring. These glazing profile segments may have various cross-sections, each of them covering a specific range of angles of incidence of the window panes, e.g. 0°-9°, 9°-18°, 18°-27°, 27°-36° and 36°-45°. Additional synthetic support blocks may absorb a smaller torsion in the rebates. This principle may be applied in aluminium or synthetic profiles.

In addition to complex logistics, time-consuming production and assembly, all consequences of the large number of different components, problems occur because in the corners of the window frames, fillers of various shapes and orientation do not connect well. Drawing 1 shows a mullion and a transom to be connected. The fillers do not fit accurately at a corner, nor do the rectangular profiles at varying distances from the glass panel. By facetting a multitude of undesirable connection variants is introduced. Therefore, the facet approach has been abandoned.

Problem definition
How can the connection between glass panels and window frames of a twisted façade be combined with a building structure (e.g. floors and/or columns) that meets the façade at varying angles?

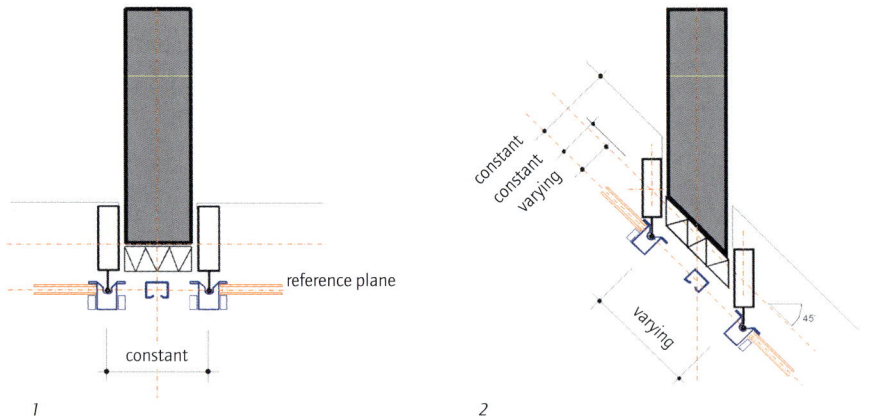

reference plane

constant

1

constant
constant
varying

varying

45

2

THE TWIST SYSTEM

This new window frame system offers a solution for all the aforementioned problems. The frame profile was divided into a torsion-soft glazing profile and a rigid supporting profile.

With the cylindrical contact surface between the parts, the window frame system combines a parallel connection to the twisted or possibly double-curved glass panel with an adjustable support. This implies a standard connection to the building's superstructure, generally speaking: horizontal surfaces for floors and parapets and parallel vertical surfaces for walls, floor beams and columns. The surfaces on the in- and outside of the façade are made from the reference surface by offset. Part dimensions follow from the intersecting lines of the reference surface with structural surfaces (the superstructure's grid surfaces). Supporting and glazing profiles only need to be shortened in one angled direction. This attunes well to current production methods.

New types of surfaces and new façade subdivisions

Basically the Twist system is suitable for any kind of façade shape and enables any type of subdivision. However, applications are restricted due to the lack of availability of freely double-curved glass.

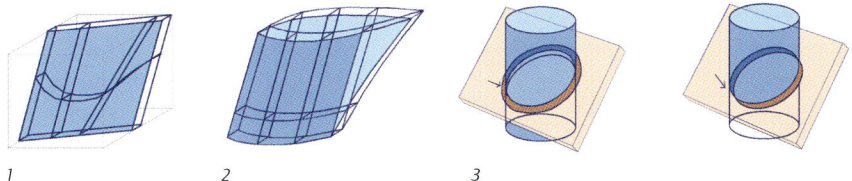

1   *2*   *3*

A small selection of applications of the Twist system with available glass, that are difficult or even impossible with other window frame systems:

1   A planar façade may lean over, while support profiles are not perpendicular to the façade.
2   A singly curved vertical or inclining façade can be connected to another surface, for example, a cylindrical one. The choice of façade contours is free. Bending the support profile in a free 3D curve, however, will be expensive. A 2D curve is much easier to achieve.

3   The support profile can be bent with its longer side parallel or perpendicular to a flat surface. Twisting the profile in the drawn example is necessary, due to the varying inclination angle of the glass.

The Twist system allows constructing high-rise buildings with inclined curved facades that connect to the superstructure by window frames. To date, glass façades with varying angles of inclination have only appeared in atriums and entrance halls, where the connection to the building was narrowed down to a line. This could simply be sealed and did not have to comply with the strict sound and fire prevention requirements for high-rise buildings.

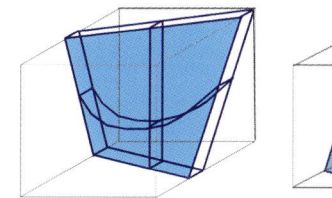 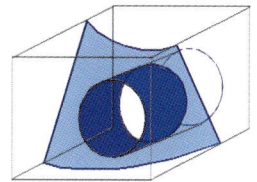 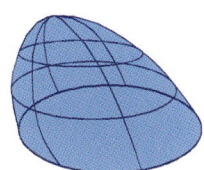 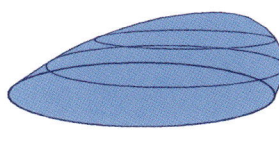

Twisted surfaces   *Freely double-curved surfaces or volumes ('blobs')*

Just like in the ship-building industry, where beams almost always are in flat surfaces, a freely double-curved glass roof is easier to make when the supporting structure only needs to be curved in one direction. This has been done before, with comparable profiles, both manually and by computer.

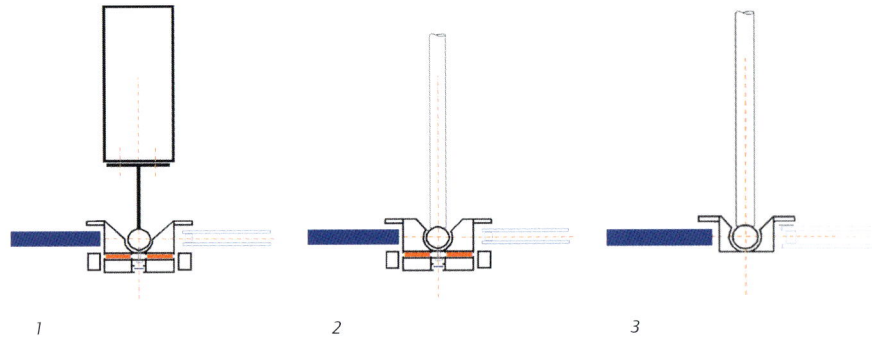

1   2   3

PRELIMINARY DESIGN

Alternatives for supporting construction

Glazing profiles may also be applied without supporting profiles, fastened locally to a supporting construction:

1   Braces connected to a tube, e.g. with a rectangular cross-section.
2   Rod protruding from supporting construction that allows adjustment.
3   Glazing profile, flush with façade outside.

Structural glazing with fixed points

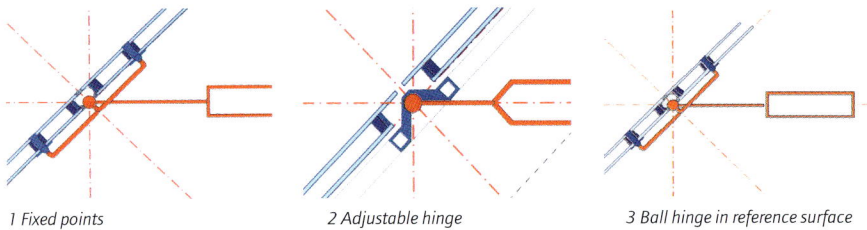

1 Fixed points   2 Adjustable hinge   3 Ball hinge in reference surface

1   The glass panels are secured mechanically in the corners. Each panel has holes at different positions, or, alternatively, the hinge is asymmetrical. The connection will vary both vertically and horizontally for every hinge.
2   The part connecting to panels may be adjustable (in two directions), so that holes in the panels are always in the same position.
3   By placing the pin joint of a ball hinge in the reference surface, the holes can be positioned identically in panel corners, and all hinges are the same. The window pane connection must be adjustable, for instance through a mechanical fixture.

Symmetrical and asymmetrical profile

A symmetrical profile is easier to dimension systematically than an asymmetrical one. With an asymmetrical profile, the two sides of a supporting profile are different. If the profile axis is always at an equal distance from the structural axis, or at an equal distance from the wall, the connections can be standardized quite easily. The distance from the window frame to the wall can be adjusted to standardize connections. But this is not attractive, because of variations.

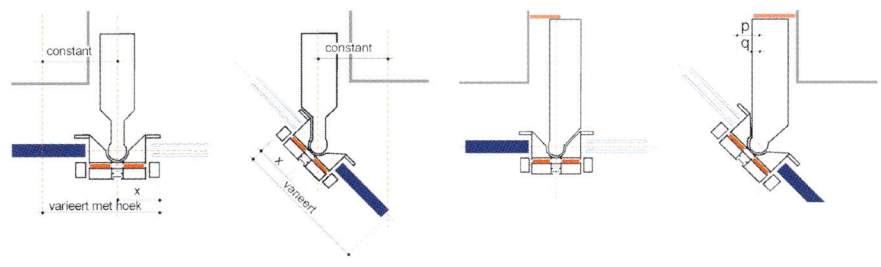

Symmetrical profile   *Asymmetrical profile*

The profile can be shifted not only in transoms, but also in mullions, using different combinations for each bay of the façade. Recessed areas, or inaccessible corners must be avoided to allow cleaning.

Hollow connections, small and large

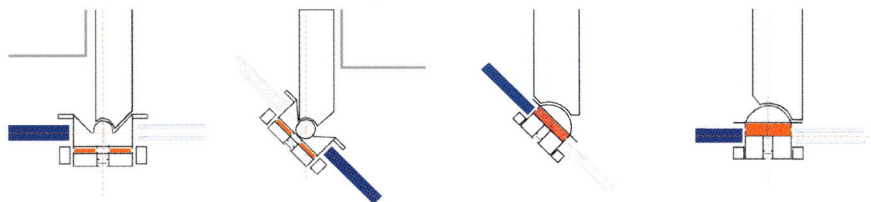

A support profile with a concave connection to the glazing profile has an adjacent torsion axis.

Round glazing profile with symmetrical support profile

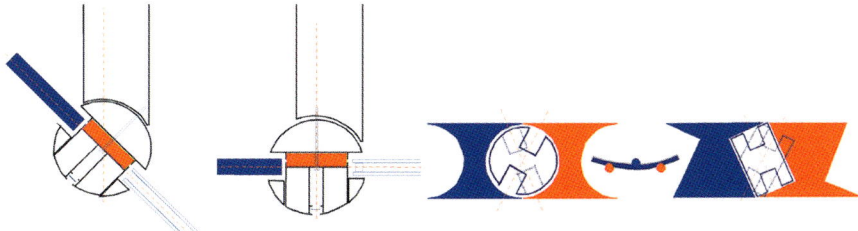

Round glazing profile   *Bending jig for a round, and a rectangular profile*

Glazing profiles connect lengthwise at a varying angle to the support profile, which is either straight or singly curved. A round glazing profile is easier to bend accurately than a square one that stands at varying angles on its side. A twisted oblique square meets a bending jig with a varying application side. The transformation back to its original shape will vary due to the rectangular profile's changing slope. This not only complicates manual, but also computerized bending. A profile that can easily be transformed by hand is preferable.

Window frame with round glazing profiles

The supporting transom profiles are in horizontal surfaces; the mullions are in parallel vertical ones. The round glazing profiles twist along with the glass sheets. The twisting becomes visible where the (red) rebate varies in width.

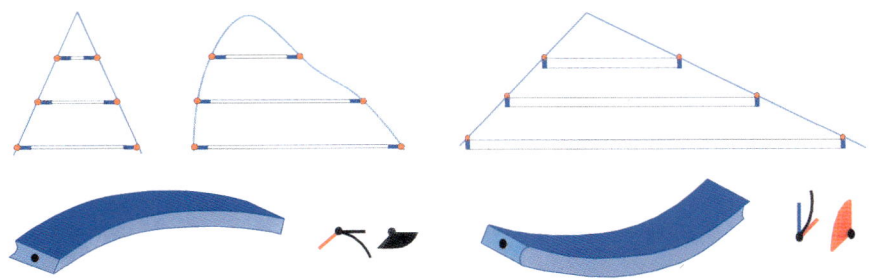

The supporting profiles are either straight or singly curved. In the latter case, they are curved along either the long or the short side. Their curvature depends on the façade's inclination.

At the junction of supporting profiles, it is necessary to locally spindle the surface because of the angled connection. Otherwise, round glazing profiles would not fit against them. To avoid creating an opening, they have a larger thickness at the side that connects to the glazing profile. This also avoids the necessity to machine the connecting element between mullions and transoms inside the profiles. The varying profile thickness makes it even more difficult to bend. For the extrusion process to follow a regular course, the aluminium should be symmetrical. The massive parts of a window frame increase costs, due to extra material usage.

Connections

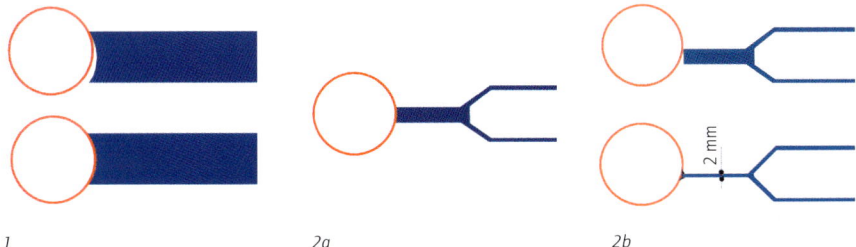

1   2a   2b

1   A flat contact surface allows a shift sideways; this cannot be achieved with a protruding part that fits into a groove. The connection between two round profiles is, therefore, sensitive to size deviations.

2   If the contact surface is relatively narrow, size variations need not show.

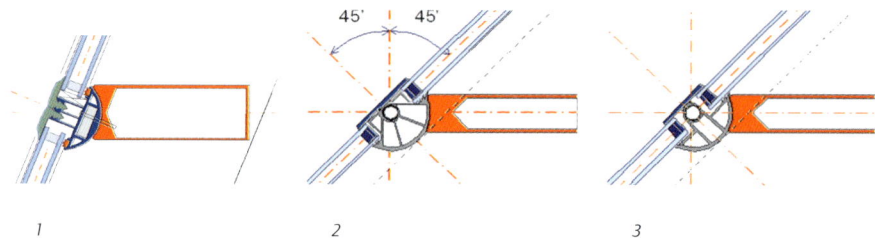

1   2   3

Synthetic glazing profiles

1   The glass panels are fastened with rubber profiles. Connecting pieces that fit in rectangular hollow spaces of the glazing profile, ensure a secure joint.

2   Profile with supporting bracket for the glass sheet and a wide cover strip. It can be fastened with a screw. The supporting bracket may be removed locally to allow drainage.

3   Symmetrical profile with narrow cover strip.

An aluminium tube in the centre serves as a reinforcement. The tube does not have to pass through the corners, but can be interrupted. The rubber profile can be transformed by hand.

The length of the void walls determines heat insulation by the rubber profile. The synthetic coating on the viewing side can be extruded in any colour.

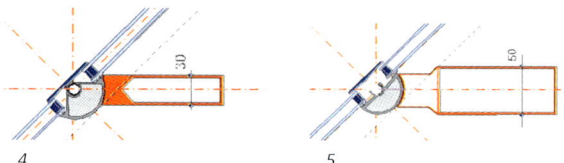

4   5

4   Rubber profile with glass sheets centred on the reference surface

5   Ditto against the reference surface

Due to the spongy, constant structure of the profile's inner side, the screws can always be fastened in the required direction. Because of compression differences between the inside and outside, the screws must be tightened properly to ensure a waterproof seal. Sections of a half-tube can be used to fasten the glazing profile.

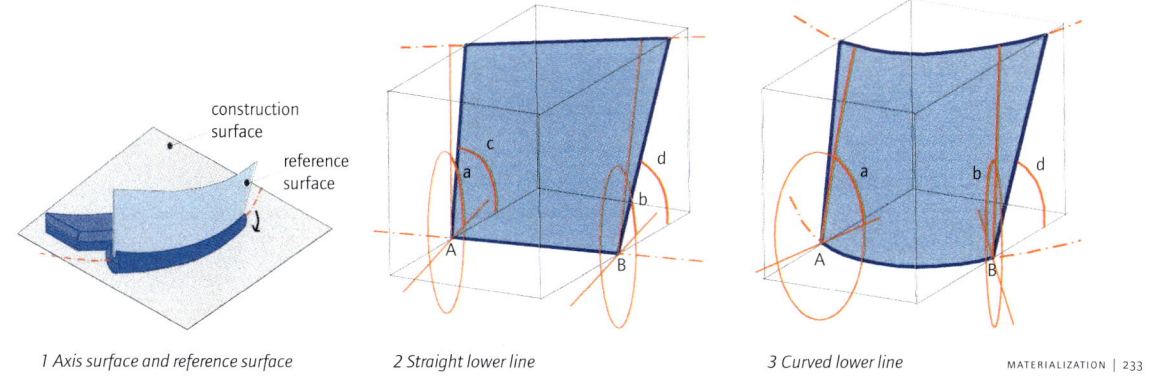

Drainage

Mullions and transoms, respectively, can be in vertical and horizontal, but also in sloping surfaces. Water that runs into the groove, despite the rubber sealing at the top,
must be drained. Façades with a varying inclination allow water inside a twisted profile to flow down in a natural way. An outward self-draining profile with a strong dis-
charge would be ideal. However, within one transom the groove may lean both inward
and outward, through torsion. This can result in varying directions of drainage. A general solution would be a rubber slab that connects the sealing profile at the inside of
the upper glass sheet, to the outer sealing profile of the lower glass sheet.

Elaboration of the twist system geometry

The surface containing the axis runs through the centres of the support and the glazing profile. The former is usually straight or singly curved, whereas the latter does not
just follow the shape of the supporting profile, but also connects to the glass sheet's
varying directions, and for that purpose contains an additional twist. The flat axis surface, coincides with the building structure's surface. Generally speaking, the angle
between the reference surface and the axle surface varies.

Viewed from the outside, and from A to B, clockwise torsion is positive. In the drawing, the fat blue lines are the straight base lines at the sides. The vertical red lines, in
surfaces perpendicular to the profile axis, are curved. The angles of incidence a and b
are the angles under which the straight lines in points A and B enter the horizontal
line, measured relative to the axis surface, at the inside of the building. They were
measured in surfaces perpendicular to the lower line. The angles c and d were measured in the cube's side surfaces. A surface has a starting-angle of incidence a and an
end-angle of incidence b. The varying torsion may generally be replaced by an average torsion, due to the absorption capacity of the rubber profiles in the grooves, for
small deviations.

The torsion angle (a-b) is the difference between two angles of incidence on a line.

The base line torsion angle (c-d) is the angle difference between two base lines that
may be are in parallel surfaces. It need not be equal to the torsion angle of the profile
or of the surface.

The average torsion angle ($v = t/p$ degrees per metre length of the lower line).

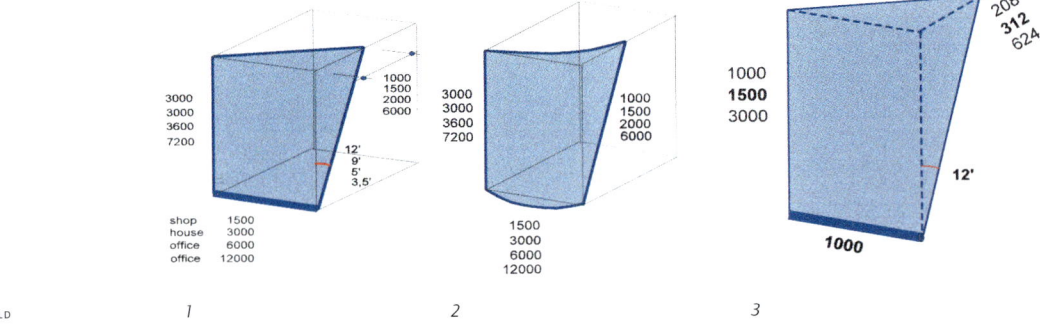

shop	1500
house	3000
office	6000
office	12000

3000
3000
3600
7200

1000
1500
2000
6000

12'
9'
5'
3,5'

1500
3000
6000
12000

3000
3000
3600
7200

1000
1500
2000
6000

1000
1500
3000

208
312
624

12'

1000

1   2   3

1 Ruled surface, hypar

2 Ruled surface, conoid

3 The sizes of the window frame
   prototype are in bold type

Maximum torsion angle of a profile in various applications

Read from top to bottom the dimensions in the drawings indicate rather extreme torsion angles of window panes in a corner of a shop front, a home, an office, and an entrance hall with double height.

It is hard to predict what torsion angles or surface sizes the market will demand. Although, almost by definition, designers search for limits, the majority will remain within standard applications. Torsion per element in large façades usually is modest. The general rule is: the larger the total dimensions are, the smaller the torsion per metre needs to be to make a spectacular impression.

In Tordo 1, the torsion per element is very small: in the northern façade the straight transoms twist about 6° over the 18 metre (shortest) transom: 0.33° per metre. In all other, longer transoms it is even less.

Prototype window frame 1 is 2 x 2 metres with a large degree of torsion; over a length of 1 metre, the centre transom twists 18° approximately.

Research models for the Twist window frames

Physical characteristics can be described in formulae, but it is difficult to specify preconditions. There are many more options than the simplicity of formulae suggests. One can derive an endless range of variants from preconditions. Many possibilities are overlooked, since preconditions seem to be obvious. Examples: shearing resistance can be eliminated by facetting a profile (many straight segments with a slight positional rotation between them), or by assembling it from rods (or line-shaped elements). In addition, a profile can be composed of different materials, exploiting their individual qualities. Some models are described, each with its own variants:

A Models obeying the laws of physics, where variants are developed on the basis of formulae.

B Ideal models, meeting the physical definition of torsion, e.g. twisted profiles that have an equal cross-section over the entire length.

C The monolithic model, consisting of one piece of material

D Composite models: the glazing profile is composed of various elements.
   For example: metal parts can be mutually connected by a plastic medium.
   Profiles can also be split into linear elements, that can slide along each other.
   Once the parts are in correct position, they can be mutually fixed using a sealant.

E   Practical models: the behaviour in practical tests is described and torsion qualities
    of profiles and materials are examined in test models.

The physical model

Torsion stress $\tau_t = \dfrac{M_t}{T_t}$

Torsion moment $M_t = \dfrac{P}{\omega} = \dfrac{P}{2\,\pi.\eta} = F.d$

Torsion angle
(of a tube) $\varphi = \dfrac{M_t . l}{I_p . G} = \dfrac{180°}{\pi} \times \dfrac{M_t . l}{I_p . G}(z.e^5)$

T = moment of resistance
P = power
d = distance between edge fibres and point of gravity
F = force
l = tube length
I_p = polar moment of inertia
G = Young's module (a constant factor)

In torsion statics, physical qualities of a profile are placed in mutual relationship
under the condition of elastic deformation. From the formulae can, however, be
deducted how the torsion angle can be enlarged plastically. It can be done by:
1   Enlarging the moment. With a constant radius this implies the increase of force.
    The stronger the force, the larger the twist. If the radius decreases, with a constant
    force, the moment increases. In other words: more slender means easier to twist.
2   Extending the length. Less rotation has to be absorbed per unit of length.
3   Decreasing the second torsion moment of area of cross section It. To design a
    weak torsion profile, the material must be as close to the torsion axis as possible
    and the material be split up lengthwise into various strips, each of which have a
    low It.
4   Reducing the resisting moment by using a material with low Young's module.
By applying a combination of materials, they will complement each other's qualities.

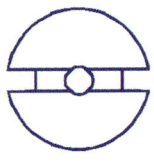

1 Extruded with a twist

2 Spindled

The ideal model
Twisting a profile changes the thickness of the material locally, so theoretically, the twisting option is unfeasible. Remaining possibilities are:

1 Extruded with a twist.
2 Spindled from a massive bar.

The monolithic model

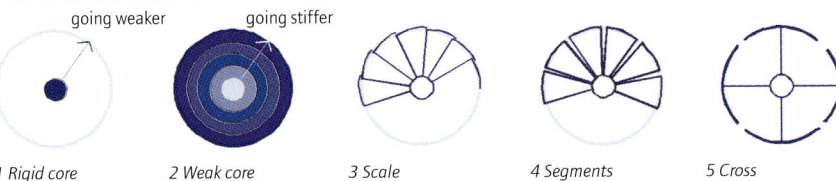

going weaker   going stiffer

1 Rigid core *2 Weak core* *3 Scale* *4 Segments* *5 Cross*

Monolithic models have many options. With a compression-resistant core, the outer side shortens different from the inner side. The straight lines at the outside are changed into helixes, forcing the material to be divided over a longer distance. The material resists. The outside of a twisted bar is under strain of tension and becomes shorter. Tension at the edge is compensated by compression in the core.

The composite model

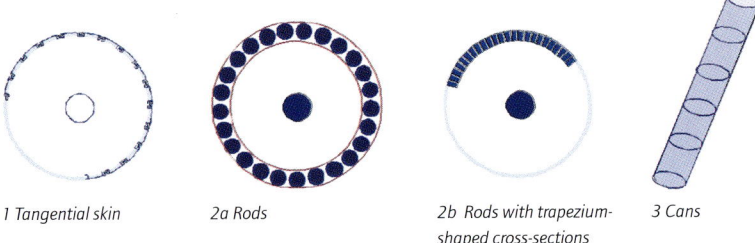

1 Tangential skin   *2a Rods*   *2b Rods with trapezium-shaped cross-sections*   *3 Cans*

In composite models, the glazing profile is composed of various elements, the outer ring being divided into sections to diminish the torsion resistance. The profile can consist of a number of elements, all of the same material, mutually connected by, e.g. temporary sliding connections.

The following distinctions are made:
1 Composite models in which various materials are combined to absorb local forces and distortions, e.g. elastic media between rigid rods.
2 Rod models. The outside becomes shorter and constricts when twisting. If the rods are kept together by a different material, then this is a composite model. The diameter of the rods can be round or trapezium-shaped.
3 Can models, composed of segments. One can compare this to a pile of beer cans, the label being turned a little further on each can. They slide along each other in the contact planes without friction, thus forming a facetted torsion. If the connections are flexible, and the number of short sections is infinite, a twisted profile occurs.

THE REYNO-TWIST WINDOW FRAME SYSTEM

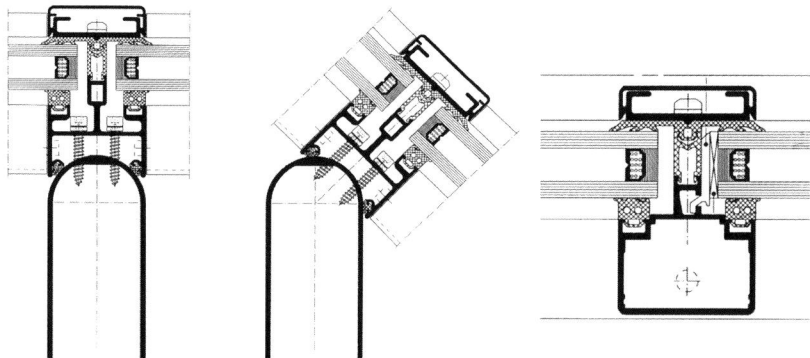

In cooperation with Reynolds Architectuursystemen, Harderwijk, NL, an aluminium frame system was developed. It employs standardized components, that are part of their new frame system for the European market. Prototypes built with this system, can be found in chapter 7.

GLASS

Since the widespread introduction of computers, the application of double-curved surfaces has increased. This project aims to contribute to the development of a computerized mold for twisted window panes. A series of glass transformations have been described, and some have been tested with prototypes:

- A window frame with several cold-bent insulating glass panes, singly curved, with a varying radius. The planar opening hinged window panes are cold-bent by closing them.
- A window frame with one slightly twisted annealed (hot-transformed) window pane.
- A large segment of a cold-bent façade, that approximates a twisted surface.
- A hypar-shaped window frame encasing four annealed panes twisted to a considerable extent.

During the development of the prototypes, building models were designed that demonstrate application options (see Chapter 5).

MARKET AND BUILDING TECHNOLOGY

The demand for twisted glass is difficult to assess, because the product was not available prior to this research. No market survey with prototypes could be carried out. There are many opportunities for applying twisted glass; e.g. in entrance halls and atriums, exhibition and conference centres, or shopping arcades. Façades can be assembled in various ways, e.g. single, laminated or insulating glass, different kinds of glass, e.g. coloured, reflecting. Also a market will appear for twisted skylights, balustrades and, not to be underestimated, interior products like furniture.

A demand will no doubt emerge, with new structural applications, because curved elements require less material, due to greater rigidity. The increasing number of publications on projects with twisted surfaces fuels the expectation that architects will apply it on a large scale. The price, an important criterion, strongly depends on the industrialization of the process. As a result of the limited demand and protected market, twisted glass will initially be produced by manual labour. Adjusting a mold is presently very time-consuming, particularly when air-cooling grates for tempering are installed separately. As demand increases, economic interests will grow. To lower the price, the production will be optimized.

GLASS PANELS AND THEIR PROCESSING

For the test project, adjustment of the mold by hand sufficed. However, adjustment of a glass mold can, largely, be instigated by computers. For this purpose, existing software only needs to be adapted. For example, adjustment data as obtained by the 'pin jigs' command can be used (see Chapter 6). Now that it has proved feasible to twist glass, the mold and furnace techniques must be improved. This will be done in several stages to limit costs, and to map out technical developments.

Visual distortion of glass

The regularity of glass distortion in architecture need not meet such high standards as in the car industry. Currently, relatively large deviations are accepted in tempered planar and bent architectural glass. In insulating glass these are often even amplified, since pressure differences due to changes in temperature in the cavity, cause additional deformations. Where a clear view through the pane is required, the surface quality must be at least as good as that of a conventionally produced flat sheet. With a large radius, single-curved glass will show no optical distortion. Nor will twisted glass. Visual distortion due to stretch or butt, e.g. differences in sheet gauge, is negligible.

Computer simulations

Cold-bent surfaces do not take on the exact singly-curved or twisted surfaces, but can approximate them. The division of forces over a cold-bent glass sheet is complex; its manual calculation is highly labour-intensive. Computerized calculation, however, provides a rapid insight. The calculated values can be tested on models. The cold-bending stresses in the test sheets were verified with a Gauge measuring device. The stresses that occur along the edges of cold-bent glass sheets, when used in double-glazing, were calculated by computer. The outcome provided glueing requirements.

Dimensioning and manufacturing twisted window panes

If window panes have different corner angles, cutting the sheets to size digitally is a logical way to save labour and reduce size tolerances during production. Cutting after distortion of the window pane, is only possible with annealed glass, not with tempered glass. This is an additional process and should, therefore, be avoided.

Size changes resulting from stretch and butt, are not only related to geometry (e.g. surface dimensions, degree of twisting), but also to the transformation process, for example the temperature division in the furnace. Just a few tests will probably provide sufficient insight into the progress of a specific process. The size changes resulting from torsion compared to double-bending, are small.

This project only aims to prove the structural feasibility of a twisted building element. Optimizing the production process is up to the industries themselves.

Mutual adaptation of window frame and glass panel

For a test model of a window frame (and of a specific façade), the distortion of sheet and frame can be attuned to each other. The window shape may deviate from a twisted surface, for example for reasons of production. But deviations are undesirable, because then each building component may have its own tolerances, which will complicate process control.

The reproduction of a reference surface with a mold demands considerable accuracy. In the case of a hypar, this is a surface with straight lines in both directions. For glass sheets, this implies that the reference surface is in the centre or on one of the outer surfaces, and not on an offset surface, simply because it would be easier to produce.

This project is aimed at minimizing the deviations from a twisted shape and, therefore, when making insulating glass, a reference surface in the centre of the window panes is preferred. The sheets are then an offset of the reference surface. Deviations are so small that they can be ignored with regard to production tolerances of the panels themselves and of the window frame. The deviations can be absorbed by the synthetic profile in the groove.

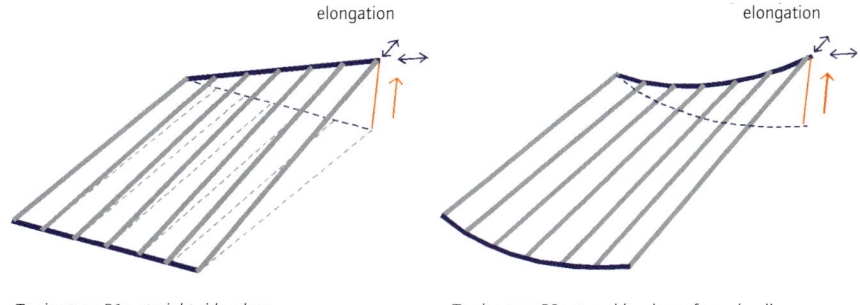

Torsion type R1a, straight side edges   Torsion type R3a, two side edges of equal radius

THE ADJUSTABLE MOLD

Varying lengths of main girders and supporting profiles

The mold may consist of rods. Using jigs these can be manually adjusted for height. Computerized adjustment will enable the shape to be changed in a matter of seconds. The above mold is suitable for ortho-hypars, in which straight lines are in parallel vertical or horizontal surfaces. Sliding up and down will alter the lengths of supporting profiles. The length of the main girders also varies.

Dimensions and adjustment of a parallel mold

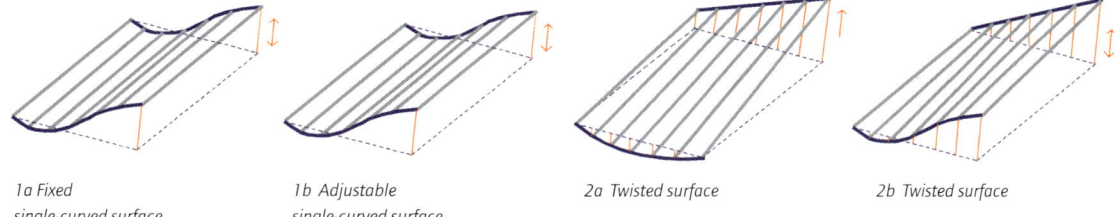

1a Fixed
single-curved surface

1b Adjustable
single-curved surface

2a Twisted surface

2b Twisted surface

1a For single-curved surfaces, it suffices to support the ends of a main girder to which supporting profiles are connected.

1b Supporting profiles can also be independently adjusted in height.

2   Ditto, for twisted surfaces. Ruled surfaces R1a, R2a and R3, will be produced on a 'parallel' mold, i.e. a mold with supporting profiles that move in parallel surfaces.

40 pipes 21.3x2.11 h.t.h. 50

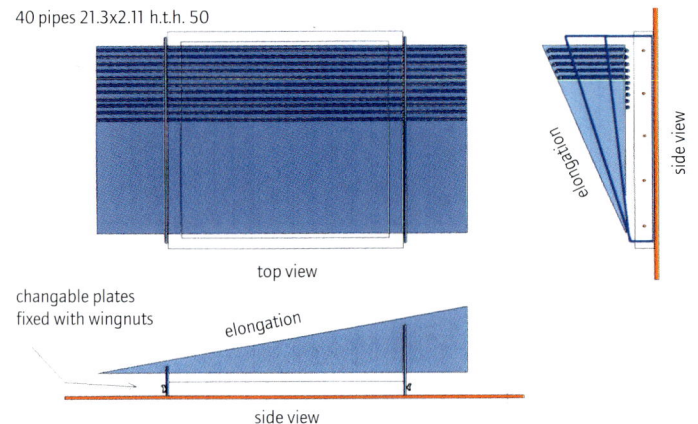

top view

side view

elongation

changable plates
fixed with wingnuts

elongation

side view

Drawing of plate jig
Examples of base plates for straight and curved side edges

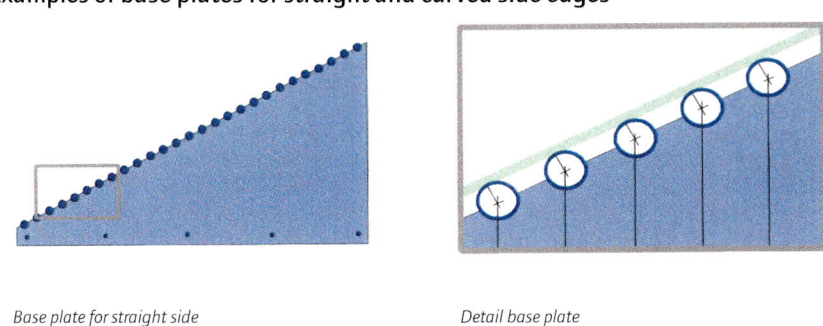

Base plate for straight side

Detail base plate

Example of base plate, curved side edge

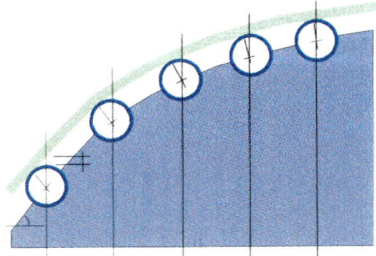

If the inclination of a window pane is large, the distance between supporting profiles will increase, and the mold may have to be very high. A plate jig will decrease these distances quite simply: by averaging the height of the plates on either side of the jig. This cannot be achieved with a parallel mold. With tempering, similar problems arise. The distance between the cooling air supply outlets will also increase when the inclination of the window pane is increased. This will cause an unequal division of the cooling air over the window pane.

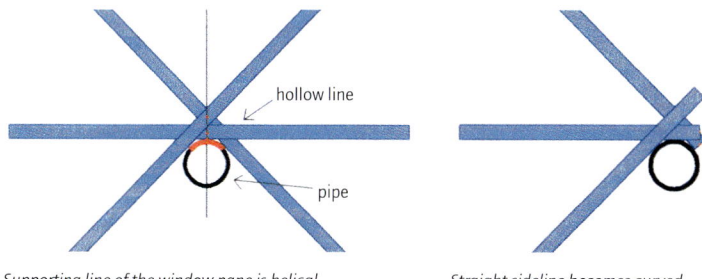

hollow line		
pipe		

Supporting line of the window pane is helical *Straight sideline becomes curved*

Deviation of the reference surface when using supporting rods

If the mold is composed of straight rods, the supporting line of the window pane is not straight, but helical on the rod, due to sheet twisting. With a small rotation, deviations can be ignored. Minimizing the diameter of the rod also minimizes deviations. They are equally divided and hardly visible, but can cause problems, in particular at edges where the window pane must connect to adjacent parts.

The surfaces on either side of a curved window pane differ in size. Deviations with regard to the reference surface in the centre are determined by the diameter of the mold rods, as well as by the degree of torsion. The position of the window pane with regard to the reference surface can be chosen freely. For the sake of adjustment, it would be advantageous to have it coincide with the lower side of the horizontal pane and thus, with the supporting plane of the mold.

Curve of side edge when bearing on rods

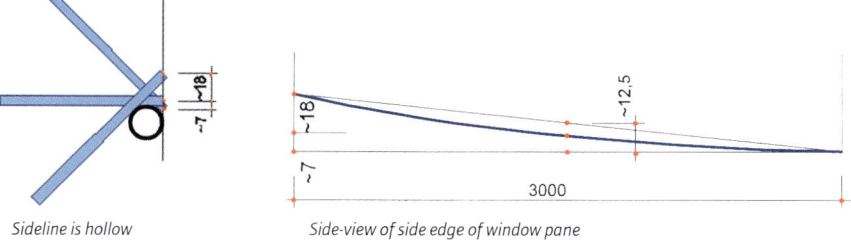

Sideline is hollow *Side-view of side edge of window pane*

If the window pane has a length of say 3,000 mm, the height of the panel, with a regularly divided torsion of 90°, should be equidistant between the extremities. But, in the drawn mold with rods, it is 12.5 - 7 = 5.5 mm away from the centre. This deviation of the reference surface is caused by the diameter of the rods. The smaller it is, the straighter the bearing and the smaller the deviation. In practice, the rotation is less, 45° at the most, instead of the drawn 90°, so the deviation will be less than 2.75 mm.

Deviations at the edges

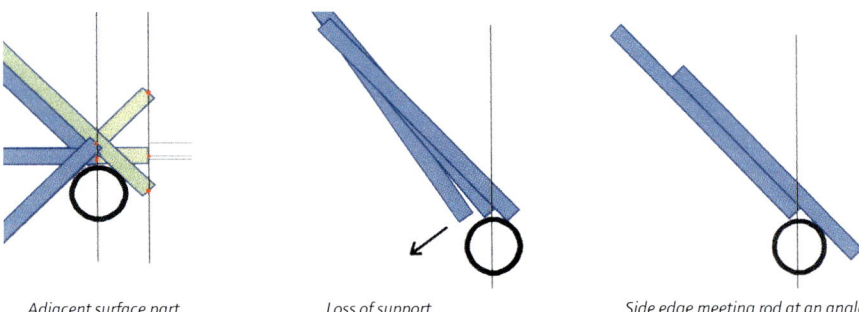

Adjacent surface part   *Loss of support*   *Side edge meeting rod at an angle*

Directly above the rod the curvature of the side edge is minimal. If the edge protrudes beyond the rod, increasing the cantilever will also increase the curvature. Generally, the torsion per window pane and the curvature of the side edge is very small. If the rod diameter decreases, deviations from the reference surface will also decrease. If the distance between the rods becomes too large, the glass will sag between the supports during heating. The window pane will also sag if it has a large cantilever, or if its edge is crooked above the rod.

Straight surface lines and curved rods

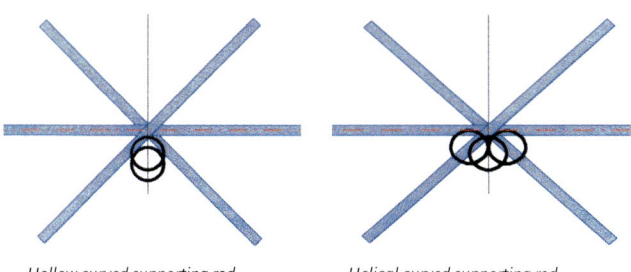

Hollow curved supporting rod   *Helical curved supporting rod*

In order to ensure that the lines of the twisted surface remain straight, the supporting rods have to be curved, each one differently. Of course, bending stiff rods is expensive and critical as far as accuracy is concerned. A computerized mold can correct the bending, if the rod can be slightly curved and adjusted in height at various points, or when, instead of a rod, a row of supporting points is applied. Generally, size deviation due to the twisting of a window pane, can be ignored.

All the above-mentioned problems can be prevented if one uses line-shaped rather than tubular supports, e.g. if the glass is placed on a grid, using pointed instead of spherical supports.

07

PROTOTYPES

The prototypes have proven that the façade designs were feasible. Material transformations and measuring were tested in a range of models of increasing complexity, described and drawn by the author.

First a wooden single-curved window frame (with varying radii) was designed, with cold-bent sheets combined into insulating glass. D3BN Engineers, The Hague, calculated the forces on the seal. This was a cheap way of producing a small series of glass panels curved to varying degrees. Since breaking glass might cause injuries, this model did not come to realization. Instead an adjustable mold for annealed single-curved and twisted glass was designed. Subsequently the glass, produced by Van Tetterode Glasatelier, Voorthuizen, was introduced onto the market by Eijkelkamp, Goor (subsidiary of Glaverbel). Simultaneously an aluminium window frame system for the twisted glass panes was designed and introduced onto the market in cooperation with Reynolds Architectuursystemen, Harderwijk. The author was granted a patent for the system in Europe, and the USA. Next a mock-up (two sheets wide and three sheets high) of Twister 3 was built by Van Dool Constructies, De Lier. With slightly transformed cold-bent glass and cold-bent profiles, it is a relatively cheap option for modestly twisted façades. Subsequently the firm tendered the façade. Cold-bent glass in laminated form, offers opportunities for building developable surfaces, particularly non-rectangular, single-curved and conical sheets.

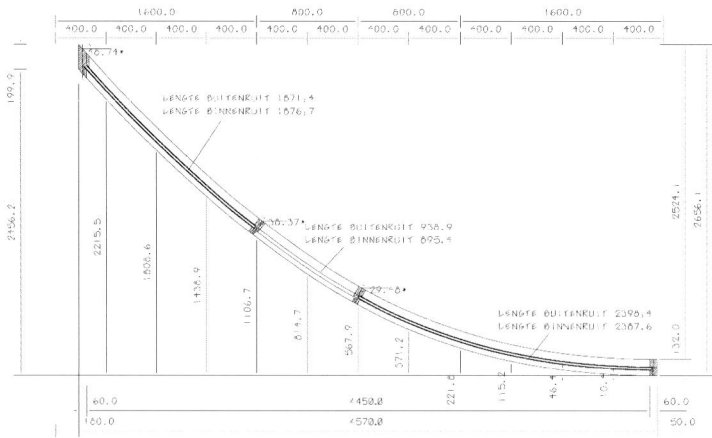

Ground plan and frontal views

PROTOTYPE WINDOW FRAME 00, SINGLE-CURVED (NOT EXECUTED)

Ground plan and frontal views

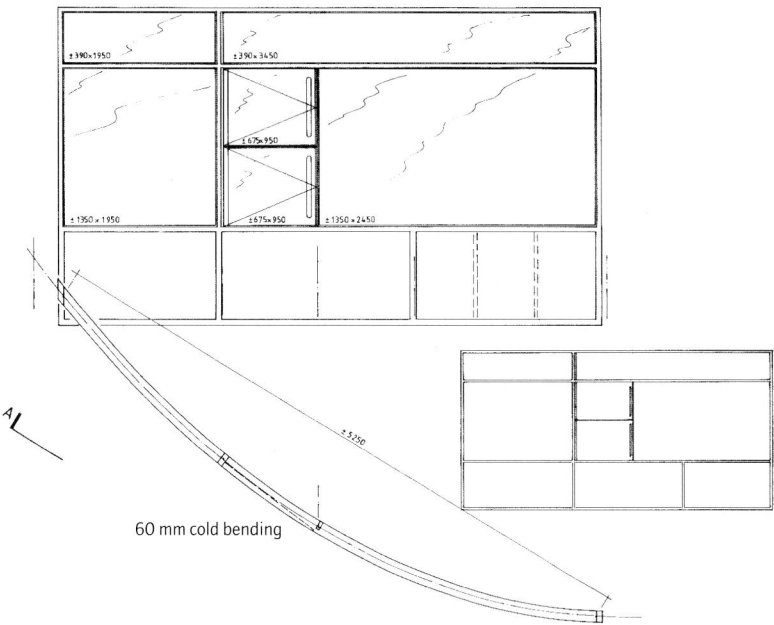

60 mm cold bending

This single-curved window frame has varying curvature. The heat-strengthened insulating window panes are composed of two cold-bent sheets, glued together. [7-1] The opening windows consist of two separately hinging chemically strengthened glass sheets. [7-2] In opened position, they are flat, and in closed position bent against the window frame. The forces in the sheets necessitate making appropriate window fittings, to prevent a kid being catapulted out when opening the window.

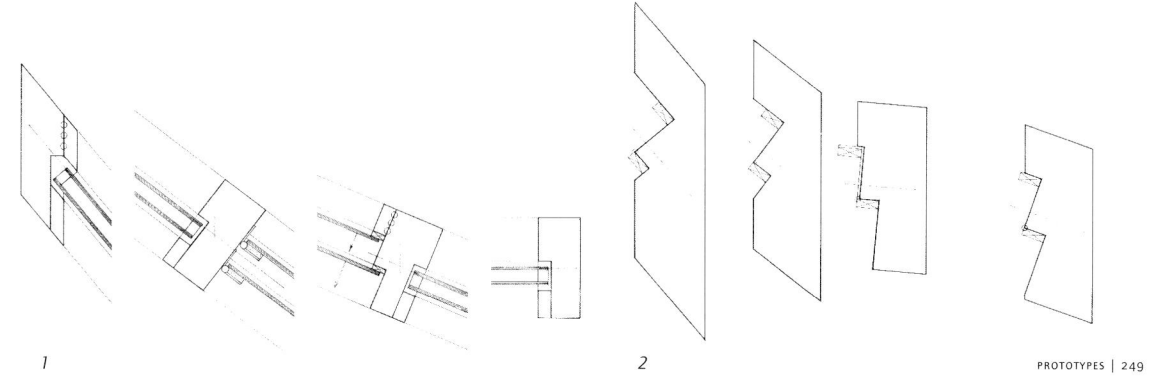

Horizontal cross-sections

1   The massive wooden mullions at both sides of the window are perpendicular to the outer edge of the transoms.
2   Inside, all mullions on the one side connect perpendicularly to the wall. On the other side, where they connect at an angle, grooves must be made, parallel to the glass.

Horizontal cross-sections
  of prototype 00

Horizontal cross-sections
  of mullions of houses ABCD

Vertical cross-sections

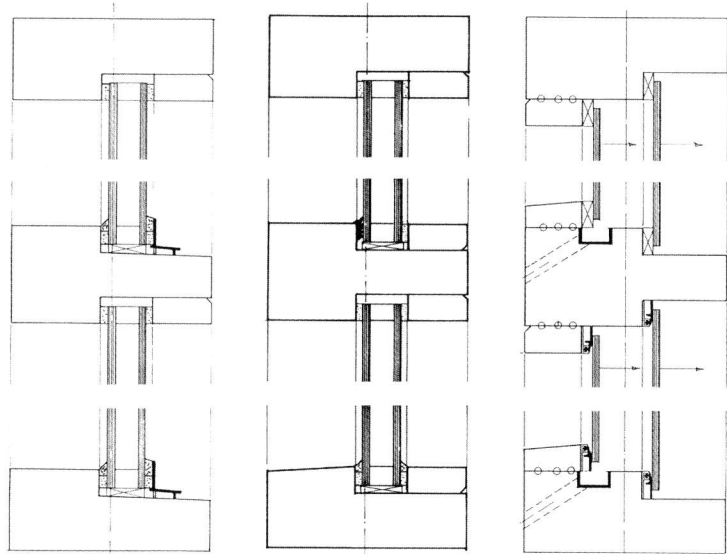

Cross-section with fixed window panes

Inside and outside can be interchanged by providing the wooden profiles with both a weather drip and an inclined upper surface to provide natural drainage.

INSULATING GLASS OF COLD-BENT HEAT-STREGNTHENED WINDOW PANES

Heat-strengthened glass was chosen because of its general availability in the Netherlands, and the large dimensions required.

The upper window pane (420 x 3,360 mm) is 6 mm thick, because a thinner sheet of such proportions would not have the required flatness after tempering. Flatness must be balanced against the weaker bending forces in glass with a 4 mm gauge. The lower window pane (1,420 x 2,400 mm) is 5 mm thick.

Hair cracks along the edges often lead to breakage. Therefore edges are ground down. To further reduce risks it is preferable to apply the largest possible sheets, because in this way, circumferential edge lengths are kept to a minimum. It is advisable to consider the air and bath sides of the sheet when determining direction of curvature. The side of the glass that rests upon the nickel bath during production, has a smoother structure than the air side as well as less thermal pollution and is, therefore, the best side to withstand tension.

The laths provide a mechanical way of locking the bent sheet and protect the seal against ultraviolet light. By applying bent-glass only on the ground floor, the chance of injury due to breakage will be limited. Because the straight lines in the bent surface are vertical, dead-weight hardly influences bending forces.

HINGING WINDOWS OF COLD-BENT CHEMICALLY STRENGTHENED GLASS
The opening windows are a variation on a system with two flat glass sheets, fastened without casing to the window frame by hinges. When open, the sheets are flat, but when closed they are curved against the window frame. They have a 3mm gauge and are chemically strengthened, which implies they can absorb greater tensile stresses than heat-strengthened glass. Their thickness is minimized, as bending forces in thin glass are considerably lower. Operating convenience is also increased, and load on the seal of window fittings as well as compression of rubber rebate profiles are reduced. The window panes are bent along the long sides. This is easier than along the short sides. The panes are made to size, and perforated by water jet. This reduces production tolerances, while less damage may occur along the edges, than with drilling. Limiting the number of perforations is important too, because this considerably reduces the risk of breakage during production. A profile that envelopes the sheet at the hinge side is to be considered, since it would make perforations unnecessary, and secure the sheet in a safe position in case the glued joint gives way.

INSULATING GLASS OF COLD-BENT SHEETS

Panes are usually joined with silicone sealant and thiocol. Silicone sealant is UV-resistant and has a short bonding time. The insulation value of insulating glass is considerably higher if the cavity is filled with an insulating gas, rather than with air. Silicone has a high rate of vapour migration. Therefore it should be combined with a buffer, e.g. butylene or thiocol, applied between the glass and the aluminium spacer. The latter is itself vapour-proof. The layer must be as thin as possible, to minimize the permeable surface. Usually thiocol is used, because its vapour permeability is half that of butylene which, by the way, is more likely to leak.

For the structural connection, silicone is used most often. It has a faster rate of bonding than polyurethane (PUR). But PUR, on the other hand, is preferred for its better filling qualities and its flexibility with full bonding. PUR glues require water vapour as a catalyst. Therefore, drying may take a few days. Fast-cure PUR glues were developed for fast functioning. 7.3 They are highly reactive with a quick skin formation. Fast-cure sealant achieves sufficient strength after half-an-hour in an 80° furnace. Polyurethane is a good gas buffer, and is, therefore, used as a sealant in gas meters. This seal has some flexibility, but must be applied to a thickness of at least 1.5 mm. As thickness decreases with compression, the model was designed with a 2.5 mm layer. Special profiling of both sides of the spacer may be considered, to prevent the layer from being compressed too much. The glue can absorb temporary strain and shrinkage, but a continuous tension load may cause problems. Therefore, a mechanical lock is advisable.

By having a series of molds on which one can leave the panels to dry, one avoids becoming dependent on bonding time or on obtaining sufficient capacity for tension load. An enveloping U-profile to keep sheets together may influence the duration of closure of the cavity seal negatively, by trapping water in the joint. Local clamps, free from the sealant, may cause fewer problems.

During assembly, some movement of the sheets is permissible, but after three to four years, the sealant structure becomes rigid. By then, the glass must have stopped moving, otherwise leakage may occur. After ten years, the 1.4 insulation value of insulating glass will have decreased to 1.8, due to vapour permeability in both directions. The technical life-span of insulating glass is guaranteed for approximately 10 years, but is estimated at 40 years.

Gluing window fittings

Window fittings (hinges and window latches) can be glued. The size of the connecting area determines the forces that can be absorbed. A hinge extending along the entire sheet provides a large surface for gluing and spreads forces evenly. The shearing force in the glue layer is important. It depends on the weight of the glass relative to the surface of the glued joint. Horizontal application of the window panes – to ease bending – has the disadvantage that it increases the shearing moment in the glue layer. Weight decreases with thinner sheets, resulting in less load on the hinges. Both aluminium and stainless steel can be glued to glass directly. To improve adhesion, the glass can be etched. UV-light affects the sealant. Therefore, it is advisable to put metal primer on the glass, before attaching the fittings. To meet requirements, it is advisable to have all fittings glued in the factory under controlled conditions.

Calculations

ABT Engineers, Velp, demonstrated in computer calculations, that glass of the suggested gauges can be bent without exceeding the maximum tension forces. [7-4] Manual calculations of Van den Heuvel Glashandel, Rotterdam, confirmed this.

PROTOTYPE WINDOW FRAME O

Geometry of transoms and mullions

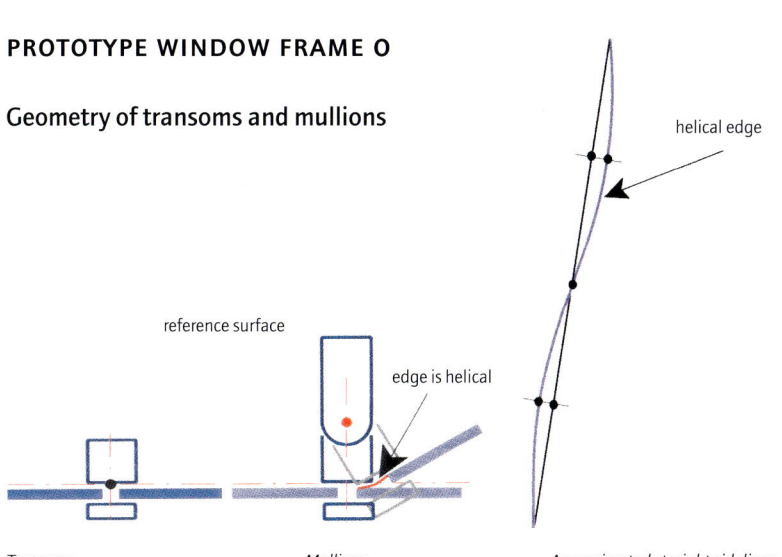

Transoms   Mullions   Approximated straight sidelines

The torsion angle of the rules in a hypar varies, and a hypar offset is not a twisted sur-face, (see Chapter 5). With the prototype window frame O, that uses existing compo-nents of Reynolds' latest window frame system, only the mullions have supporting profiles. These are not twisted. The mullion torsion differs from that of the transoms. This also applies to their maximum connecting angles and average degree of torsion. Characteristics:

- Transoms only consist of a glazing profile. They have a torsion axis within the pro-file and are not additionally bent.
- Mullions' glazing profiles have an adjacent point of rotation. They are both bent and twisted.

The grooves must meet exactly, to ensure water-proof connections. To this end, the reference surface is positioned to coincide with the rebate's inner surface. Since the window panes are offsets, the edges are helical. The edges of panes with small offset distances are hardly curved. They can be considered straight.

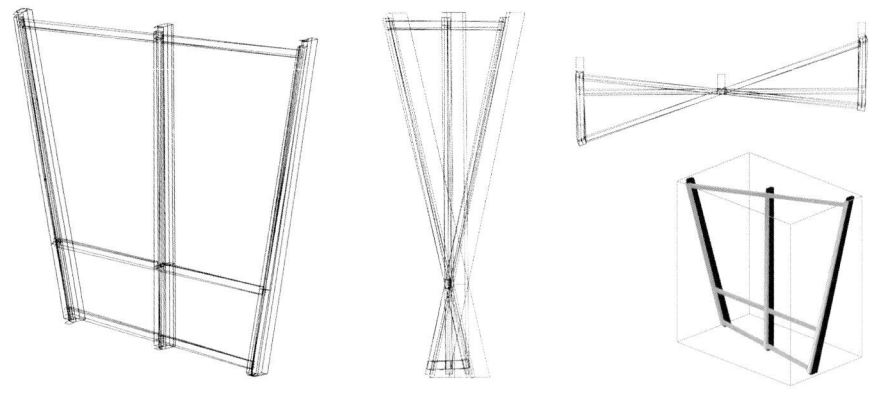

Drawings of Prototype 1

PROTOTYPE WINDOW FRAME 1

The shape of this window frame is an ortho-hypar. The surface, (2 x 2 metres), is divided into four pieces by a vertical centre mullion and a horizontal intermediate transom. The one side of the mullion leans 470 mm backwards, the other forwards over the same distance. The supporting mullion profiles in the prototype are in parallel surfaces, but they can each be rotated in different directions.

The spatial qualities of a twisted surface are clearly visible, making this model suitable for showrooms, to investigate market demand. It already served to test the assembly procedure and production accuracy.

Development drawings were made of the four window panes including transformation and a pin-bed for the left upper window pane 1Rb. The pin-bed's grid is 75 x 75 mm. Supporting points along the edges of the sheet are also indicated (see Chapter 6). A list of the pin-bed's adjustment coordinates was generated (the height of pins and the position of supporting surfaces in two directions). The data, calculated by computer, establish the support locations in the glass mold. The drawings of this window frame are similar to those shown for window frame 3.

The window frame measures, in frontal view, 2,000 x 2,000 mm. The mullions incline 470 mm, at the one side forward, at the other side backward. The mullion in the middle is vertical. The supporting profiles of the mullions lie in parallel surfaces, but may be rotated in any required direction.

PROTOTYPE WINDOW FRAME 2

The 150 metre high Tordo 4 has a cold-bent façade. A trial set-up was used to test assembly procedure, accuracy of profile positioning and handling torsion rigidity. One corner of the set-up (2,400 mm. wide and 4,800 mm. high) bends 84 mm out of a planar surface. This façade has been tendered by the manufacturers involved.

As each floor rotates 1° further, the geometry differs from that of common façades. Helical positioning of the mullions is unusual and specialists have to design a special procedure. Whether mullions are helical or straight, the problems are identical. The ends of the straight profiles must also connect to a helix. Accuracy of positioning is of major importance. The helix at a corner of the building is double-curved. If the helix is approximated with straight storey-high mullions (with their endings upon the helix), the meeting angle of 179.9° between storey-high mullions (approx. 3,200 mm.) is imperceivable. With double-height straight mullions (approx. 6,400 mm.), the mutual angle of 179.7° is also invisible. Such an angle will occur with the facetting of a circle of approximately 2.5 kilometres radius(!).

The mullions and transoms differ in torsion rigidity. The transoms, fixed between the mullions, are torsion-weak. Their maximum rotation is 1.11°/m. A slight variation in torsion of the panes can be absorbed by the rubber stop profiles in the rebate. A slight variation will, therefore, not influence water-proofing. Torsion is applied to the transoms by pulling them into the right position compared to the mullions by means of a screw fixture. The design may deliberately allow some play in the connections. A mullion, in contrast to transoms, is bend- and torsion-rigid, but due to its length still easy to twist and, at its greatest width, easy to bend. Cold-bending causes a deviation of between + and − 3 mm. from the twisted reference surface. At the outset of this research project, the author was not familiar with applications of cold-bent insulating glass to a façade, as guaranteed by producers.

Tordo 4 has an enormous recurrence of elements, but this is not essential for guarantee. When tendering Tordo 4, different applications in other (possibly freely double-curved) designs should also be guaranteed. The importance of this should not be underestimated. However, when applying cold-bent glass, designers must consider restrictions, in particular with respect to distortion and proportions.

Prototype 2 has cold-bent glass and profiles

Drawings of Prototype 3

PROTOTYPE WINDOW FRAME 3 (NOT YET EXECUTED)

This window frame has curved transoms, in contrast to window frame 1, which has straight ones. Their curvature makes measuring, processing and assembly considerably more complex.

Measurement drawings of the window frame

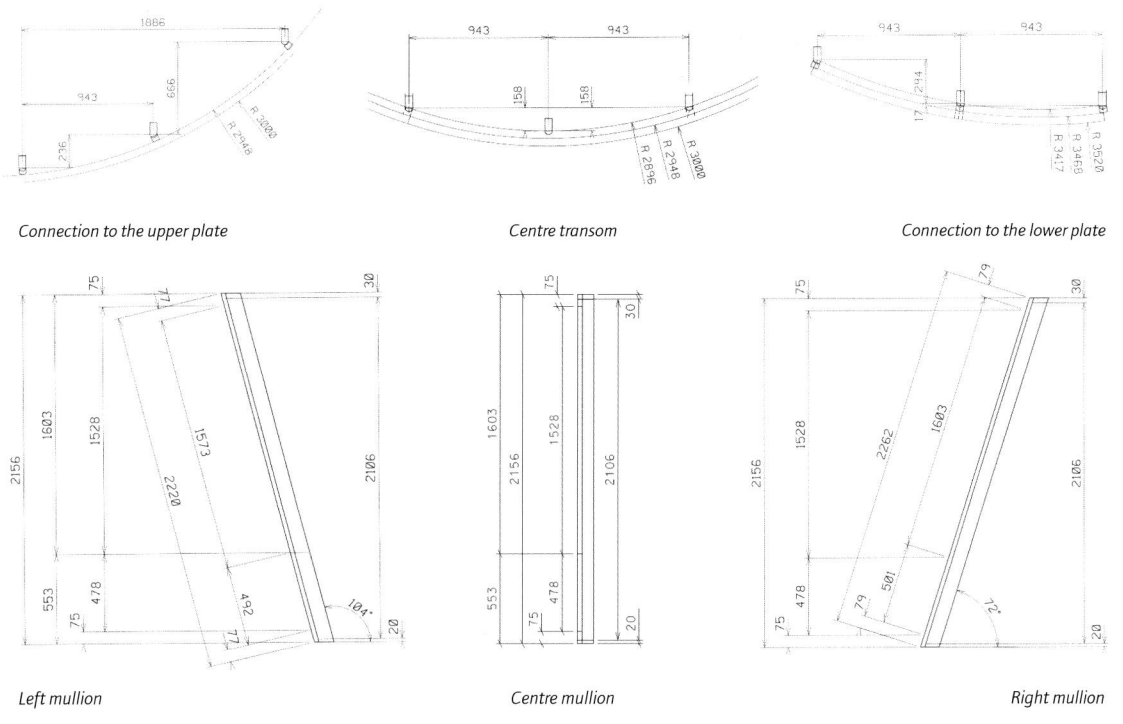

Connection to the upper plate

Centre transom

Connection to the lower plate

Left mullion

Centre mullion

Right mullion

08

CONCLUSIONS AND RECOMMENDATIONS

Conclusions

This study covers many aspects of twisted façades in architecture. Starting in architectural culture and town planning, the quest for twisted facades has led me through architecture, to building technology, production technology and material technology, and when all research topics were adequately covered, back to production and building technology, architecture and town planning. The quest has been a classic cycle of research and development assisting architectural design. The specific characteristics of torsion have been briefly described and schematised, in order to provide insight and to allow optimal integration. They are to be elaborated in later studies. Detailing examples has helped to elucidate the geometry of twisted shapes. Tangible models, e.g. the window frame prototype and the building scale models, have proved that it is feasible to produce twisted building elements industrially. They have acted as important aids in visualizing the various distortions that occur with twisting. The new Twist system as utilised in the window frame, by longitudinal twisting of a torsion weak glazing profile along a rigid profile, offers a sound solution for industrial manufacturing twisted and other double-curved façades. Its importance for double-curved façades, may be similar to that of the principle of a wheel turning around an axis for mobility. Architects, as well as the building industry, are now able to recognize this surface type and optimize usage in buildings, production and processing.

Recommendations

The use of twisted surfaces in architecture, and the innovation of products will be stimulated if steps are taken at various industrial levels. Of major importance are:

CONTROL OVER GEOMETRY
When making use of torsion, one must have knowledge of geometrical implications, since they determine production and processing. It is essential to have a manual available that describes the geometry of twisted surfaces. Specific programmes must be written for working with twisted surfaces. If the computer is used correctly, arithmetical work will no longer be necessary, and it will be quite easy to draw and manipulate complicated surfaces. These drawing programmes must be attuned to both design and manufacture of twisted surfaces. The classification schemes of surfaces and shapes may be elaborated in a follow-up study by introducing a notation system to indicate the degree of shift and rotation. Extending the shape classification schemes with those that result (characteristically) from computer manipulations, may be elaborated, e.g. by stretching (points on) a surface in one or more directions. New typological variations will probably be found.

BRIDGING THE GAP BY 3D DISCIPLINE

It is the duty of an architect who designs a geometrically complex building to provide the building team with clear drawings of the building where not only the overall geometry will be established but also the sizes and topologies of the different components and their 3D connections. For that reason the work of the architect has to go into further depths than usual in order to bridge the gap which is created in the building team between architects and the production and building members. The 3D drawing grid will be supplied to the producing parties who get fixed 'slot times' to work in more detail on the model, before sending their contribution over to other participants. It will show the need for a discipline of 3D CAD drawings.

TWISTED SHAPES AND ARCHITECTURE

The use of twisted surfaces in architecture may be manifold. The series of models as developed in this study, touches upon many architectural aspects, ranging from shaping of buildings to consequences of the use of twisted surfaces within a building. The typological research, e.g. into the varying inter-positioning of elements like stairs and elevators, or core and outer façades, or of separate building volumes, should be elaborated in a follow-up study. This could well result in new architectural variations.

INSTIGATING THE INNOVATION OF PRODUCTS AND THEIR PROCESSING

For the past decade, development of twisted (and in general double-curved) glass has been stimulated by clients and architects who show by design that this product adds value to the built environment. There will be a world-wide market for the first supplier who is able to offer twisted glass. Furnace engineers will have to put up a good fight: they will have to demonstrate that the product can be developed. The development of a tempering furnace for twisted glass costs approximately 5 million Euros. However, until one of the parties introduces tempered double-curved glass onto the market, the incentive to the remaining parties (glass processors or furnace producers) to invest in such an innovation is, obviously, too weak. From an economic point of view, considering the risk of such a new product and the slow start of a new market, it is understandable. But it is bad for the industry as a whole. Apart from the self-interest of glass producers and processors, there is an even greater interest at stake for the allied branches of the industry. Through the application of double-curved glass, many other products will be drawn into the innovation process, e.g. twisted steel panels. Twisted surfaces make great demands on production, logistics and assembly. Glass is a strong stimulus for the computerization of the building industry, but this interest does not count for the glass industry when they are considering whether to invest large amounts of money themselves. The innovation of the shaping process of glass will gain momentum with growing demand. Architects operate individually and design in different styles. Therefore the demand will be put forward as small series of expensive complex shaped freely-curved surfaces and large series of relatively cheap ruled surfaces for buildings as developed in this study: Twisters.

09

Notes

1-1   Donat, 1965, pp. 24-27

1-2   Xenakis, 1965

1-3   Wachsman, 1961

1-4   Tzonis, 1984, pp. 27-42

1-5   Interview of the author with J. van de Beek, Groningen, 14.12.2000

1-6   Interview of the author with D. van der Waarden, Amsterdam, 18.12.2000
      She told me all twisted spires in the region have been designed by one architect,
      and that similar towers have been built in the Dordogne region, France.

1-7   Van der Heide, Molema, Tomlow, 1979
      Gaudí made extensive use of the advantages of straight lines in ruled surfaces,
      with regard to dimensioning, assembly and flow of forces, for example in the
      Sagrada Familia in Barcelona, Spain.

1-8   Zerbst, 1987

1-9   De Vries, 2000

1-10 Elger, 1984

1-11 Gabo, 1957

1-12 Nash, 1985

1-13 Argan, 1988

1-14 Lootsma, 1984, p. 20
      Lootsma, 1984, pp. 10-17
      Xenakis produced musical compositions that, as a diagram, have similarities
      with ruled surfaces, in particular his first important composition, Menastaseis,
      1954. He found sources of inspiration in the glissandi in his musical composi-
      tions. His notation system for polyvalent (or multi-linear) music was not equiva-
      lent to the building' s geometry, yet both exhibit tendencies towards displacing
      simple linear horizontal progressions across inclined staves.

1-15 Frampton, 1992, pp. 44-45

1-16 Bloc, 1964, pp. 190-191

1-17   Faber, 1963

1-18   Bouwkundig woordenboek, 1997

1-19   Bouwkundig vertaalboek, 1997

1-20   The *Grote Winkler Prins Encyclopedie*, Elsevier, Amsterdam, 8th edition 1983, describes the twist's characteristic hip, arm and leg movements as drying the buttocks with an imaginary towel while grinding out an imaginary cigarette with one foot.

1-21   A cat is more supple (than man) in its ability to twist its body. If it falls from a great height, it will often land on its feet, because it can twist its body/ by making use of a changing inertia moment. By retracting and stretching the forelegs and hindlegs, respectively, it can rotate into the right position to make a more comfortable landing.

1-22   Lynn, 1998

1-23   Dal Co, 1998

1-24   Interview of the author with Mr Francesc Arbós Bellapart, at the Batimat Building Fair in Paris, France, 10.11.1999

2-1   Realistic Manifesto, 1920.

2-2   Peissi, 1961

2-3   Gabo, 1957

2-4   Janssen, 1964, p. 95

2-5   Neumann, 1959, p. 32

2-6   Hammacher, 1968

2-7   Escher, 1959

2-8   Jencks, 1997, p. 51

2-9   Sharp, 1996

2-10   Zerbst, 1987

2-11   Grino, 2000, pp. 71-81

2-12 Izzo, 1981

2-13 Kloos, 1984, pp. 18-19

2-14 Frampton, 1981, pp. 44-45

2-15 Lootsma, 1984, p. 20

2-16 Faber, 1963

2-17 Engineering News Record, August 1, 1968 pp. 46-47

2-18 *Engineering News Record*, January 7, 1971, pp. 22-23, and
      L'Architecture d'Aujourd'hui, no. 156, 1971, pp. 94-95

2-19 De Kort, 1977

2-20 Albrecht, 1998, pp. 538-544

2-21 Johnson, 1996

2-22 De Bever, 1991, pp. 68-69

2-23 Zardini, 1996

3-1   Le Roux, 1993, pp. 52-55

3-2   Hendricks, 1975

4-1   Engel, 1977

5-1   I performed this research in co-operation with Bart Weggeman, one of my
      students at the HTS in Amsterdam. As an exercise in 'architecture and
      construction', I had him and a fellow student examine the building methods of
      multihulls (catamarans and trimarans).

5-2   Property developer and contractor SBB, Beverwijk, promised Grondbedrijf
      (Public Developments) in Rotterdam to realize the project, provided we would
      get a location there. Eventually, no piece of land was allocated, because a
      higher building density was required than that of the designed model.
      The Dutch participants made the following commitments:
      • Hoogovens, IJmuiden: to supply free of charge the corrugated steel roof
        plates, in the colour we wanted, because of the new application with the
        profiling running across the curved ridge.
      • Prince Cladding, Zoeterwoude : to assemble the corrugated roof and create
        a trial set up.

- Property developer and contractor SBB, Beverwijk: the Grondbedrijf in Rotterdam to realize the project, provided a location was allocated there.
- ABT Engineers, Velp: they performed the calculations for the cold-bent glass, and made a model for a computerized calculation and drawing of the concrete floor reinforcement, which was different for each house.
- Glaverned, Tiel: they supplied tempered glass sheets for the testing models.
- The concrete for the 8 houses was to be supplied free of charge by the organisation of Dutch concrete industries VNC, Den Bosch. They also asked whether they could make the parapets, which were designed in brickwork, with concrete, cast in an adjustable shuttering. Due to the limited technical problems of their request, I decided to turn this into research into twisted concrete structures. They sponsored a part of the preliminary investigation.

5-3 Bart Weggeman made these folded models.

5-4 When working for YRM Partnership in London, Mr. R. Aish M Des (RCA), PhD, also wrote associative geometry routines for detailing the double-curved arched roof of Waterloo Station, London, where all arches are a slightly different variation of the original prototype.

5-5 Photos by Hans Werlemann, Rotterdam

5-6 Initially, I had the naive, but inspiring, conviction that twisted surfaces could be produced without stretch or butt, and only needed to be bent. I was also convinced that the shipbuilding industry (cad) designers with whom I conversed about the characteristics of torsion, were wrong and echoing each other and their study books, which in my opinion were based on incorrect theories. It was only during the detailing of tower Tordo 1, while having a conversation with the yacht designer Gerard Dijkstra, that I began to doubt my premises. As a test, a blacksmith made a twisted steel frame for me against which we, subsequently, tried to push a large plate of hardboard. No way, of course! Apparently, the cardboard tower models made so far, because they were only slightly transformed, had been assembled from developable surfaces. These approximated twisted surfaces very closely, partly due to the intermediate seams.
This coincided with the fact that the first models left the option open to fall back on straight or flat elements, for the various components. In the subsequent reports the description of the geometry was correct.

5-7 Reichhart, 2000

7-1 Because of the danger of glass breakage, Mr. R. van Keer, at the time sales director of Glaverbel, Brussels, internally notified his co-workers on 29.11.1993 not to co-operate with the cold-bent applications in this project. In the mean time, this research has resulted in laminated cold-bent glass, which was introduced onto the market as Ellips Glas, by Eijkelkamp, Goor, NL, subsidiary of Glaverbel

7-2 This is a variant on the Fentolat system of Maasglas, where two flat, tempered glass sheets are hung side to side, each with its own hinge.

7-3 An example is Sikaflex, type 255FC PUR of Sika.

7-4 Mr. B. Nieuwpoort of D3BN Engineers, The Hague, performed the calculations with the Diana programme

9-1 De Jong, 2000

Literature

Albrecht, Peer: 'Der neue Zollhof in Düsseldorf, Innovative Schalung für ein aussergewöhnliches Bauprojekt': *Beton* no. 48, 1998, pp. 538-544

Argan, Guilio Carlo: *Henri Moore*, Atrium, Alphen aan de Rijn 1988

Bever, Stefan de (et al.): 'Gedraaide toren, Rotterdam': *Bouwen met Staal* no. 102, 1991, pp. 68-69

Bloc, André (ed): 'Un siècle d'Architecture': *Architecture d'aujourd'hui* 113-114, 1964, pp. 190-191

Dal Co, Francesco, Kurt W. Forster: *Frank O. Gehry, The complete works*, The Monacelli Press, New York 1998

Davidson, Cynthia C. ed.: *Iannis Xenakis & Le Corbusier, Philips Pavilion*, Architecture New York, no. 5, pp. 34-35, 1994

Donat, John (ed): 'Noriako Kurakawa, Helix City': *World Architecture no. 2*, 1965, pp. 24-27

Elger, Dietmar: *Der Merzbau, eine Werkmonographie*, Walther König, Köln 1984

Engel, Heino: *Tragsysteme*, Deutsche Verlags-Anstalt, Stuttgart, 1977

Engineering News Record, August 1, 1968 pp. 46-47

Escher, M.C.: M.C. *Escher, Grafiek en tekeningen, ingeleid en toegelicht door de graficus*, De Koninklijke Erven, Zwolle 1959

Faber, Colin: *Candela/ The Shell Builder*, Reinhold Publishing Company, New York 1963

Frampton, Kenneth, Silvia Kolbowski (ed.): *Le Corbusier's Firminy Church*, Institute for Urban Studies, Rizzoli International Publications, New York 1981, pp. 44-45, 92

Gabo, Naum: *Gabo, Constructions, Sculpture, Paintings, Drawings, Engravings*, Lund Humphries, London 1957

Grino, Silvia (etal.): 'Eladio Dieste 34° elatitude sud': AMC no. 107, 2000, pp. 71-81

Hammacher, H.M.: *Barbara Hepworth*, Thames and Hudson, London 1968

Hendricks, Gordon: *Eadward Muybridge, The Father of the Motion Picture*, Secker & Warburg, London 1975

Izzo, Alberto, Camillo Gubitos (ed): *Marcel Breuer, Architectura 1921-1980*, Stampa, Florence 1981

Janssen, Pierre: *Kunstgrepen*, De Bezige Bij, Amsterdam 1964

Jencks, Charles: *The architecture of the jumping Universe*, p. 51, Academy Editions, London 1997

Johnson, Philip: 'What I would like to have built': *Wiederhall* no.19, 1996

Jong, T.M. (ed) (et al.): *Ways to study architectural, urban and technical design*, Delft University Press, Delft 2000

Kloos, Maarten: 'Iannis Xenakis: muziek, architectuur, ruimte': *Wonen TABK* no. 2, p.18-19, 1984

Kort, J. de, J.M. Gerrits, *Hangars voor wide-body vliegtuigen, Draagkonstrukties van gebouwen*, Gebouwendokumentatie, deel 1, TU Delft, Delft 1977

Lootsma, Bart: 'Le Poème Électronique, Het verlangen naar synthese': *Wonen TABK* no. 2, 1984, p.20

Lootsma, Bart: 'Een ode van Philips aan de vooruitgang': *Wonen TABK* no. 2, 1984, pp.10-17

Lynn, Greg: *Animate Form*, Princeton Architectural Press, New York 1979

Molema, Jan (et al.): *Gaudí, Rationalist met perfecte materiaalbeheersing*, Delft University Press, Delft 1979

Nash, Steven, J. Merkert (ed): *Naum Gabo, Sixty Years of Constructivism*, Prestel Verlag, Berlin 1985, p.35

Neumann, Erich: The archetypal world of Henry Moore, Routledge & Keegan Paul, London 1959, 32

Peissi, Pierre: *Antoine Pevsner*, Editions du Friffon, Neuchâtel 1961

Reichart, A.: 'Specifity of shells made of elestic deformed profiled metal sheets', in: *Bridge between civil engineering and architecture*, Delft University of Technology, Delft 2000

Roux, F. Le, J. van Muylwijck: *Strip & Cartoon tekenen*, Teleac, Delft 1993 pp. 52-55

Sharp, Dennis (ed): 'Santiago Calatrava': *Architectural Monographs* no. 46, 1996

Tzonis, Alexander, Liane Levaivre: 'The Question of Autonomy in Architecture': *The harvard Review* no.18, 1984, pp. 27-42

Vries, Peter de: Morphology and structural behaviour of the hyperbolic lattice, in: *Bridge between civil engineering and architecture*, Delft University of technology, Delft 2000

Wachsman, Konrad, *The Turning Point of Building, Structure and Design*, Reinhold Publishing Company, New York 1961

Xenakis, Iannis: 'A Utopian project for 'cosmic cities', 5 km in height': *L'Urbanisme, Utopies et Réalités*, 1965

Zardini, Mirko: *Santiago Calatrava, Secret Sketchbook*, The Monacelli Press, New York 1996

Zerbst, Rainer: *Antoni Gaudí*, Tachen/ Librero, Köln 1987

Supplement 1 Research by design

In order to describe this study's procedure, a diagram was used as described in Ways to study, architectural, urban and technical design. [9-1] It describes the process of 'research by design', by interaction between object and context, which is already perceivable in the design process: first the object is the subject matter, and then the context. Designing is carried out on various scales and hence, with various legends simultaneously. The point is to change presumptions about the context and subsequently study the effects on the design, that are fed back to context. The notion 'context' depends on scale and aspect.

In an academic environment designing on various scales can be taken to considerable lengths. Scale confrontations between individual problems of component details and larger-scaled concepts in building designs, may occur and interact systematically during the design. Time and again, presumptions about larger-scale concepts are omitted, in order to better conceive parts and, vice versa, presumptions about products are dropped to acquire a better large-scale concept. Prototypes of each of the scale levels (for instance a glass sheet or a building model) do not have to meet a context-regulated list of requirements, to which they would be exposed in reality. An experimental design has its own constraints, as far as the test's context is concerned. For example, the first developed building models in this study did not necessarily have to be built with twisted parts. On the other hand, only a few applications of twistable components were known.

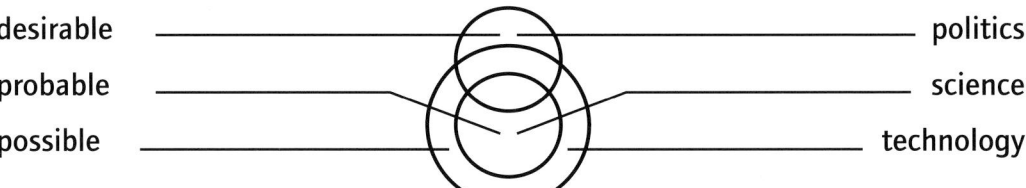

desirable — politics
probable — science
possible — technology

If a design could be predicted on the basis of causal connections, via laws of probability, it would no longer be a design. The probable will happen anyway. The designer's duty is to explore unlikely occurrences, in particular when the most probable development is not desirable. These incidents will not be predicted because of their improbability: they have to be designed. In the diagram, the difference between absolute science and technology is outlined as a difference in orientation towards probable and possible futures. What is probable, is by definition also possible, but not all that is possible will actually happen. Therefore, the domain of the technician is basically broader and for that reason, some common academic profundity has to be abandoned. After all, the desirable future concerns us all. It is the domain of politics.

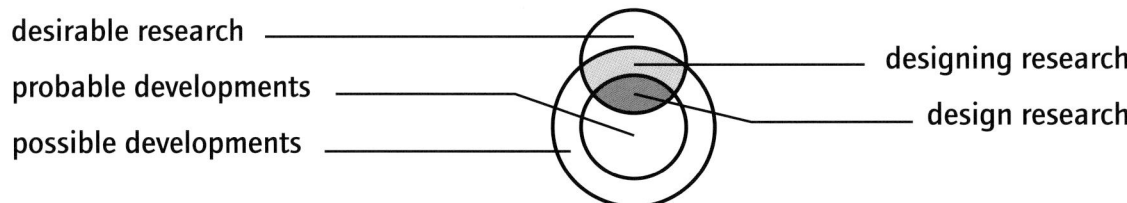

desirable research — designing research
probable developments — design research
possible developments

'Reseach by design' studies conditional changes. Under specific conditions something may happen, with a specific cause something is bound to happen. Conditional logic does not always disclose the probable, but it will disclose the possible. Just as cause and effect chains exist, there are conditional chains in which, under certain conditions, patterns and processes may not be very predictable, but rather conceivable.
This conceivability can be introspectively checked with the test: if A can be conceived without B, but not B without A, then A is a condition for B. Within the design process, results from certain design stages are conditions for further development. Specific data in the preliminary design may, for instance, be a condition designing a façade component.

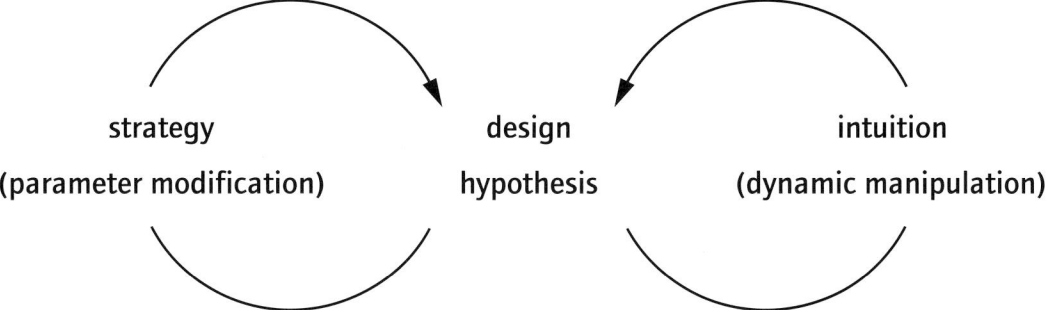

strategy   design   intuition

(parameter modification)   hypothesis   (dynamic manipulation)

The study of context and object conditions does not exclusively follow the linear logic of causal thinking. A building may be designed from a detail, to do maximum justice to its operational mechanism. From the shape of a building, on the other hand, an unforeseen urban development quality may arise. When testing quality, it is not the design process followed that matters, but rather the meeting of certain demands that can be described in retrospect.
In 'research by design', the designer must anticipate the variations he wishes to examine, in order to subsequently study, devise and test the interrelations. It is unlikely that the complex figuration of the design process can be satisfactorily encoded in an all-encompassing system. A better approach is to create separate application sub-systems and subsequently manipulate parametric systems, in an intuitive as well as a strategic manner. One may experiment intuitively with variations in configurations of parameters, and introduce or remove parameters. Strategic manipulations allow the actor to change the value of key parameters and to observe the propagation of this change on dependent expressions and hence dependent configurations. As an example: the strategic manipulation in geometry is the design of the dependency relation between the geometric objects. These dependencies are geometric (tangency, parallelism, orthogonality, etc.) or expressions (typically involving distance and angular measurements).

Research by design does not result in just one solution,
but in a collection of potential ones.

Supplement 2 Time schedule

ACTIVITY QUARTER

PHASE

PRELIMINARY RESEARCH INTO SINGLE-CURVED SURFACES

00 selection/purchase of hard/software
design/detailing of project Cad on a roof

RESEARCH INTO TWISTED BUILDING ELEMENTS

01 Description of motivation and research objectives
Inventory of aspects of torsion
Analysis of design aspects of Twisters and Tordos
Classification scheme of twisted surfaces
Defining of strategy

02 Design of Tordo 1; elaboration production aspects

03 Dimensioning of trial project per element

04 Description applications of new glass transformations

05 Window frame - description of alternatives
                      - detailed window frame system
      Glass   - consultation/visits specialists/manufacturers
                      - selection of industrial participants
      Concrete   - design of adjustable shuttering
                      - description of twisted elements

06 Window frame - drawing of 3 prototypes
                      - production of mould
      Glass   - design/optimization of adjustable mould
                      - calculation of forces in cold-bent applications

07 Design of Twisters 1 and 2

08 Design and elaboration construction of Twister 3
production trial set-up of cold-bent façade

09 Design of Twisters 4and 5 and Low-rise tordos

10 NOT YET REALIZED
Window frame: - optimization of window frame profile
      Glass   - production of tempered twisted panels
                      - design of mould for double-curved glass

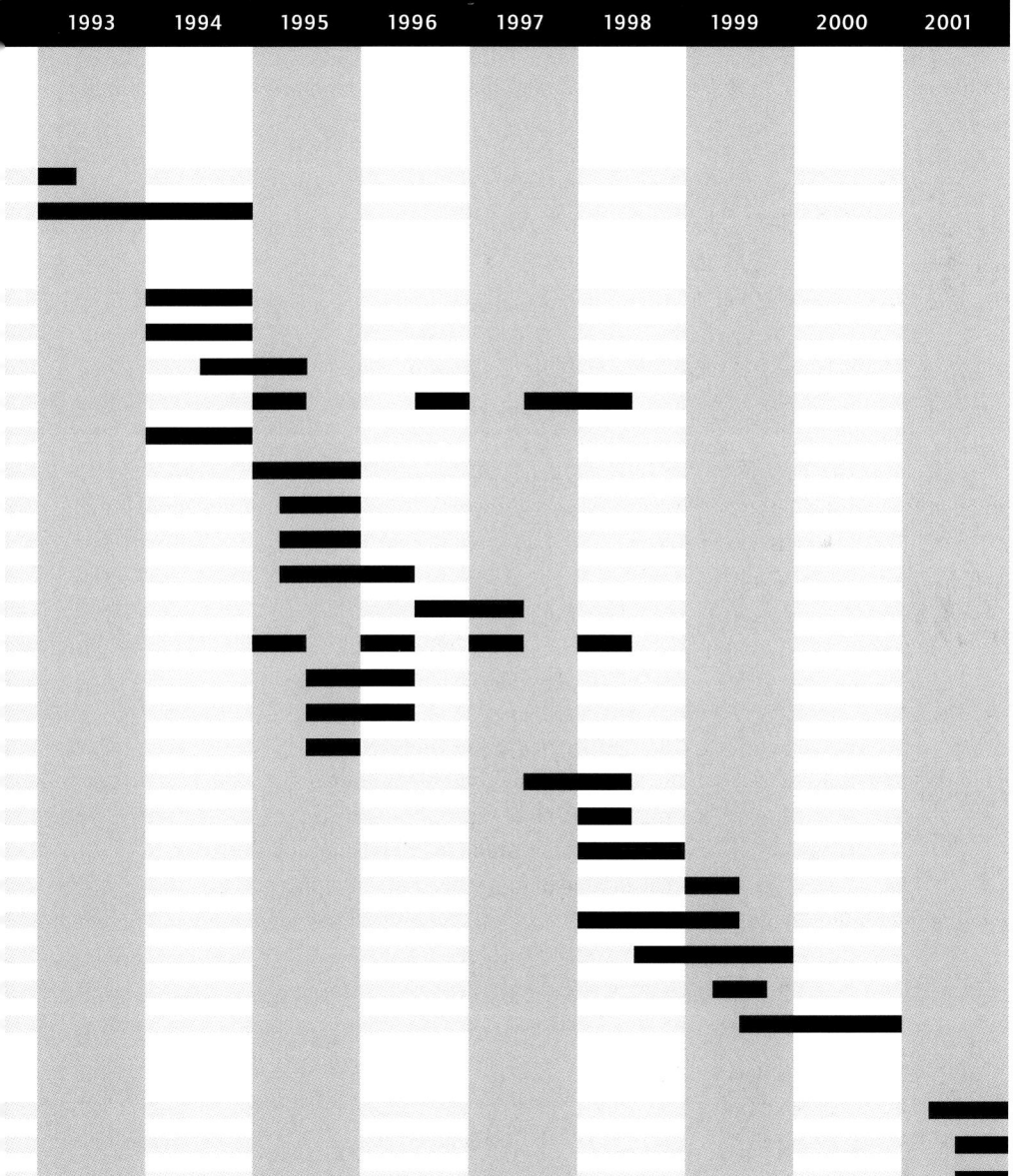

| 1993 | 1994 | 1995 | 1996 | 1997 | 1998 | 1999 | 2000 | 2001 |

Supplement 3

Description of activities, per field of research and per phase

Preliminary study of single-curved surfaces

PHASE 0
- In cooperation with the InnovatieCentrum Amsterdam and the Dutch scientific research organisation TNO CAD-Centrum, Delft, software and hardware was selected, appropriate for drawing and dimensioning intersecting single-curved surfaces, making development drawings and Cad-Cam (the use of digital data to instigate production means).
- Followed drawing and system management courses at Intergraph for EMS-software. This software, based on solid modelling, enables development drawings of double-curved surfaces.
- Purchase of Intergraph hardware and Microstation software.
- Robert Aish (at the time working as programwriter at Bentley, the manufacturer of Microstation and EMS software, and currently its director of R & D) wrote associative geometry routines for manipulating single-curved surfaces.
- Visit to Brazil to study curved shapes in the work of the architect Oscar Niemeyer and to interview him. This resulted in a number of publications on his work.
- Bart Weggeman, assisted with the research into geometrical aspects of the distortion of a plate with curved folding lines.
- Design of a trial project for 8 houses in which single-curved lines and surfaces were integrally incorporated in the shape (walls, roofs, parapets and balconies). Prepared a scale model and had it photographed by Hans Werleman, NL.
- Assembled the designed housing types into urban models.
- Structural detailing of single-curved window panes, window frames, parapets and roof surfaces and approached Dutch building participants.
- Start of the co-operation with Gobel Hellevoort, Amsterdam who made the computer drawings from then on.

PHASE 1 RESEARCH INTO TWISTED SURFACES
- Description of motivation and objectives.
- Prepared an inventory of existing architectural applications in which torsions occur.
- Investigation of dimensioning and production of twisted elements in other fields.
- Devised a scheme in which all twisted surface types are named. Investigated which twisted surfaces within that outline would be interesting as firstlings for the building industry.
- Literature research into the use of twisted surfaces in architecture.
- Description of the design aspects of twisting at various levels:
  - drawing actions, when designing with computer.
  - manipulations of façade elements, to compose a façade.
  - manipulations of floor plans, which result in buildings, and examination of mutual connection of their façades. Set up a building typology for this purpose.
  - tudy of the consequences of twisted façades for floor plans.
- Drawing of various building types and comparing their optical and geometrical characteristics.

- Selection of two building models for detailing.
- Made arrangements for a research plan that must result in an industrial production of twisted building elements.
- Delivered a lecture on the work of Oscar Niemeyer and on new techniques with which twisted and double-curved shapes can be built, at the First Architectural Biennale of Recife, in Brazil.

PHASE 2 GENERAL: TORDO 1

- Design of research model.
- Study of reflections and contour effects of twisted façades.
- Developed the shape sequentogram, see chapter 3.
- Made a scale model and had it photographed by Hans Werleman.
- Approached possible participants for the structural detailing and introduction onto the market of the glass, window frames and concrete parapets. Explained technical and aesthetical aspects of the prototype and described possible market for twisted elements.
- Established four study groups (CAD, Window frame, Glass and Concrete), to carry out sub-studies. Initially instigated their work, and subsequently delegated the coordination of activities to the firms, to stimulate their commitment to developing the various products.

PHASE 3 GENERAL

- Requested the Grondbedrijf in Rotterdam, to allocate a building location for the twisted tower. The chance of realization increased the interest of the participating parties and tested the investigations compared to reality. The project team of the Hook of Holland, NL, included the plan in their urban development proposal as a possible completion.

PHASE 3 CAD

- Made a drawing, in cooperation with ship's designer Gerard Dijkstra, of an approximation of a twisted surface with developable surfaces (for appropriate software this is a standard command).
- Had a metal frame made (1 x 1.5 metres) with a torsion of 0.15 metres, to 'manually' examine the forces, needed to press a hardboard plate against the twisted mould, and to 'visualize' the behaviour of the material.
- Used Intergraph to make development drawings of twisted surfaces.
- Measured the designed tower model Tordo 1; also the most important façade segments. Presented this to the participants as the geometry to pursue for their prototype.

PHASE 3 WINDOW FRAME, GLASS, CONCRETE
- Elaborated measuring and production aspects with manufacturers.

PHASE 4 GENERAL
- Drew examples of twisted glass roofs, to motivate the building industry to invest in developing new ways of transforming glass and window frames.
- Presented a description of the scale-less transition of associative meanings in curved lines, the influence of the reading vector.

PHASE 4 CAD
- To get myself used to the geometrical shapes, line manipulations of a straight, respectively, curved line, were drawn by shifting and rotating (using WordPerfect).

- The result was a new classification scheme with shapes composed of the above-mentioned lines. The diagram is based on pictorial symbols that represent manipulations by computer, instead of mathematical formulae. Distinguished, within the group 'twisted surfaces', besides the 'ruled surfaces' (=twisted surfaces composed of straight lines), the new notion 'curve surfaces' (=ditto of curves) and schematized these in the order of their distortions.
- Description of mathematical characteristics of the surfaces in the new diagram. For example the conditions under which sliding, roller, respectively, ball-and-socket joint window panes occur in planar, spherical, and twisted surfaces.

PHASE 5 GENERAL
- Prepared a summary of the geometry of the model Tordo 1, so that new participants can acquire a rapid insight into their sub-problems, while avoiding confronting problems of others.
- Visit to Marianne Peretti in Recife, Brazil. She uses a very freely curved lining in her works of art, with a great interaction between adjacent, differently curved lines. I have described certain aspects of her work in sub-studies.

PHASE 5 CAD
- Additional software placed at my disposal by Bentley Systems, manufacturer of the Microstation programme, to accelerate the drawing process and achieve greater accuracy.

PHASE 5 WINDOW FRAME
- Description of geometrical problems of twisted window frames. The designed system also proved to be suitable for freely double-curved façades.
- Applied for and was granted a patent in the Netherlands for the technical principle of the 'Twist window frame'; also applied for a PCT (=world-wide claim for 18 months).
- Further development of the window frame, in co-operation with Reynolds Architectuursystemen, Harderwijk, NL. The 'Twist window frame system' connects to their latest profiles, designed for the European market, and makes use of a great number of moulds, already designed by them for this purpose. Reynolds starts with the sponsoring of my research.

PHASE 5 GLASS
- Consultations with Dutch glass specialists, e.g. the research centre TNO, Delft, and constructors.
- Visited glass and furnace manufacturers in the Netherlands, Belgium, Germany, England and Switzerland; consultations with their (technical and/or commercial) managing directors.
- Description of various possible glass applications, anticipating designs of glass moulds:
  - cold-bent glass for developable surfaces in laminated and/or insulating glass.
  - annealed glass for developable and twisted surfaces.
  - tempered glass for twisted and double-curved glass, with the help of a computerized mould.

Assembled a powerful combination of firms for development and marketing of the new glass types. Had solicitors draw up co-operation contracts.

PHASE 5 CONCRETE
- Schematization of façade elements in size, zone and connection to the other building elements.
- Description of the geometry of twisted parapets. Designed an appropriate adjustable shuttering. Various Dutch concrete element manufacturers remarked they would gladly realize this project: Kemper Oosthoek, Schokbeton, Betonson. The choice will be determined later, in co-operation with the project developer.

PHASE 6 GLASS
- Optimized the glass mould for annealed twisted glass. The quality of test window pane 0 suffices for the market.
- Eijkelkamp produced a market plan for the cold-bent glass, as a follow-up to the plan produced in phase 2.
- Glaverned, Tiel, measured the tensions in the cold-bent glass. Tensions proved to correspond with those calculated by hand.
- The Dutch research centre TNO, Delft, carried out durability tests for laminating cold-bent sheets assembled into window panes. Eijkelkamp coordinated these tests.
- Calculation of the forces on gluing when assembling two cold-bent window panes into a insulating window pane, carried out by D3BN.

PHASE 6 WINDOW FRAME
- Drew and measured prototype window frames 0, 1 and 3. The drawing and measuring of twisted profiles was time-consuming. Window frame 0 envelops the window pane 0 of approximately 1,100 x 1,900 mm. with a torsion of 200 mm.
- Reynolds Architectuursystemen had a matrix produced for the profiles. Van Campen Aluminium Productie, Lelystad, assembled window frames 0 and 1.
- Window frames 1 and 3 each consist of 4 window panes and measure, in frontal view, approximately 2,000 x 2,000 mm. Window frame 1 has a torsion of approximately 940 mm. and straight contours. Window frame 3 has a total torsion of approximately 1,200 mm., curved lower and upper contours and straight sides.

PHASE 7 GENERAL: TWISTERS 1 AND 2

- Design of two 90° twisted towers (twisters), with rectangular floor plans; constructed scale models and drew frontal views to study optical aspects. These towers have a greater repetition of elements than the earlier model and they can no longer fall back on straight profiles or flat plates for their elements. The geometrical qualities of these twisters are more apparent than that of the lesser transformed earlier model Tordo 1.
- Measured material distortions of façade elements of both towers.

PHASE 7 CAD, GLASS AND WINDOW FRAME

- Was granted a scholarship by the Stimuleringsfonds voor de Architektuur to describe associative aspects and spatial effects of curved lines and surfaces, and to examine spatial composition of double-curved surfaces, when varying only a few parameters.
- Schelde Scheepsnieuwbouw, Vlissingen, drew the development drawings of the window panes for prototype window frame 1 and generated a list with numeric information on pinbed jigs, as a preparation for developing a mould for freely double-curved glass.
- Transferred the PCT into a patent for the Netherlands, Belgium, Great Britain, Germany, France, and Denmark. The patent for the USA was granted in the year 2000.

PHASE 8 GENERAL: TWISTER 4

- Designed a cross-shaped tower, 150 metres in height and fitted this into the urban plan for South-East Amsterdam, together with the Dutch architect Pi de Bruijn. Due to the greater number of floors and the four identical wings, the tower has a greater recurrence than the previously designed towers Twister 1 and 2. The building is less extreme in distortion and usage than the previous models and connects, therefore, relatively easily to current building practice.
- Investigated various degrees of torsions and turning directions, in drawings and scale models.
- Detailed core and wing floor plans; the varying of mutual connections is new and very functional with twisted buildings.
  Produced a presentation booklet in which the building has been detailed with regard to measuring and building technical aspects.
- The superstructure was developed in consultation with Mr. R. Nijsse of ABT Engineers, Velp.
- Consultations with various developers and investors. Eventually property developer Volker Wessels Stevin, Amersfoort, was selected.
- Made a mould in co-operation with Van Tetterode Glas, Voorthuizen to examine the approximation of the twisted window pane shape if cold-bent glass, instead of hot-bent glass, were applied.
- Drew a vertical trial set up (2.4 x 4.8 metres) of the façade. It was realized by Van Dool Constructies, De Lier; Glaverbel/Eijkelkamp, Goor, supplied the glass. The window frames, composed of linear profiles and planar tempered insulating glass sheets, are cold-distorted. A cold-distorted façade of such a scale has not been

tendered before. This implies that different surface types, with an identical degree of cold distortion, can also be tendered.

PHASE 9 GENERAL: TWISTER 5
• This tower is assembled from two building wings that turn around a vertical cylinder in opposite directions. The main structure makes use of mirror symmetry in the shape.

PHASE 10 GLASS AND WINDOW FRAME (NOT REALIZED TO DATE)
• Have a trial window pane made of tempered twisted glass, of a rectangular glass sheet (approx. 1.200 x 2.000 mm.) with a torsion of respectively 100 and 150 mm.

• Draw exemplary window frame 4, for the façade part with the greatest distortion of Twister 2.
• Production of tempered twisted window panes for window frame 4, and fit it in a frame.
• To write a program of requirements for a computerized mould, with market prognosis, market plan, development schedule and plan of activities.

PHASE 10 CONCRETE (NOT REALIZED TO DATE)
• To draw a concrete twisted façade element for tower Twister 2 and have it produced.

About the author

Karel Vollers (Redhill, UK, 1951) studied at the Faculty of Architecture of Delft University of Technology. In 1978 he obtained his Master's degree in Architecture. From 1980-1981 he worked on competitions and conversions of shopping centres at several architect offices in Berlin. After returning to the Netherlands, he abandoned working on architecture in the years 1982 and 1983, to design, manufacture and market, light emitting jewelry.

After that adventure he worked for several architects, among them Peter Gerssen and Kas Oosterhuis. An architectural tour through Brazil in 1986, was followed by almost yearly visits, to study the use of free curves in architecture, especially in the work of Oscar Niemeyer. In 1991 he worked for Van Berkel & Bos Architects in Amsterdam as project leader for the Erasmus bridge in Rotterdam, supervising the structural and architectural elaboration of the preliminary design of bridge and landings until the feasibility of the construction was proven and the project was commissioned by the Mayor and Councilors of Rotterdam. 1992 saw the start of his own practice 'Vollers Architekten' in Amsterdam.

He is a regular speaker at conferences, teaches at the Amsterdam High School and works as a researcher at the Faculty of Architecture of Delft University of Technology. Karel Vollers is author of a number of publications about Brazilian architects.

Samenvatting Twist&Build

TWIST&BUILD

*Het realiseren van een te torderen gevelsysteem voor de architectuur
vanuit een wisselwerking tussen materiaalonderzoek en gebouwontwerp.*

Vanuit interactie tussen materiaalonderzoek en gebouwontwerp is een beschrijving gemaakt die voor diverse doelgroepen (fabrikanten, constructeurs, architekten, opdrachtgevers/gebruikers) inzicht geeft in de vervormings- en toepassingsmogelijkheden van getordeerde gevels en bouwelementen. Er zijn industriële samenwerkingsverbanden gerealiseerd die de getordeerde materialen produceren en op de markt offreren. Als tastbaar resultaat is een 1:1 voorbeeldmodel gemaakt van een getordeerd kozijn met getordeerd glas.

Context en probleemstelling

Sinds 1980 zijn met de invoering van computers in de bouw de vormgevings- en de productiemogelijkheden aanzienlijk toegenomen. Aanvankelijk werd de computer ingezet om bestaande handelingen in het bouwproces te automatiseren. Hij verminderde arbeidskosten, verhoogde de productiesnelheid en minimaliseerde menselijke fouten. De invloed van de computer op de vormgeving van gebouwen was daarbij beperkt: zij bleven orthogonaal. Vanaf 1985 groeide met het beschikbaar komen van relatief goedkope en eenvoudig bedienbare modelleerprogramma's de interesse voor vrij vervormde dubbelgekromde vlakken. Een belangrijke stimulans voor het onderzoeken van dergelijke vormen was, dat met het (vaak om economische redenen) steeds vlakker detailleren van gevels, steeds meer aandacht werd gevestigd op de visueel-associatieve werking van vlakken en contouren.

Na 1990 richtten meerdere architekten hun aandacht op het toepassen van getordeerde vlakken. Men ontdekte dat deze veel ruimtelijke kwaliteiten gemeen hebben met dubbelgebogen vlakken, maar veel eenvoudiger te realiseren zijn. Het begrip torderen dekt een heleboel typen vervormingen, maar de tot nu toe gebruikte typologische benamingen ervan zijn te algemeen van aard. Daarnaast zijn de meeste hedendaagse bouwkundigen niet meer gewend op wiskundige wijze de vlakken te beschrijven.

Verder zijn tot nu toe getordeerde vlakken alleen in staal, metselwerk of beton gerealiseerd, nog niet in glasplaten. Een groot deel van veel gevels is niettemin gemaakt van glas. Een driedimensionaal vervormde gevel zal het kleinste buitenoppervlak - inclusief materiaalgebruik en energieverlies - hebben, als alle onderdelen de gewenste gebogen vorm exact volgen. Omdat zulk glas niet verkrijgbaar is, wordt doorgaans een met vlakke ruiten gefacetteerde oplossing gekozen.

De industrie kon niet voor een aanvaardbare prijs en op korte termijn, getordeerd glas leveren, laat staan vrij dubbelgebogen glazen panelen. De motivatie tot innovatie van de technieken om glas ondersteunende geveldelen als kozijnen, en paneelvullingen driedimensionaal te vervormen, is gering zolang geen dubbelgebogen glas verkrijgbaar is.

Ontwerpend onderzoek

Stedenbouwkundige inpassing, gebouwontwerp en technisch en economisch haalbare materiaalverwerking zijn in dit proefschrift met elkaar in verband gebracht. Om met materialen die in de huidige staat van ontwikkeling complex te bewerken zijn, tot marktconform geprijsde producten te komen, is gezocht naar bestaande industriële productieprocessen en zijn deze vervolgens geïnnoveerd. Industriële samenwerkingsverbanden zijn geïnitieerd en in afspraken bestendigd, om de producten met kwaliteitsgarantie op de markt te brengen. Dit integreren is wellicht één van de belangrijkste onderdelen van het ontwikkelingsproces, en zeer tijdrovend.

De volgorde van de ontwerpactiviteiten varieerde per gebouwmodel. Omdat er geen bindende tijdlimiet was of een opdrachtsituatie, kon een resultaat nagestreefd worden dat niet door gangbare economische-, politieke- of maatschappelijke processen werd gedomineerd en konden de diverse aspecten van het torderen naar eigen inzicht op de diverse planniveaus op elkaar worden afgestemd.

Enkele gebouwontwerpen zijn tot in detail uitgewerkt. Daarbij zijn de consequenties beschreven die getordeerde gevels hebben op de diverse aspecten van een gebouw, zoals gebruiksmogelijkheden, ruimtelijke kenmerken, kosten en techniek. Door de van gangbare gebouwen afwijkende onderdelen exact te bematen, zijn de plannings- en kostentechnische onzekerheden van een nieuwe geometrie tot aanvaardbare grootheden gereduceerd.

Resultaten

Uit de vele aspecten die tijdens het onderzoek bestudeerd zijn, kwamen nieuwe schema's, vormen en theorieën voort. Dit betreft zowel technische- als expressieve aspecten. Veel van de beschrijvingen zijn nieuw. Diverse van de gesignaleerde en in algemene termen beschreven aspecten, zijn nog niet uitgewerkt.

Zij kunnen worden gezien als aanzetten tot later te verrichten verder onderzoek. Het schematiseren was bedoeld om inzicht te krijgen in de mogelijkheden en om de diverse onderzoeksgebieden optimaal te kunnen integreren.

Met het industrieel geproduceerde gevelstramienvullende bouwdeel, hebben de deelnemende industrieën nu een richtmodel waarbinnen zij hun onderdeel kunnen optimaliseren. Bedrijven uit al dan niet verwante bedrijfstakken kunnen hierop 'aanhaken' door vanuit hun specifieke kennis alternatieven voor te stellen en wellicht het model ingrijpend te innoveren. Daarnaast biedt het proefmodel de bouwwereld zicht op een nieuw product, zodat zij daar nieuwe toepassingen voor kan ontwerpen en een nieuwe vraag op gang kan brengen.